THE WORD WINDOW
The Bible Word Reference Book

Dedicated to Lionel Harris, Sr.

With all of the words I could draw from my vocabulary, and with any of the languages I could use, I could never come up with any to fully express the impact you left on my life.

Acknowledgements

To God be the glory for the great and wonderful thing He has done

To my wife Rosa, who had the wherewithal to keep and maintain every word that was sent out from the emails that started the Word Window

To my family for all the spiritual support and encouragement any one could receive.

To Bishop Clifford M. Johnson, Jr., for his leadership, guidance, and love for words and the Word.

To Rosanna Mollett for her divine design.

To Demetrius Wright, Vince Clark, and Stanley Blackwell, for their editing and advice.

And to all who supported me by providing the words and feedback through the development of The Word Window from the offset, your committment to the Word, strengthened my committment to the words.

THE WORD WINDOW

VOLUME ONE

The Bible Word Reference Book

- A Look at the Bible from God's view
- Good for self study, group study, and life application
- Including words that are regularly used in and around Church
- Meanings, definitions, and explanations from various sources and resources
- Used by Interpreters, Preachers, Teachers, Lay Persons, and Students (young and old)

LIONEL HARRIS, JR.

© 2009 Lionel Harris
Published by DAHU Publishing
5506 McCormick Avenue, Baltimore, MD 21206

You can arrange to have Lionel Harris speak, present, or train, by contacting him through DAHU Publishing, 5506 McCormick Avenue, Baltimore, MD 21206, by telephone 443-794-5233 or at dahuincc@aol.com.

All rights reserved. No part of this publication may be reproduced, stored in a retrieval system, or transmitted in any form or by any means, electronic, mechanical, photocopying, recording or otherwise, without the prior written permission of the publisher. Printed in the United States of America. Every effort has been made to locate copyright and permission information.

Design: Rosanna Mollett. Cover Art: stockxpert.com.

Library of Congress Control Number: 2009904336
ISBN 978-0-615-28230-5

FOREWORD

Books which deal with the definition and use of biblical words steadily appear. They serve and meet the needs of preachers, teachers, and saints of God who are looking for insight, inspiration, and encouragement as they study the Word of God. For twenty five years, God has afforded me the great privilege of preaching and teaching His word. In that time, I've come to appreciate and understand the value of how a single word in a passage of scripture can affect the meaning and the interpretation of that passage. Through the years there has been any number of bible dictionaries and exhaustive concordances that gives insight as to how the words of scripture are used.

By means of the present book, Minister Lionel Harris, himself a seasoned and respected preacher, and communicator has joined the ranks of those concerned with helping the saints of God gain a deeper understanding of the word of God. The insights that he shares in *The Word Window* have been gathered from his own first hand research as he has labored to serve the body of Christ by preaching the word from the pulpit, and years of study and reflection and service by teaching sign language as part of his ministry of communicating the gospel of Jesus Christ to the deaf.

The Word Window is a user friendly resource, yet it gives the reader an in-depth look into the etymology of the words. This book by Minister Lionel Harris now takes its place among a growing number of resources that God has provided for the body of Christ as we seek a deeper understanding and a growing relationship with God and our fellow man.

If you're looking for a USER FRIENDLY resource that gives an in-depth insight into the etymology into the words of scripture, I suggest this work by Minister Harris.

Franklin Peterson Jr.
Senior Pastor, Faith United Baptist Church
Baltimore, Maryland

HOW TO USE THIS BOOK

The words have been listed in alphabetical order, with definitions in either/or English, Hebrew and Greek. Most words regardless of the source, seem to be tied to the Strong's Concordance, therefore so are these. In many cases a number is written before the meaning (judge: Greek 2919 - krino - try or sentence, condemn, punish; 350 - anakrino - investigate, ask question, examine, search out; 1252 - diakrino - to separate). A number could also correspond with a number with definition in the Hebrew as well as the Greek.

At times you will not get a English definition, because the Hebrew or Greek is better, or you will get English only (ex. C.E. & B.C.E.).

Read the word, examine the definition, consider the usage, and apply it to your study and your life.

Abbreviations

A.D.	in the year of the Lord, i.e., the Christian Era
B.C.	Before Christ
Cf.	cross reference
Der.	derived
Fig.	figuratively
KJV	King James Version 1611
Lit.	literally
Mss.	manuscripts
Mt.	Mount
NASB	New American Standard Bible
NIV	New International Version
NT	New Testament
OT	Old Testament
RSV	Revised Standard Version
Sept.	Septuagint
Song.	Song of Solomon

ABASE
Hebrew:
6031: anab (aw-naw), through the idea of looking down or browbeating; to depress lit. or fig.: abase, self, afflict, chasten self, deal hardly with, defile—Isaiah 31:4

8213: shaphel (shaw-fale), to depress or sink (espec. to humiliate):- abase, bring (cast, put) down, debase, humble (self), be (bring, lay, make, put) lower—Job 42:11; Eze. 21:26

8214: shephal (shef-al), abase, humble, put down, subdue —Dan. 4:37

Greek:
5013: tapeinoo (tap-i-no-o), signifies to make low, "bring low," (a) of bringing to the ground making level, reducing to a plain as in Luke 3:5; (b) metaphorically in the active voice, to bring to a humble condition, "to abase," 2 Cor. 11:7, and in the passive, "to be abased," Phil. 4:12; in Matt. 23:12; Luke 14:11; 18:14, the KJV has "shall be abased," the RV "shall be humbled," in Matt. 18:4; 2 Cor. 12:21 and Phil. 2:8.

ACCOMPLISHED
ACCOMPLISHED (focus on Acts 21:5)
Greek:
1822: exartizo (ex-ar-tid'-zo), from 1537 and a der. of 739; to finish out (time); fig. to equip fully (a teacher): accomplish, thoroughly furnish. From the intens. ex (see ek, [1357]), from, and artios (739), complete. The verb artizo, to put in appropriate condition. To complete entirely, spoken of time (Acts 21:5), to furnish, or fit completely (2 Tim. 3:17). Deriv. katartizo (2675), to put a thing in its appropriate position, establish, set up.

ADDICTED

Greek:

5021: *tasso (tas'so)*, to arrange, assign, is translated "set (under authority) in Luke 7:8. In I Cor. 16:15, RV, "have set (themselves)," KJV, "addicted." To appoint, order (Matt. 28:16; Acts 22:10; 28:23); to set in order or in its proper category (Luke 7:8); to dispose, adapt, an order, regular method, to regulate, issue orderly and detailed instructions, a specific command for a specific person; to place under; submission; unruly (I Thess. 5:14); to behave in a disorderly manner (2 Thess. 3:6, 11).

All the deriv. have inherent in them order and categorization, classification.

ADO

English:

a do: noun. Bustle; fuss; trouble; bother. [Middle English from the phrase at do, "to do": at, from Old Norse at (used with infinitive), to do]

Greek:

2350: *thorubeo (thor-oo-beh'-o)* from 2351 (a disturbance); to be in tumult, i.e. disturb, clamor: make ado (a noise), trouble self, set on an uproar. "To make an uproar, to throw into confusion, or to wail tumultuously," is rendered "make .... ado," in Mark 5:39; elsewhere in Matthew 9:23; Acts 17:5; 20:10.

ADOPTION

Greek:

5206: *huiothesia (hwee-oth-es-ee'-ah)* from *huios*, "a son," and *thesis*, "a placing," akin to *thithemi*, "to place," signifies the place and condition of a son given to one to whom it does not naturally belong. The word is used by the apostle Paul only.

In Rom. 8:15, believers are said to have received "the Spirit of adoption," that is, the Holy Spirit who, given as the Firstfruits of all that is to be theirs, produces in them the realization of sonship and th attitude belonging to sons. In Gal. 4:5 they are said to receive "the adoption of sons," i.e., sonship bestowed in distinction from a relationship consequent merely upon birth. Two contrast - 1) between the sonship of the believer and the unoriginated sonship of Christ, 2) between the freedom enjoyed by the believer and bondage, whether of Gentile natural condition, or of Israel under the Law.

God does not "adopt" believers as children; they are begotten as such by His Holy Spirit through faith.

"Adoption" is a term involving the dignity of the relationship of believers as sons; it is not a putting into the family by spiritual birth, but a putting into the position of sons. In Rom. 9:4 "adoption" is spoken of as belonging to Israel, in accordance with the statement in Exodus 4:12, "Israel is My Son." Cf. Hos. 11:1. Israel was brought into a special relation with God, a collective relationship, not enjoyed by other nations, Deut. 14:1; Jer. 31:9, etc.

Two clear cases of adoption, taking another's child into one's own family, are noted in the OT. Moses was adopted by Pharaoh's daughter, and Esther by Mordecai (Ex. 2:10; Est. 2:7, 15).

In the NT "adoption" is a figure of speech which expresses the relation of either the Israelites to God or individuals who have a certain type of faith to God. These are spiritual relations of sonship and not physical or creation relationships.

These who are adopted through faith are subject to God's control, have his Spirit dwelling within them, receive his corrective chastisement in this life, and his inheritance in the world to come (Gal. 4:6; Heb. 12:5; Rom. 8:23). God redeemed Israel from the bondage of Egypt and made them His sons. So God redeems from the bondage of sin all those who have faith in Christ as Savior and Lord, and ultimately by resurrection he redeems them from death itself.

AGAIN (EMPHASIS ON - BE BORN AGAIN)

1364: *dis (dece)*, the ordinary numeral adverb signifying twice, is rendered "again" in Phil. 4:16, "ye sent once and again unto my need," and in I Thess. 2:18, where Paul states that he would have come to the Thessalonians "once and again" that is, twice at least he had attempted to do so.

3825: *palin (pal'-in)*, the regular word for "again," is used chiefly in two senses, (a) with reference to repeated action; (b) rhetorically, in the sense of "moreover" or "further," indicating a statement to be added in the course of an argument, e.g., Matt. 5:33 or with the meaning "on the other hand, in turn," Luke 6:43.

Other words are rendered "again" in the KJV, which the RV corrects, namely, deuteras and anothen. Deuteros signifies "a second time," John 9:24; Acts 11:9.

509: *anothen (an'-o-then)*, an adv. of place or time, from ana, above, and the suffix - then denoting from.

From above (John 3:31; James 1:17), from the beginning (Luke 1:3); again, anew, as before (John 3:3,7; Gal. 4:9). In these two passages it is plain that it means again, and not the literal meaning of from above. Nicodemus understood the Lord to mean again because in John 3:4 he mentions being born for the second time. With a prep. as in Matt. 27:51; Mark 15:38, it is used in the sense of a noun meaning the top or upper part. See ana (507), up. (from the Greek Lexicon)

Anathen signifies "from above, or anew." See the RV version of John 3:3, 7, and the KJV and RV of v 31. Nicidemus was not puzzled about birth from heaven; what perplexed him was that a person must be born a second time. This context makes it clear. This is really the meaning in Gal. 4:9, where it is associated with palin, "over again." The idea is "anew," for, though the bondage would be the same in essence and effect, it would be new in not being in bondage to idols but to the Law. Anathen may mean "from the first," in Luke 1:3 and Acts 26:5. For the meaning of "from above," see James 1:17; 3:15, 17. (from Vine's Complete Expository Dictionary).

AGNOSTIC

A person who doesn't know there is a God, and may believe it is impossible ever to know. In contrast a theist believes there is a God, and an ATHEIST believes there is no God.

noun - A thinker who disclaims any knowledge of God. adj. - Pertaining to the agnostics or their doctrines.

ALTAR

Hebrew:

4196 - mizbeah (miz-bay-akh) "altar", Noun has cognates in Aramaic, Syriac, and Arabic. In each of these languages the consonantal root is mdbh. Mizbeah occurs about 396 times in the OT.

The word signifies a raised place where a sacrifice was made. It is derived from the Hebrew verb zabah, which literally means "to slaughter for food" or "to slaughter for sacrifice." Another OT noun derived from zabah is zebah (162 times), which usually refers to a sacrifice that establishes communion between God and those who eat the thing offered.

"altar" for the God of Israel had to be built from earth or from unhewn stone and could not be so high that it required steps to reach its top (Ex. 20:24-26). In early biblical times some were to commemorate the appearance of deity or to mark an important event (Gen. 12:7)

741 ari'eyl (ar-ee-ale') the orthodox var. for 2025; the altar of the Temple:- altar —Ezek.43:15

To ANOINT

Hebrew:

masah (4886) - consecrate, smear, illustrates the idea of anointing something or someone as an act of consecration. the basic meaning is simply to smear something on an object. A special setting apart for an office or function.

ANOINTED ONE

MASIAH (4899) gives us the term messiah —- the New Testament word Christ is derived from the Greek word Christos which is exactly equivalent to the Hebrew word masiah, for it is rooted in the idea of "to smear with oil". So the term Christ emphasizes the special anointing of Jesus of Nazareth for His role as God's chosen one.

ANOINTING

Hebrew - 4888 mishchah or moshchah - from unction (the act), a consecratory gift: to be anointed.
8081 shemen - from root word to shine, to be or make oily, to be or to make fat, grease especially liquid (as from the olive), often perfumed), figurtively used as richness (fat things, fruitful)
5480 cuwk (sook) - meaning to smear over (with oil)
1101 - balal - to over flow (especially with oil) to mix; also to fodder: anoint, confound, mingle

Verb usage:
Greek - 21 aleipho - from joint words meaning as "a particle of union" and the base meaning "to oil" (with perfume) —- used as anointing of any kind
5548 chrio - confined to sacred and symbolical anointings (as Christ as the "Anointed" of God
1472 enchrio - to rub in, to besmear, to anoint is used metaphorically in the command to the church in Laodicea to "anoint" their eyes with eye-salve. It is used of the anointing of the eyes with a view to beautifying them.
2025 epichrio - to rub ON or upon, is used of the blind man whose eyes Christ "anointed" and indicates the manner in which the "anointing" was done.
3462 murizo - is used of anointing the body for burial THE NOUN USAGE:
5545 chrisma - corresponds with chrio (5548) and signifies an unguent or anointing. It was prepared from oil and aromatic herbs. Used only metaphorically in the New Testament; of the Holy Spirit, I John 2:20, and verse 27 twice. When we say that believers have "an anointing from the Holy One" indicates that this anointing renders them holy, separating them to God. This teaches that the gift of the Holy Spirit is the all efficient means of enabling believers to possess a knowledge of the truth. It is used of the oil for anointing the high priest. It stands for the anointed one - Christ. It stands for the person Himself, as for the Holy Spirit in I John 2.

examples:
4886 - Ex. 28:41; 5480 - Deut 28:40; 1101 - Ps. 92:10; 218 - Mt. 6:17.

APOCRYPHA -

A Greek word in the plural meaning "hidden" (things), applied first to works considered not suitable for circulation, but coming to mean "spurious" (lacking authenticity or validity in essence or origin; not genuine; false) noncanonical (books). For Roman Catholics the term indicates the books which the protestants call Pseudepigrapha (spurious writings, esp. writings falsely attributed to biblical characters or times) while Protestants understand by the term the books outside of the Hebrew included in the Septuagint and the Vulgate.

When canon of the Hebrew Bible was fixed at the Council of Jamnia (A.D. 90) the books of the Apocrypha were excluded for one of the following reasons: some books survived only in Greek after the Hebrew or Aramaic original was lost (Tobit, Judith); others were written later than Ezra, after whom prophecy, and consequently inspired writings, were believed to have ceased (I Maccabees, Ecclesiasticus); others had been written in Greek (Wisdom of Solomon), II Maccabees). But in Alexandria this chronological limitation was unknown:

All writings translated from the Hebrew or Aramaic were included in the Canonical Scriptures in Greek, and even some Jewish books written in Greek were regarded as inspired.

*The Apocrypha consists of 15 books or parts of books. The writings date from about 200 B.C. to A.D. 100. The titles in the Apocrypha differ in various editions of the Bible. The following list gives the titles and order of the books in the Revised Standard Version.

I Esdras; II Esdras; Tobit; Judith; Additions to the Book of Esther; Wisdom of Solomon; Ecclesiasticus, or the Wisdom of Jesus the Son of Sirach; Baruch; Letter of Jeremiah; Prayer of Azariah and the Song of the Three Young Men; Susanna; Bel and the Dragon; Prayer of Manasseh; I Maccabees; II Maccabees.

Some Bibles include the Letter of Jeremiah in Baruch, reducing the number of books to 14.

The Hebrew Bible excludes all the books of the Apocrypha. The Roman Catholic Church places I and II Esdras and the Prayer of Manasseh after the NT. It distributes the remaining 12 books throughout the OT either as separate titles or as part of other books. Some Protestant Bibles place the entire Apocrypha between the OT and NT. A few place it after the NT. Some Protestant churches omit the Apocrypha completely from their versions of the Bible.

APPLE
Hebrew:

380 - iyshown (ee-shone), dimin. from 376; the little man of the eye; the pupil or ball; hence the middle (of the night):- apple [of the eye], black obscure—Deut. 32:10

892 - babah (baw-baw'), fem. act. part. of an unused root mean. to hollow out; something hollowed (as a gate), i.e. the pupil of the eye: - apple [of the eye].—Zec. 2:8

1323 - bath (bath), from 1129 (as fem); a daughter (used in the same wide sense as other terms of relationship, lit. and fig.):- apple [of the eye], branch, company, daughter—Ps. 17:8; Lam. 2:18

8598 - tappuwach (tap-poo'-akh), from 5301; an apple (from fragrance), i.e. the fruit or the tree (pro. includ. others of the pome order, as the quince, the orange, etc.): - apple (tree).—Song. 2:3, 8:5; Joel 1:12

APPREHEND & APPREHENDED
Greek:

2638 - katalambano (kat-al-am-ban'-o), from kata (2596), an intens. prep. and lambano (2983), to take.

To seize (Mark 9:18), to lay hold of, apprehend, in a figurative sense (Phil. 3:12); to receive, admit (John 1:5), meaning the darkness did not admit or receive the light, cf. vv. 10-12; 3:19); to take, catch unawares (John 8:3); to come upon, overtake (John 12:35; I Thess. 5:4); to attain, obtain (Rom. 9:30; I Cor. 9:24); to comprehend mentally (Eph. 3:18). In the middle voice, katalambanomai, to perceive, understand, find (Acts 4:13; 25:25)

4084 - piazo (pee-ad'-zo), to squeeze, i.e. seize (gently by the hand, or officially [arrest], or in hunting [capture]): - apprehend, catch, lay hand on, take.

AUTHOR
Greek:

159 - aitios (ah-ee-tee-os), an adjective (cf. aitia, a cause), denotes "that which causes something." Translated "author" in Hebrews. Aitios, in Heb. 5:9, descirbes Christ as the "Author of eternal salvation unto all them that obey Him," signifying that Christ, exalted and glorified as our High Priest, on the ground of His finished work on earth, has become the personal mediating cause (RV, margin) of eternal salvation. It is difficult to find an adequate English equivalent to express the meaning here. Christ is not the merely formal cause of our salvation, He is the concrete and active cause of it. He has not merely caused or effected it, He is, as His name, "Jesus," implies, our salvation itself, Luke 2:30; 3:6.

747 - archegos (ar-khay-gos), beginning or rule. Beginning, originating as a substitute it means originator, founder, leader, chief, prince. Jesus Christ is called the arch egos of life (Acts 3:15); of faith (Heb. 12:2); of salvation (Heb. 2:10). He is also called the aparche (536), firstfruits, of them that sleep, the originator of the resurrection of those who are going to be raised from the dead. Archegos occurs also in Acts 5 :31.

B

BAAL

Hebrew:

896 - baal (bay-uhl) a false god (Num. 22:41). Baalim is the plural (Judges 2:11). The Canaanite word for husband, Lord, and master. The male god worshiped by the people of Canaan and Phoenicia and sometimes by Israelites. The god was supposed to cause people and things to be fertile. The worship involved self-torture, child sacrifice, and sinful sexual practices outside of marriages.

The supreme male divinity of the Phoenician and Canaantish Nations, as Astoreth was their supreme female divinity.

see- Baal-Berith, Baale, Baal-Gad, Baal-Hammon, Baal-Hanan, Baal-Hazor, Pear, Baal Perazim, Baal-Shishha, Baal Tamar.

1167 & 1168 - baal (bah'-ale), "master; baal." In Akkadian, the noun belu ("lord") gave rise to the verb belu ("to rule"). In other northwest Semitic languages, the noun ba'al differs somewhat in meaning, as other words have taken over the meaning of "sir" or "lord." The Hebrew word ba'al seems to have been related to these homonyms.

The word ba'al occurs 84 times in the Hebrew OT, 15 times with the meaning of "husband" and 50 times as a reference to a deity. The first occurrence of the noun ba'al is in Gen. 14:13: "And there came one that had escaped, and told Abram the Hebrew; for he escaped, dwelt in the plain of Mamre the Amorite, brother for Eshcol, and brother of Aner: and these were confederate with [literally, "ba'al's of a covenant with"] Abram."

The primary meaning of ba' al is "possessor." Denotes deity other than God of Israel. A common name given to the god of fertility in Canaan. The god of the Canannites.

1168 - ba'al - A city in Simeon

A descendant of Reuben, A descendant of Benjamin

THE WORD WINDOW

BESEECH
Greek:
3870- parakaleo (par-ak-al-eh-o) the most frequent word with this meaning, is used as "to call to one's side," hence, "to call to one's aid." It is used for every kind of calling to a person which is meant to produce a particular effect, hence, with various meanings, such as "comfort, exhort, desire, call for," in addition to its significance "to beseech", which has a stronger force than (ask).

2065 - erotao (er-o-tah-o) often translated by the verb "to beseech", in the Gospels, is elsewhere rendered "beseech," in I Thess. 4:1; 5:12; II Thess. 2:1

1189 - deomai (deh-om-ahee), to desire, "to desire, to long for" usually representing the word "need" is sometimes translated "beseech," e.g., Luke 5:12; Acts 21:39. It is used of prayer to God, in Matt. 9:38; Luke 10:2; 21:36.

NOTE— 3870 - parakaleo - from (3844), by the side, and kaleo, to call (2564); to call to one's side, hence aid (Mark 1:40). Deriv.: paraklesis (3874), a calling to one's side and aid, hence an appeal (II Cor. 8:4), an encouragement, exhortation (Acts 4:36; Romans 12:8), consolation, comfort (Rom. 15:4); parakletos (3875), one called to one's side and aid counsel for the defense, an advocate, comforter (John 14:16); sumparakaleo (4837), with, sun (4862), together, to comfort together (Romans 1:12).

BIBLE VERSIONS (MOST READ)
Ancient Versions Aramaic Targums

Septuagint (LXX). 70 to 72 translated the Hebrew Scriptures into Greek. This version was often used by the NT authors. It is often used as the bridge between Hebrew thought and the NT. There were other OT translations Aquila's, Symmachus's and Theodotion's.

English versions.

Old Latin - Versions of the OT and NT prior to Jerome's Vulgate. The OT based on the LXX, not the Hebrew OT. Vulgate - In A.D. 383 Eusebius Hieronymus, known today as Jerome, was asked to make a revision of the Old Latin versions, both OT and NT.

Old Syriac - a dialect of Aramaic, from the second century. Peshitta - was new Syriac from the fourth century.

Coptic - A later form of Egyptian (from the hieroglypic), developed in the Christian Era, written in Greek alphabet. Gothic - Ufilas in about AD. 375 translated the Scripture into the Gothic (a Germanic tribe).

Miscellaneous - Armenian, Georgian, Ethiopic, Slavonic, Arabic, Persian, Frankish, and many others

Wyclifs - The first English Bible, completed in 1382. For 150 years was widely used and was the only Bible that was complete. It was an extremely literal rendering of the Latin Vulgate.

Tyndales - In 1525 his NT was based on the Greek text and hence, according to his opponents, in "error" with the Vulgate rendering. He was a great scholar. A great deal of KJV NT follows the Tyndale version.

Coverdale's - In 1535 translated by Myles Coverdale, actually a revision of Tyndale's work.

Matthew's - In 1537 a revision of Tyndale's version by one pen named Thomas Matthew (actually John Rogers). Taverner's - A revision of Matthew's Bible by Richard Taverner.

The Great Bible - In 1539 a revision was made of the Matthew's Bible by Coverdale, supported by Cromwell. It was called the Geat Bible because of its size. It became a popular version with the laity.

Geneva Bible - In 1560 this was a revision of the Great Bible with Tyndale's clear influence. This was the version used by the Pilgrims, John Bunyan, and King James himself.

Bishop's Bible - In 1568 was the revision of the Great Bible by Bishops, not nearly as popular as the Geneva Bible.

Douai-Rheims. In 1609 a Roman Catholic version.

King James Bible - In 1611 King James sanctioned a new version to be made. Forty-seven scholars were commissioned to do the work. This version was to have no marginal notes (the Reformer's notes were sometimes too radical for the status quo) and was to be used in all the churches of England only in time of divine service. The Bishop's Bible was to be the basis of the work. Though not accepted for the first 50 years, this version has endured over the centuries to the present day.

Some committee-made versions after the King James Bible.

English Revised Version - ERV - 1881, a committee work by 51 to 65 British and American scholars. The American Standard Version - ASV, 1901. The American rendition of the 1881 version.

The Revised Standard Version - RSV, 1946. Revision of the KJV, 1881, and 1901 versions.

The New Revised Standard Version - NRSV, 1990 is a revision of the RSV.

The New American Standard - 1960. This was a revision, done by 58 translators, of the ASV, 1901. The New English Bible - NEB, 1961. Joint church committees from England, Scotland, and Ireland.

The Jerusalem Bible - the JB, 1966; (New Jerusalem Bible), 1985). An English adaption of the French La Bible de Jerusalem.

The New International Version - NIV, 1978. This version is a completely new translation, a tran-denominational effort by 115 translators in conjunction with the New York International Bible Society.

The New King James Version - NKJV, 1982. A partial revision of the KJV, done by 119 "translators," who removed some archaic word forms while maintaining essentially the same original text of the KJV.

Tanakh - a single volume published in 1985. This is a work of the threefold Jewish canon of Sciputre, known to Christians as the OT. Fourteen translators and editors were involved over the last three decades in producing this work.

BIBLICAL PRAYERS

Confession - acknowledging sin and helplessness and seeking God's mercy— OT - Ps. 51; NT - Luke18:13; Jesus' teaching - Luke 15:11-24 & Luke 18:10-24

Praise - adoring God for for who he is—OT - I Chron. 29:10-13; NT - Luke 1:46-55; Jesus' teach -Matt. 6:9. Thanksgiving - expressing gratitude to God for what he has done - OT - Ps. 105: 1-7; NT -I Thess. 5:16-18; Jesus' teaching - Luke 17:11-19

Petition - making personal request of God - OT - Gen. 24:12-14; NT - Acts 1:24-24; Jesus's teaching Matt. 7:7-12

Intercession - making request of God on behalf of another - OT Exod. 32:11-13; NT - Phil. 1:9-11; Jesus' teaching - John 17:9, 20-21

Commitment - expressing loyalty to God and His work - OT - I Kings 8:56-61; NT - Acts 4:24-30; Jesus' teaching - Matt. 6:10; Luke 6:46-49

Forgiveness - seeking mercy for personal sin or the sin of others - OT - Dan. 9:4-19; NT - Acts 7:60; Jesus' teaching - Matt. 6:12; Luke 6:27-36

Confidence - affirming God's all-sufficiency and the believers's security in His love - OT - Ps 23; NT - Luke 2:29-32; Jesus' teaching - Matt. 6:5-15; 7:11

Benediction - a request for God's blessing - Num. 6:24-26; NT - Jude 24;

BIND UP (FOCUS ON ISAIAH 61)

Hebrew:

2280 - chabash (khaw-bash'), to bind on, wrap around; bind up (a wound), bandage; to saddle; to cover, envelope, enclose; to govern, rule (Exod. 29:9; I Kings 2:40).

Isaiah 61 : ... hath anointed me to preach good tidings unto the meek; he hath sent me to bind up the broken hearted, to proclaim liberty ....

BOAST

Hebrew:

559- amar (aw-mar) to say (used with great latitude): answer, bid, boast self, call, certify, challenge

1984 - halal (haw-lal) to be clear, to shine; hence to make a show, to boast; and thus to be foolish; to rave, to celebrate, glory, sing praises

3235 - to change places, to exchange

3513 - to glory, to be heavy (in a bad way - burdensome), (in a good way, rich or honorable), boast, be chargeable, in honor (self), promote, sore, stop

6286 - paar (paw-ar) to gleam, embellish, to boast, also to explain (to make clear) oneself, beautify, boast, glorify (self), vaunt self

Greek:

2620 -katakauchaomai (kat- ak- ow - khah - om -ahee) to exult against, boast (against), glory, rejoice against

2744 - kauchaomai, (kow - khah - om -ahee) to vaunt (in a good or bad sense): (make) boast, glory, joy, rejoice

3166 megaulaucheo (meg-al-ow-kheh-o) to boast, to talk big, (arrogant), egotistic, boast great things

examples:
Hebrew:
559 - psalm 94:4; 1984 - I kings 20:11; 3235 - Is. 61:6;
3513 - II Chron. 25:9
Greek:
2620 - Rom 11:18; 2744 -II Cor. 10:13
Eph.2:9
3166 - to lift up the neck, hence, "to boast" is found in some texts of James 3:5. It indicates any kind of haught speech which stirs up strife or provokes others. In Acts 5:36, the verb lego, "to say", is used "as boasting" in the King James; but in the Revised Version its "giving out"

BOAZ

Hebrew:

1162 - boaz (bo-az), an ancestor of David; also a name in front of the temple.

Boaz was a half-blooded Bethlehemite whose mother was an offspring of Ham and whose father was of the Hebrew "stock".

Boaz was a wealthy landowner who capitalized in grain. One day as he toured his fields, he saw a beautiful Moabitess named Ruth gleaning his crops. He showed her considerate kindness and gave her privileges beyond that of a gleaner.

Boaz afterward married Ruth, and she bore him a son, Obed, the great-grandsire of King Solomon.

According to Barbot, Jews in Spain and Portugal were so black that whites often mistook all Jews to be black. How erroneous, he says, "The Jews in Germany and Prague are as white as their counterparts";

- M. Fishberg, who visited Africa during the early 1900's, says that while strolling the streets of Algiers, he couldn't distinguish the Jews from the Mohammedans, and that many were of the Negro type;
- N. Slouschz, the white Jewish rabbi, says that down the eastern borders of Algeria settled large group of black Jews;
- A. Godbey said that in Algeria, in the range of 350 miles from the Mediterranean Sea, existed an area of Jews who were black as Negroes.

Ruth 4:13, 20-22; Matt. 1:5-6

BORN/BEGET/BEGAT/BEAR

Hebrew:

3205 - yalad (yaw-lad) to bear young, to act as a midwife, to bring forth (children), to show lineage

Greek:

1080 - gennao (ghen-nah-o) from word genos (ghen-os) which means "kin", born, country, diversity, generation, kind(red), nation, offspring, stock. It means to procreate (properly of the father, but by extension of the mother); fig. to regenerate: - bear, beget, be born, bring forth, conceive, be delivered of, gender, make, spring

BREATH, BREATHE

Air drawn into the body to sustain life. Since breathing is the most obvious sign of life, the phrase breath of life is used frequently in the Bible to mean "alive" or "living" (Gen. 2:7; 6:17). Breath is recognized as the gift of God to His creatures (Job 12:10). But since breath is usually invisible, it also may symbolize something without substance or a temporary state of existence (Ps. 144:4).

In a different sense, the "breath of God" (Job 37:10) signifies God's power. This stands in striking contrast to heathen gods, which have neither power nor life. The word breath may be used figuratively, as when Jesus "breathed" the Holy Spirit upon His disciples (John 20:22).

Hebrew:

1892 -hebel (heh-bel) "breath; vanity; idol." Cognates of this noun occur in Syriac, late Aramaic, and Arabic. All but 4 of its 72 occurrences are in the poetry (37 in Ecclesiastes). First, the word represents human "breath" as a transitory thing: "I loathe it; I would not live always: let me alone; for my days are vanity [literally, but a breath]" Job 7:16. Second, hebel means something meaningless and purposeless: "Vanity of vanities, saith the Preacher, vanity of vanities; all is vanity" Eccl. 1:2.

Third, this word signifies an "idol," which is unsubstantial, worthless, and vain: "They have moved me to jealousy with that which is not God; they have provoked me to anger with their vanities" Deut. 32:21.

Greek:
Nouns
4157 - pnoe (pno-ay) akin to pneo, "to blow," lit., "a blowing," signifies (a) "breath, the breath of life," Acts 17:25; (b) "wind," Acts 2:2.
4151 - pneuma (pnyoo-mah) "spirit," also denotes "breath," Rev. 11:11 and 13:15, RV. In II Thess. 2:8, the KJV has "spirit" for RV, breath.
Verbs
1709 - empneo (emp-neh-o) lit., "to breathe in, or on," is used in Acts 9:1, indicting that threatening and slaughter were, so to speak, the elements from which Saul drew and expelled his breath.
1720 - emphusao (em-foo-sah-o) "to breathe upon," is used of the symbolic act of the Lord Jesus in breathing upon His apostles the communication of the Holy Spirit, John 20:22.

BRUISED

Hebrew:
1792 - dhakha (daw-kaw) to be cast down, be humbled; to break, crush, oppress, humble, tread down, to be broken in pieces, crushed, humbled, afflicted.
This verb is used only in Hebrew poetry and is applicable only to people. God is often the agent (the one doing the bruising).

BUFFET

Greek:
2852 - kolaphizo (kol-af-id'zo), signifies "to strike with clenched hands, to buffet with the fist" (kolapos, "a fist"), buffet —Matt. 26:67; Mark 14:65; I Cor. 4:11; 2 Cor. 12:7; I Pet. 2:20.
5299 - hupopiazo (hoop-o-pee-ad'-zo), lit., "to strike under the eye" (from hupopion, "the part of the face below the eye'" hupo, "under," ops, "an eye"), hence, to beat the face black and blue (to give a black eye), is used metaphorically, and translated "buffet" in I Cor. 9:27 (KJV, "keep under),
of Paul's suppressive treatment of his body, in order to keep himself spiritually fit (RV marg., "bruise"); to tease or annoy (into compliance), subdue (one's passion): - keep under, weary

THE WORD WINDOW

English:
a blow or cuff with or as if with the hand. To hit or club especially repeatedly. To strike against forcefully; to batter. To force (one's way) with or as if with crude blows. To struggle; contend. To force one's way by struggling.

*note: Though Satan should buffet, though trials may come, let this blest assurance control that Christ has regarded my helpless estate, and has shed His own blood for my soul

"It is well with my soul"—Horatio G. Spafford

BULWARKS
Hebrew:
2426 - cheyl (khale), an army; also an intrenchment-army; bulwark, hot, rampart, trench, wall—Is. 26:1

2430 - cheylah (khay-law), intrenchment-bulwark—Psalm 48:15

4685 - matsowd (maw-tsode), a net (for capturing animals or fishes); also a fastness or (besieging) tower:- bulwark, hold, munition, net, snare—Ecc. 9:14

4692 - matsowr (maw-tsore) or matsuwr (maw-tsoor), something hemming in, a mound (of besiegers), a seige, (fig) distress; fenced; fortress, strong (hold) tower—Deut. 20:20

6438 - pinnah (pin-naw), an angle; by implication a pinnacle; fig. a chieftain:- bulwark, chief, corner, stay, tower—2 Chron. 26:15

English:
a wall of earth or other material built for defense; rampart any protection against external danger, injury, annoyance; any person or thing giving strong support or encouragement in time of need, danger, or doubt (ex. Religion was his bulwark)

Nautical use: a solid wall enclosing the perimeter of weather or main deck to fortify or protect with a bulwark; secure by or as if by a fortication

BURDEN
Greek -
922 - baros -(bar-os) from the root word meaning to walk (through the notion of going down), weight; in the New Testament only fig. as a load, abundance, authority: - burden (some),

5413 - phortion - (for-tee-on) an invoice (as part of freight) , a task or service: burden, something carried - always used as a metaphor except in Acts 27:10.

The difference between baros and phortion is, that phortion is simply something to be carried, without reference to weight, but baros always suggests what is heavy or burdensome.

1117 - gomos - (gom'os) - full, or heavy, to be full

916 - bareo - (bar-eh'o) used of the effect of drowsiness (were heavy - Matt. 26:43), effects of gluttony (Luke 21:34)

1912 - epibareo (ep-ee-bar-eh'o) - to burden heavily, is said of material resources, to be chargeable to, of the effect of spiritual admonition and discipline

example:
5413 - Matt. 11:30
922 - Matt. 20:12 and Gal. 6:5

CANAAN

Hebrew:

    3667 - Kenaan (ken-ah'-an) humiliated; Kenaan, youngest son of Ham; also the country inhabited by him:

Canaan (89x); merchant (3x); traffick (1x); traffickers (11x)

    He fathered eleven nations, seven of which fell under the hands of Israel. During their dispersion from Babel, Canaan did not follow his three brothers to Africa. Instead, he traveled southwest, settling in a region known today as Palestine.

    When Canaan entered the land, it was uninhabited. But as time passed, smaller groups entered who were not of Canaan (Philistines). During Israel's invasions, they showed minor resistance, but the chief strength existed among Canaan's descendants since they were greater in number and more established culturally. Some of the largest fortresses were controlled by them, such as Ai and Jericho. The Bible refers to this land, and its adjacent territories as Ham's (Gen. 9:22; 14:5; Deut. 2:10; I Chron. 4:40).

    Canaan is the most talked-about black character in the Bible. The Sidonians, Hittites, Jebusites, Amorites, Girgasites, Hivites, Arkites, Sinites, Arvadites, Zemarites ... , and Hamathites who also occupied and comanded the principal city of upper Syria (Gen. 10:18) were all black nations living in the land during Israel's invasion. These Blacks dwelt in Canaan Land with the Israelites for centuries, where it has been revealed in the Scriptures that the Hebrews were the blacks' closest relatives through genealogy (Judg.1:21; 3:5 -6; Ezra 9:1-2; 10:14; 16,19, 44; Ezek. 16:1- 3).

    The Canaanites were an ingenious race and were early developers of arts and sciences. The construction of their cities was superior to later Hebrew edifices; they were talented in ceramic arts, music, musical instruments, architecture, and military warfare.

    One of Jesus' twelve disciples was a Negro called Simon the Canaanite. He was called a Canaanite because of his descent from the black man Canaan (Matt. 10:1-4; Luke 6:12-16; Acts 1:1-14; Mark 3:18-19).

Noah prophetically placed a curse on "Canaan" because his father had stared at Noah's nakedness and reported it grossly to his brothers. Ham's sin, deeply rooted in his youngest son, is observable in the Canaanites in the succeeding history.

Gen: 9:25-27 stamps a theological significance on "Canaan" from the beginning: "Cursed be Canaan; a servant of servants shall he be unto his brethren .... Blessed be the Lord God of Shem; and Canaan shall be his servant."

For years many people have said that Ham (which is Black) was black because of this curse; however, scripture shows the curse was put on Canaan, not on Ham. Meaning it had nothing to do with color.

CANON

The word canon comes from a Greek word that means "measuring stick." Over time, the word eventually came to be used metaphorically of books that were "measured" and thereby recognized as being God's Word. When we talk about the "canon of Scripture" today, we are referring to all the biblical books that collectively constitute God's Word.

The canon is the official list of books included in the Bible. The NT contains 27 books - the 4 Gospels, the Acts of the Apostles, twenty-one Epistles, and the Revelation. The books of the NT were written over a period of about fifty years, from A.D. 40 to 90. The Gospels were written in order to provide an account of the life and ministry of Jesus, and the Epistles were letters that were written (mostly by Paul) to specific churches or groups of Christians. These letters were widely copied and circulated, and over time the letters written by the Apsotles or immediate disciples of the apostles were accepted by the church as havng divine authority and having been inspired by God.

There was no single point in history when the canon was offically established. Over the first several hundred years of Church History, various groupings of Gospels and letters were given prominence.

The NT canon in its present form was largely in place by about A.D. 200, and the first exact listing of the twenty-seven books we now know as the NT was included in a letter of Athanasius in A.D. 367.

The same was published shortly thereafter by two different Church Councils.

CAPHTOR - KAPHTOR

3731 - Kaphtor (kaf-tore), also Caphtor "a crown"; the seventh son of Mizraim (Egypt), grandson of Ham, and father of the black Philistines (Jer. 47:4; Amos 9:7).

During the break up of Babel, Caphtor and his offspring journeyed to the island of Crete, but were later forced off the island by a ruinous change in the earth (earthquakes). They migrated from Crete to Canaan (their great "uncle") and settled southwest of Canaan's land. They built the cities of Gaza, Ashod, Ashkelon, Ekron, Gittite and Avite. For many years each of those cities was governed by an axis lord (Josh. 13:3; I Sam. 29:7).

When Israel entered Canaan, three of the Philistines' strongholds were seized by the tribe of Judah; however, the Philistines were never destroyed by Israel, because of their great warriors and wide advancement in war equipment, for they had war chariots with iron scythes (Judg. 1:18-19).

The Philistines remained prominent and powerful throughout the Davidic-Solomonic empire. Many of them even married into the Hebrew race (Neh. 13:23).

The most popular black Philistines in the Bible are Delilah and Goliath. Gen. 10:6, 13-14; Judg. 16:1-31; I Sam. 17:23-24.

C.E. AND B.C.E.

The abbreviation "C. E." is a standard way of denoting dates in scholarly literature.

C.E. means "Common Era" and B.C.E denotes "Before the Common Era." The year 1 C.E. is the same as the year 1 A.D.

Many people do not appreciate the fact that the abbreviations AD and BC profess the Christian faith:

Anno Domini, meaning "in the year of Our Lord", states the belief that Jesus is the Lord, and BC states that Jesus is the Christ (Messiah). Religious scholars, many of whom are non-Christian, are keenly aware of this, so a neutral way of denoting the year was devised.

Just like AD, the CE system counts the birth of Jesus as year 1.

In fact, we do not know what year Jesus was born. The Gospels indicate he was born near the end of the reign of Herod the Great. The AD system thus takes the last year of Herod's rule as the birth year of Jesus. Because of a counting error, this year turns out to be, in the modern calendar, 4 BC/BCE, not 1 AD/CE.

Not even scholar's appreciate the fact that our calendar does not count from the first year of Jesus, which is unknown, but from the last year of Herod, which is known. Thus the entire AD/BC system is based on the reign of the last great Jewish king!

"G. J. Goldberg states "my own proposal is that non-Christian scholars can indeed use AD and BC in good conscious, as long as they interpret AD to mean "After the Death of Herod" and BC to mean "Before Caesar:, i.e., before the Jewish state was partitioned by Augustus Caesar upon the death of Herod."

CHASTEN/CHASTENING/CHASTISE/CHASTISEMENT

Hebrew:

3256 - yasar (yaw-sar), to chastise, lit. (with blows) or fig. (with words); to reprove, discipline, chasten, instruct; to be chastised; to learn reproof; to take a warning; to punish, correct, admonish; to be instructed. This Hebr. root has the definite connotation of either physical enforcement or verbal reinforcement. One becomes educated when the proper amount of training and correction are imposed. The purpose of God's discipline is reformation. Man must learn from God's mighty acts.

The Lord's discipline tests His children (Deut. 8:5). Jehovah is like a father (Ex. 4:22; Deut. 1:31; Is. 1:2). Therefore, He disciplines us as a father would discipline his son (Heb. 12:5-11); it is a sign of His love Prov. 1:7,8; The prophets dev. the theme of discipline (Is. 8:11); Jesus took man's chastisement (Is. 53:5)

3198 - yakach (yaw-kahh'), to be right (i.e. correct); to argue; to decide, justify or convict:-appoint, chasten, convince, correct (ion), dispute, judge, maintain, plead reason (together), rebuke, reprove, surely, in any wise—2 Sam. 7:14

4148 - muwcar (moo-sawr'), from 3256 chastisement; fig. reproof. warning or instruction; also restraint: bond, chastening, chastisement, check, correction, discipline, doctrine, rebuke—Prov. 13:24.

6031 - anah (aw-naw'), through the idea of looking down or browbeating; to depress lit. or fig., trans. or intrans. as follows: - abase self, afflict, answer, chasten self, deal hardly with, defile, exercise force, gentleness, humble (self), hurt, ravish, submit self, weaken in any way—Dan. 10:12

8433 - towkechah (to-kay-khaw'), chastisement; fig. (by words), refutation, proof (even in defense): argument, chastened, correction, reasoning, rebuke, reproof, reproved—Ps. 73:14

Greek:

3811 - paideuo (pahee-dyoo'o) denotes "to train children," suggesting the broad idea of education (pais, "a child"), Acts 7:22; 22:3; see also Titus 2:12, "instructing" (RV), here of a training gracious and firm grace, which brings salvation, employs means to give us full possession of it; hence, "to chastise," this being part of the training, whether (a) by correcting with words, reproving, and admonishing, I Tim. 1:20; 2 Tim. 2:25, or (b) by "chastening" by the infliction of evils and calamities, I Cor. 11:32. The verb also has the meaning "to chastise with blows, to scourge,"—Heb. 12:6,7; Luke 23:16

CHRISTMAS

- The word Christmas comes from the words Cristes maesse, or "Christ's Mass". Christmas is the celebration of the birth of Jesus for members of the Christian religion. Most historians peg the first celebration of Christmas to Rome 336 A.D.
- Christmas is both a holiday and a holy day. In America it is one of the biggest events of the year, and for members of the Christian religions it is an important day on the religious calendar. The federal government, all state governments all schools/colleges/universities and the vast majority of businesses in America give employees one or two days off at Christmas, making it an important holiday.
- According to the 1994 "Britanica Book of the year" there are 1.8 billion Christians in a total world population of 5.5 billion, making it the largest religion in the world. In America, 241 million out of a total population of 281 million people are Christians —that's 85%. Because Christians follow Jesus, the birth of Jesus is important to them (us).
- Why do people give gifts - the tradition of gifts seem to have started with the gifts that the wise men (the magi) brought to Jesus. They came, bowed down, and they worshipped him. Then they opened their treasures and presented him with gifts of gold, incense, and myrrh.
- No one was really in the habit of exchanging elaborate gifts until late 1800's. The Santa Claus story combined with an amazing retailing phenomenon that has grown since the turn of the century, has made gift giving a central focus of the Christmas tradition.
- No one knows on what day Christ was born. What is known is that Christian leaders in 336 C.E. set the date to December 25 in an attempt to eclipse a popular pagan holiday in Rome (Saturnalia) that celebrated Natalis Solis Invincti, or "Birthday of the invincible Sun God," on the Winter Solstice.
- One mid-fourth century church theologian later wrote "we hold this day holy, not like the pagans because of the birth of the sun, but because of him who made it".
- Originally, the celebration of Christmas involved a simple mass, but over time Christmas has replaced a number of other holidays in many other countries, and a large number of traditions have been absorbed into the celebration in the process.
- The Christmas tree originally a German tradition, started as early as 700 A.D. In the 1800's the tradition of a Christmas tree was widespread in Germany, then moved to England and then to America through Pennsylvanian German immigrants.

According to the book "Did You ever Wonder" by Jeff Rovin, the word for Christ in Greek is Xristo. The use of the shortened form "Xmas" became popular in Europe in the 1500's. The word Xmas is so common in advertising most likely because "Xmas" and "sale" have the same number of letters, and "Xmas" is significantly shorter than Christmas.

The Christian leaders set December 25th to eclipse their holiday and I personally would say it worked. The pagans celebrated" Birthday of the Invincible Sun God" but it has been over shadowed by our celebration of "the birth day of the invincible Son of God"

CHURCH

Greek:

1577 - ekklesia (ek-klay-see-a) from ek, "out of," and klesis, "a calling" (kaleo, "to call"), was used among the Greeks of a body of citizens "gathered" to discuss the affairs of state, Acts 19:39. In the Sept. it is used to designate the "gathering" of Israel, summoned for any definite purpose, or a "gathering" regarded as representative of the whole nation. In Acts 7:38 it is used of Israel; in 19:32, 41, of a riotous mob. It has two applications to companies of Christians, (a) to the whole company of the redeemed throughout the present era, the company of which Christ said, "I will build My Church," Matthew 16:18, and which is further described as "the Church which is His Body," Eph. 1:22; (b) in the singular number (e.g. Matt.18:17, RV marg., "congregation"), to a company consisting of professed believers, e.g., Acts 20:28; I Cor. 1:2; Gal. 1:13; I Thess. 1:1), and in the plural, with reference to churches in a district.

3831 - paneguris (pan-ay-goo-ris) from pan, "all," and agora, "any kind of assembly," denoted, among the Greeks, an assembly of the people in contrast to the council of national leaders, or a "gathering" of the people in honor of a god, or for some public festival, such as the Olympic games. The word is used in Heb. 12:23, coupled with the word "church", as applied to all believers who form the body of Christ.

4128 - plethos (play-thos) "a multitude, the whole number," is translated "assembly" in Acts 23:7, RV.

*The Hebrew equivalent was qahal which in a religious sense referred to Israel as a religious body. The early church carried this religious sense over to ekklesia and considered itself to be a part of the true Israel of God, those who from any background had the faith of Abraham (Rom. 4:16-18; 9:6-8).

The early believers began to organize themselves in groups or churches with various officers. Thus, it is clear that the early church thought of itself as a visible organization as well as an "invisible" one - namely, a body of all those in space and time who had come to believe in Jesus Christ (I Cor. 12:13; Col. 1:24)

CIRCUMSPECT/CIRCUMSPECTLY

(circumspect 1x in OT, circumspectly 1x in NT)
Hebrew: CIRCUMSPECT
8104 - shamar (shaw-mar) to keep, have charge of, guard, to keep guard, keep watch and ward, protect, save life, watch, watchman, to watch for, wait for, observe, refrain, treasure up (in memory), to keep within bounds, celebrate, abstain, pay heed, to keep oneself from
King James usage: keep, observe, heed, keeper, preserve, beware, mark, watchman, wait, watch, regard, save
example: Ex 23:13

Greek: CIRCUMSPECTLY
199 - akribos (ak-ree-boce) exactly, accurately, diligently
King James usage: diligently (2x), perfect, (1x), perfectly (1x), circumspectly (1x)
example: Ep. 5:15

CLEAN AND UNCLEAN

The terms referred to ritual and not physical cleanliness, ritual purity, or defilement. Certain things were declared "clean" by the law. Some things were never clean, such as the "unclean" animals. Other things had to be purified or cleansed ritually when they became unclean (Lev. 7:21; Num.19: 11, 13; Dt. 14:3-20). The ritual for cleansing is spelled out in a number of cases; for example, that for the "leper" is recorded in Lev. 14:1-9.

Paul stated that the law was to lead men to Christ, to bring men to see their need for purity and deliverance, and that once a man by faith had his sins forgiven he no longer needed this function of the law. The law had its place, but that place was not for salvation (Gal. 3:23-29). Legislation is very easily capable of legalism. Men can follow the letter of the law and are capable of legalism. Men can follow the letter of the law and sidestep the spirit of it. This accounts for the controversies between Jesus and the Pharisees (Matt. 9:10-13; Luke 11:37-52). While Jesus himself did not himself abandon the ritual purity laws (Matt. 8:2-4), his emphasis on inward (spiritual) cleanliness rather than outward (physical) cleanliness (Matt. 15:18) soon caused the Christians to abandon the OT laws of purity.

"Clean" most frequently describes the purity maintained by avoiding contact with other human beings, abstaining from eating animals, and using things that are declared ceremonially clean. Conversely cleansing results if ritual procedures symbolizing the removal of contamination are observed.

Cleansing rituals emphasized the fact that the people were conceived and born in sin. Though conception and birth were not branded immoral (just as dying itself was not sinful), a woman who had borne a child remained unclean until she submitted to the proper purification rites (Lev. 12).

After the Israelites settled in the Promised Land, some modifications were made in the regulations (Deut. 12:15,22; 15:22).

Greek:

2513 - katharos (kath-ar-os) free from impure admixture, without blemish, spotless, is used (a) physically, e.g., Matt. 23:26; 27:59; John 13:10 (where the Lord, speaking figuratively, teaches that one who has been entirely "cleansed," needs not radical renewal, but only to to be "cleansed" from every sin into which he may fall); Heb. 10:22; Rev. 15:6. (b) in a Levitical sense, Rom. 14:20 (c) ethically, with the significance free from corrupt desire, from guilt, Matt. 5:8; John 13:10-11; Acts 20:26; I Tim. 1:5; II Tim. 1:3 (d) in a combined Levitical and ethical sense ceremonially, Luke 11:41, "all things are "clean" unto you."

2511 - kathrizo (kath-ar-id-zo) to mk. clean, to cleanse (a) from physical stains and dirt, as in the case of utensils, Mat. 23:25 (b) in a moral sense from the defilement of sin, Acts 15:9.

1245 - diakatharizo (dee-ak-ath-ar-id-zo) to cleanse thoroughly, is used in Matt. 3:12 RV.

COMELY

Hebrew:

2433 - chiyn (kheen) beauty, grace —Job 41:12

3190 - yatab (yaw-tab) to be good, be pleasing, be well, be glad —Proverbs 30:29

3303 - yapheh (yaw-feh) fair, beautiful, handsome —Ecc. 5:18

4998 - na'ah (naw-aw) to be comely, be beautiful, be befitting; to be at home, to be pleasant, (or suitable) —Song. 1:10

* not to be confused with 4999 which is na'ah that comes from 4998 but means a home; fig. a pasture, pleasant place

5000 - na'veh (naw-veh) comely, beautiful, seemly —Ps. 33:1; Ps. 147:1; Song. 1:5

8389 - to'ar (to'ar) shape, form, outline, figure, appearance —I Sam. 16:18

8597 - tiph'arah (tif-aw-raw) or tiph'ereth — come from 6286. The meaning is ornament, splendor (Ex. 28:2, Is. 3:18; 52:1), beauty, magnificence, honor, glory (Jud. 4:9), glorious name (Is.63:14), glorying (Is. 10:12), a boast, renown (Deut. 26:19), majesty (poetically used of the ark of the covenant as the seat of divine majesty, Ps. 78:61). It has to do with one's rank (Esther 1:4) —Is. 4:2

Greek:

2157 - euschemousene (yoo-skhay-mos-oo-nay) elegance of figure, gracefulness, comeliness (eu, "well," shema, "a form"), is found in this sense in I Cor. 12:23.

2158 - euschemon (yoo-skhay-mone) akin to 2157 "elegance of figure, well formed, graceful," is used in I Cor. 12:24, of parts of the body (see above); in I Cor. 7:35 RV, "(that which is) "seemly," KJV, "comely"; honourable," Mark 15:43; Acts 13:50; 17:12.

COMFORT/COMFORTER/COMFORTLESS

Greek:

3870 - parakaleo (par-ak-lay-o) to call to one's side. Used for every kind of calling to a person which is intended to produce a particular effect; comfort, exhort, desire, call for, beseech (Romans 12:1)

3874 - paraklesis (par-ak-lay-sis) a calling to one's side (para, "beside", kaleo, "to call"), either an exhortation or consolation, comfort (Luke 2: 25)

3875 - parakletos (par-ak-lay-tos) called to one's side -to call hither, toward, to, to speak cheerfully to, encourage. It is properly a verbal adjective, that is, he who has been or may be called to help, a helper. Used in the Greek writers, of a legal advisor, pleader, proxy, or advocate, one who comes forward on behalf of and as the representative of another. Thus in I John 2:1, Christ is termed our substitutionary, intercessory advocate.

Christ designates the Holy Spirit as "Paraklete" (John 14:16), and He calls Him - allos- (243), another, which means another of equal quality (and not -heteros 2087 meaning another of a different quality). Therefore the Holy Spirit is designated by Jesus Christ as equal with Himself, God (I John 2:1). This new "Paraclete", the Holy Spirit, was to witness concerning Jesus Christ (John 14:26) and to glorify Him. The Holy Spirit is called a "Paraclete" because He undertakes Christ's office in the world, while Christ is away from the world as the God-Man.

He is also called the Paraclete because He acts as Christ's substitute on earth when Christ, in John 14:16, designates Himself at the same time as the "Paraklete".

The word must not be understood as applying to Christ in the same meaning of our substitutionary Advocate, but rather as He who pleads God's cause with us (John 14:7-9)

COMMODIOUS

Greek:

428 -aneuthetos (an-yoo'-the-tos), from I (as a neg. particle) and 2111; not well set, i.e. inconvenient:- "not commodius," lit., "not well-placed" (from a, "not,"

n, euphonic, eu, "well," thetos, "from" tithemi, "to put, place"), is found in Acts 27:12, where it is said of the haven at the place called Fair Havens.

English:
commodious (ke-mo'de-es), adj. 1. spacious; roomy. 2. convenient; suitable. [Middle English, from Old French commodieux], from Medieval Latin commodiosus, from Latin commodus, convenient, "(conforming) with (due) measure". commodiously = adv. commodiousness = noun

COMPLAIN

Hebrew:
596 - an an (aw-nan) to mourn, i.e. complain—Lam. 3:39—Num. 11:1
1058 - bakah (baw-kaw) to weep, mourn with tears, make lamentation—Job 31:38
7378 - riyb (reeb)
ruwb (roob) to toss, i.e. grapple; mostly fig. to wrangle, i.e. to hold a controversy chide, complain, contend, debate, plead, rebuke, strive, to defend—Jud. 21:22
7878 - siyach (see-akh) to ponder, muse aloud; to declare, speak, talk converse (aloud, or even with oneself), utter with the mouth (Job 12:8; Prov. 6:22); to complain; to pray (Ps. 55:17; 77:3), to talk disparagingly (Ps. 69:12); to meditate, especially upon divine things (Ps. 77:6, 12; 119:15,23, 27, 48, 78, 148); to sing (Ps. 105:2); to consider, think upon something (Is.53:8). This verb conveys the idea of going over a matter in one's mind (i.e. rehearsing it, whether inwardly or outwardly).

COMPROMISE

*The word itself is not in the Bible Meaning from Nave's Topical Index -
Before litigation, enjoined —- Prov. 25:8-10; Matthew 5: 25,26; Luke 12: 58,59
also see - adjudication, arbitration, justice, court
Webster -
noun - a settling of an argument or dispute in which each side gives up part of what it wants
The act of compromising - syn. bargaining, granting concessions, finding a middle course -see agreement; An action involving compromise -syn. covenant, bargain, give and take - see agreement;
verb - make concession - syn. agree, conciliate, find a middle ground, take to arbitration - see negotiate;
Damage one's honor - syn. jeopardize, hazard, imperil—endanger or yield

CONFIRMATION

Greek:

950 - bebaioo (beb-ah-yo'-o), "to make firm, establish, make secure" (The connected adjective bebaios signifies "stable, fast, firm"), is used of "confirming" a word Mark 16:20; promises Rom. 15:8; the testimony of Christ, I Cor. 1:6; the saints by the Lord Jesus Christ, I Cor. 1:8; the saints by God, 2 Cor. 1:21 ("stablisheth"); in faith, Col. 2:7; the salvation spoken through the Lord and "confirmed" by the apostles, Heb. 2:3; the heart by grace, Heb. 13:9 ("stablished").

951 - bebaiosis (beb-ah'yo-sis), akin to 950, is used in two senses (a) "of firmness, establishment," said of the "confirmation" of the gospel, Phil. 1:7; (b) "of authoritative validity imparted," said of the settlement of a dispute by an oath to produce confidence, Heb. 6:16. The word is found frequently in the papyri of the settlement of a business transaction.

1991 - episterizo (ep-ee-stay-rid'-so), confirm, "to make to lean upon, strengthen" (epi, "upon," sterix, "a prop, support"), is used of "confirming" souls, Acts 14:22; brethren, 15:32; churches, 15:41; disciples, 18:23; in some messages ("stablishing," RV, "strengthening," KJV); the most authentic messages have sterizo in 18:23.

2964 - kuroo (koo-ro'o), "to make valid, ratify, impart authority or influence" (from kuros, "might," kurios, mighty, a head, as supreme in authority), is used of spiritual love, 2 Cor. 2:8; a human covenant, Gal. 3:15.

3315 - mesiteuo (mes-it-yoo'-o), "to act as a mediator, to interpose," is rendered "confirmed," in the KJV of Heb. 6:17.

4300 - prokuroo (prok-oo-ro-o) "before" and kuroo, "to confirm or ratify before," said of the divine confirmation of a promise given originally to Abraham, Gen. 12, and "confirmed" by the vision of the furnace and torch, Gen. 15, by the birth of Isaac, Gen. 21, and by the oath of God, Gen. 22, all before the giving of the Law, Gal. 3:17.

CONFUSION (WITH FOCUS ON AUTHOR OF CONFUSION)

**Note - the word author is not found in the original text. It is best read as God is not a God of confusion, but of peace.

181 - akatastasia (ak-at-as-tah-see-ah), 5 occurrences - "confusion" twice, "tumult" twice, and "commotion" once.

1. instability, a state of disorder, disturbance, confusion—I Corinthians 14:33

4799 - sugchusis (soong-khoo-sis), translates as "confusion", once, 1. confusion, disturbance; Ia, of riotous persons—Acts 19:29

CONSECRATE
Hebrew:
- 6942 - Qadash (kaw-dash), to be clean, make clean, pronounce clean (ceremonially or morally); to hallow, dedicate, consecrate to God (Lev. 27:14), declare as holy, treat as holy; to sanctify, purify, make oneself clean (Ex. 19:22); to be regarded as holy (Lev.10:3), show oneself holy (Eze. 38:23); to seclude. This verb captures the element of being pure or devoted to God. The concept of separation is a derived meaning, not the primary one. Qadash signifies an act or a state in which people or things are set aside for the use in the worship of God, i.e. they are consecrated or made sacred for that purpose. They must be withheld from ordinary (secular) use and treated with special care as something which belongs to God (Ex. 29:21). Otherwise, defilement makes the sanctified object unusable (cf. Deut. 22:9; Eze. 44:19; 46:20). Certain things were dedicated solely for God's consecrated use. Qadash is used with various objects: the people of Israel; the altar in the temple; the mountain; the Sabbath; a new building; and a fast. Jer. 6:4 uses the term in the sense of making the proper sacred preparations (cr. Mic. 3:5). It was anything which was reserved exclusively for God (Ex. 13:2, 12, 13; Num. 18:15, 16; I Sam. 1:24). This included certain kinds of war (I Sam. 1:24). Soldiers were sometimes consecrated before battle (Is. 13:3; Jer. 51:27). Qadash is the sphere of what is considered sacred.
- 5144 - nazar (naw-zar), to hold aloof, i.e. abstain (from food and drink, from impurity, and even from divine worship (i.e. apostatize); spec. to set apart (to sacred purposes), i.e. devote:- consecrate, separate
- 2763 - charam (khaw-ram), to seclude (by ban) to devote to religious uses (espec. destruction): to be blunt as to the nose:- make accursed, consecrate, (utterly) destroy, devote, forfeit, have a flat nose

CONSECRATION
- 4394- millu (mil-loo), a fulfilling (only in plural), i.e. (lit) a setting (of gems), or (tech) consecration (also concr. a dedicatory sacrifice):- consecration, be set.

CONSIST
CONSIST (focus on Col. 1:17)
Greek:
- 1510 - eimi (i-mee'), "to be," is rendered "consist" (lit. "is") in Luke 12:15.
- 4921 - sunistemi - (soon-is'-tay-mee), to set together, i.e. (by impl.) to introduce (favorably), or (fig.) to exhibit; to constitute:-approve, commend, consist, make, stand (with); sun, "with," histemi, "to stand," denotes, in its intransitive sense, "to stand with or fall together, to be constituted, to be compact"; it is

said of the universe as upheld by the Lord, Col. 1:17, lit., "by Him all things stand together," i.e, "consist" (the Latin consisto, "to stand together," is the exact equivalent of sunistemi).

To set, place. To set or place together with. In the perf. act joined with a dat., to stand together with (Luke 9:32); to stand together (II Pet. 3:5), referring to the earth standing out of the water and in the water in its first formation (Sept.: Gen. 1:6) and at the height of the flood (Gen. 8:2); to consist, subsist (Col. 1:17); to commend, recommend or make acceptable or illustrious (Rom. 3:5; 5:8; II Cor. 4:2; 10:18; 12:11); to commend, recommend, commit to the care or kindness of another (Rom. 16:1); to show, prove, approve, manifest.(II Cor. 6:4; 7:11; Gal 2:18).

CORNERSTONE

The NT references draw their meaning from three passages in the OT. The first is Psalm 118:22 where the stone rejected by the builders has become 'the head of the corner' (Heb. 6438 -pinnah - pin-naw')

(Gr. 1137 - goinia- go-nee'-ah). In its original context this reflected the Psalmist's own jubilation at his vindication over the enemies who had rejected him, but in its liturgical setting in the Feast of Tabernacles the psalm came to refer more to national than to personal deliverance. In rabbinical exegesis it was accorded a Messianic interpretation and this prepared the way for its use by Christ of himself in Matt. 21:42; Lk. 20:17.

Peter also used the text in Acts 4:11 and I Peter 2:7 to explain Christ's rejection by the Jews and his exaltation by God to be head of the Church.

The phrase 'head of the corner' can indicate one of the large stones near the foundations of a building which by their sheer size bind together two or more rows of stones, but it is more likely to refer to the final stone which completes an arch or is laid at the top corner of a building. This idea underlies Eph. 2:20

(Gr. 204 - akrogoniaios - ak-rog-o-nee-ah'-yos), where Paul pictures the stones of the new temple as joined together by Christ who as the cornerstone give the building completeness and unity.

The second passage (Is. 28:16) probably referred originally to the massive stonework of the Temple, symbolizing the Lord's abiding presence among his people. The juxtaposition in Isaiah of the words 'foundation', and cornerstone suggests either identity or similarity of meaning, but the NT blending of this with the third passage (Is. 8:14) in Rom. 9:33 and in I Peter 2:6 has effectively weakened the link and left emphasis on Christ as a stumbling-block to those without faith, but security to those who believe.

TO COUNSEL (VERB)

3289 - ya'ats (yaw-ats) used throughout the history of the Hebrew language, this verb occurs in the Hebrew OT approximately 80 times. To advise, counsel, admonish; to direct; to resolve, decide; to devise, plan, purpose, to consult. The first occurrence of the word is in Ex. 18:19, where Jethro suggests that Moses delegate some of his responsibilities to others.

While it most often describes the "giving of good advice," the opposite is sometimes true (II Chron. 22:3).

Rehoboam rejected the wisdom of his advisers (I Kings 12:8,13), as did Absalom (II Sam. 17:14). Ps. 33:10, 11 contrasts God's counsel and that of man. His way overrides all human machinations. God's will is sovereign and eternal (Is. 46:9-11, cf. Acts 2:23; 4:28; 5; 38;

Eph. 1:11; Heb. 6:17)

noun

"Those who give counsel." Ya'ats is frequently used in its participial form, "those who give counsel," especially in connection with political and military leaders (II Sam. 15:12; I Chron. 13:1).

"Counselor." Perhaps the most familiar use of this root is the noun form found in the messianic passage, Isa. 9:6. On the basis of the syntax involved, it is probably better to translate the familiar "Wonderful Couselor" (NASB) as "Wonder-Counsellor" or Wonder of a Counsellor." The NEB renders it "in purpose wonderful." Another possibility is that of separating the terms: "Wonderful, Counselor" (KJV).

COUNTENANCE

Hebrew:

639 - 'aph (af), nostril, nose,

face, anger—Psalm 10:4

2122 - ziyv (veev), brightness, splendor—Dan. 5:6

4758 - mar'eh (mar-eh), sight, appearance, vision, spectacle, what is seen—Judges 13:6

5869 - ayin (ah-yin), eye, of physical eye, as showing mental qualities, of mental & spiritual faculties (fig), spring, fountain—I Samuel 16:12

6440 - paniym (paw-neem'), used in a great variety of applications (lit. & fig.). from panah (6437) to turn.

Though plural in form, the noun can be singular or plural in meaning. A face, surface. Paniym can refer to a human face (Gen. 38:15); the surface of body (Gen. 1:2); the blade of axe (Ecc. 10:10);

It can also indicate a position of precedence with respect to time (Ruth 4:7); or distance (Gen. 32:3); Paniym is used as a synonym for a person's appearance (Gen. 31:2); or presence (Gen. 3:8). Since the face can be an obvious indicator of human emotions, paniym is used in conjunction with expressions of anger (Gen. 4:5), or sorrow (Job 9:27). —Numbers 6:26; Deut. 28:50 and more

Greek:
3799 - opsis (op'-sis), only Rev. 1:16 has "countenance." see Appearance
4383 - prosopon (pros'-o-pn), is translated "countenance: in Luke 9:29; Acts 2:28, and in the KJV of 2 Cor. 3:7 (RV, "face"). prosopon is translated "before" (lit, "before the presence of His coming")
2397 - eidea (id-eh-ah), akin to eidon, a sight or aspect:- countenance; (fig. idea); "to see".—Matt. 28:3
4659 - skuthropos (skoo-thro-pos), "of a sad countenance", (gloomy, sad, ops, "an eye")—Matt. 6:16

COVENANT

Hebrew:
3772 - karath (kaw-rath) to cut (off, down or asunder); to destroy or consume; spec. covenant (i.e. make an alliance or bargain, originally by cutting flesh and passing between the pieces): - chewed, be conferate, fall, feller be freed, hew down, make a league (covenant)
1285 - berith or beriyth (ber-reeth) a compact (because made by passing between pieces of flesh.) Determination, stipulation, covenant. The KJV also translates it as "league" and "confederacy". The fem. noun may come from 1262. See Gen. 15:9 for the ancient custom of ratifying solemn covenants by passing between the divided parts of victims. An agreement was possible between nations (Josh. 9:6), between individuals and friends (I Sam. 18:3), or between husband and wife (Mal. 2:14).

The most important covenant was that between God and Abraham (Gen:15:18), confirmed by Moses (Ex. 24:7, 8; 34:27), and renewed and amended after Exile through the intervention of the prophets (Is. 42:6) and the Messiah (Mal. 3:1). It was a treaty, alliance of friendship, a pledge an obligation between a monarch and his subjects, a constitution. It was a contract which was accompanied by signs, sacrifices and a solemn oath which sealed the relationship with promises of blessing for obedience and curses for disobedience.

Greek:
1242 - diatheke (dee-ath-aykay) contract, devisory will, disposition of property by will or otherwise. In Hebrew it is the rendering (to cut or divide) Gen. 15:10. It is called the "new" (Heb. 9:15), the "second" (8:7), the "better" (7:22). The

English word "Testament" taken from the titles prefixed to the Latin Versions.

2476 - histemi (his-tay-mee) to stand, establish, to weigh, to place (in the balances), "they covenanted with"

4934 - suntithemai (soon-tith-em-ahee) to put together, to determine, agree (John 9:22 and Acts 23:20); to assent (Acts 24:9); to covenant (Luke 22:5)

CRUCIFIXION, CRUCIFY

4717 - stauroo (stow-ro'-o), from stauros (4716) cross. To crucify, spoken of the punishment of crucifixation. To crucify the flesh along with its affections and lusts so as to mortify them through the faith and love of the crucified Christ (Gal. 5:24).

A form of capital punishment in the Roman Empire. The criminal's hands and feet were tied or nailed to a wooden cross, which was then lifted up and inserted into a hole in the ground. Crucifixation was excruciatingly painful, and a person could survive on the cross for several days before finally dying. The victim's legs were sometimes broken to keep him from lifting himself up to breathe. This then led to death by suffocation.

Tradition tells us that Peter was crucified, but that he asked to be crucified head downward because he felt unworthy to die as Jesus had died.

When Paul says in Galatians 6:14, "The world has been crucified unto me, and I to the world," he means that so great was his regard for his crucified Savior that the world no longer had any more charm for him than the corpse of a crucified malefactor would have, nor did he take any more delight in worldly things than a person expiring on a cross would take delight in the objects around him.

DART/DARTS
Hebrew:
2671 - chets (khayts) arrow —Proverbs 7:23
4551 - macca' (mas-saw) quarry, quarrying, breaking out; missile, dart—Job 41:26
7973 - shelach (sheh-lakh) weapon, missile; sprout; shoot—II Chron. 32:5
8455 - towthach (to-thawkh) a weapon perhaps a club or mace—Job 41:29

Greek:
1002 - bolis (bol-ece) a missile, dart, javelin—Hebrews 12:20
956 - belos (bel-os) a missle, dart, javelin, arrow; an instrument of war, a light spear. "Fiery darts" (Eph. 6:16) are so called in allusion to the habit of discharging darts from the bow while they are on fire or armed with some combustible material.

DEAD SEA SCROLLS
A collection of Scrolls, Manuscripts, and manuscript fragments dating from the third century B.C. to the first century A.D. Most of them were found in 1947-1952 in caves along the northern shore of the Dead Sea. They include the Hebrew, Aramaic, and Greek manuscripts of parts of the OT and are the oldest existing manuscripts of the Bible. The Dead Seas Scrolls include an entire text of the book of Isaiah. Most of the scrolls are made of leather (some papyrus) and are believed to have been part of the library of a religious community of Essenes (an Ascetic and communal sect within Judaism) at Qumran. They were stored (or perhaps hidden) in pottery jars, where they remained for 2,000 years.

In 1947 an Arab shepherd threw a stone into a cave near the Dead Sea and heard the tinkle of breaking pottery. Seven manuscripts came out of that cave, leaving hundreds of fragments. Since then, other caves have yielded additional OT manuscripts and related Jewish material.

Non-biblical scrolls - The treasure includes two kinds of writings, the first of which are the nonbiblical scrolls. These writings show how the sect at Qumran regarded the books of the OT as the product of God by His Spirit through the prophets. Repeatedly, they refer to "the Law of Moses and the Prophets," or "what God spoke through Moses and all the Prophets." Their attitude toward the OT and their terminology is similar to that of Christ and His apostles.

Biblical scrolls - Ancient copies of manuscripts compared directly with our Hebrew Bible. They demonstrate how accurately the ancient scribes did their work.

All the OT books, except one, have been found in the caves. The book of Esther has not yet been identified. Some are represented in many copies. Some only in fragments.

DERIDE

Hebrew:

7832 - sachaq (saw-khak'), to laugh, play, mock; to laugh (usually in contempt or derision), to sport; to make sport, to jest; to play (incuding instrumental music, singing, dancing)—Hab. 1:10

*play 10x, laugh 10x, rejoice 3x, scorn 3x, sport 3x, merry 2x, mock 2x, deride 1x, derision 1x, mockers 1x

Greek:

1592 -ekmukterizo (ek-mook-ter-id'-zo), to sneer at, to scoff at—Luke 16:14; 23:35

DIADEM

Greek:

1238 - diadema (dee-ad'-ay-mah), is derived from diadeo, "to bind round." It was the kingly ornament for the head, and especially the blue band marked with white, used to bind on the turban or tiara of Persian kings. It was adopted by Alexander the Great and his successors. Among the Greeks and Romans it was the distinctive badge of royalty. Diocletian was the first Roman emperor to wear it constantly. The word is found Rev. 12:3; 13:1; 19:12, in which passages it symbolizes the rule respectively of the Dragon, the Beast, and Christ. In the Sept. Esth. 1:11; 2:17; in some mss. in 6:8 and 8:15; also in Isa. 62:3–4. "Vines Expository Dictionary"

Greek Lexicon

1238 - diadem, not a crown, but a filament of silk, linen or some related thing. Contrast stephanos (4735), crown, referring to the conquerors crown, and not a royal crown.

DISCERN

Hebrew:

995 - biyn (bene) to understand; discern, to separate mentally (or distinguish), understand,:- attend, consider, be cunning, diligently, direct, eloquent, feel, inform, instruct, have intelligence, know, look well to —I Kings 3:9

3045 - yada (yaw-dah) to know (to ascertain by seeing); used in a great variety of senses, fig., lit., euphem. and infer. (incl. observation, care, recognition; and caus. instruction, designation, punishment. etc), acknowledge, acquaintance, advise, answer, appoint discern, discover, declare understand, have understanding, comprehend, be aware endued with familiar friend, feel —II Sam. 19:35; Eze. 44:23

5234 - nakar (naw-kar) to acknowledge, to scrutinize, i.e. look intently at, perceive —Ezra 3:13; Job 4:16.

7200 - ra'ah (raw-aw) to see, lit. or fig.; advise self, appear, approve, behold, discern, consider —Mal. 3:18.

8085 - shama (shaw-mah) to hear intelligently (often with impl. of attention or obedience), tell, understand, witness —II Sam. 14:17; I Kings 3:11

Greek:

1252 - diakrino (dee-ak-ree-no) to decide; to hesitate, to separate thoroughly, to withdraw from, or oppose; fig. to discriminate, to judge, be partial, stagger, waiver —Matthew 16:3; I Cor. 11:29

1253 - diakrisis (dee-ak-ree-sis) judicial estimation: - discern, disputation — Hebrew 5:14; I Cor. 12:10.

1381 - dokimazo (dok-im-ad-zo) to test; to approve: - allow, discern, examine — Luke 12:56

350 - anakrino (an-ak-ree-no) to interrogate, determine, to scrutinize, question, discern, ask, examine, judge, search —I Cor. 2:14

DISCIPLE/DISCIPLESHIP

Hebrew:

3928 - limmud (lim-mood) instructed:-accustomed, disciple, learned, taught, used

Greek:

3101 - mathetes (math-ay-tes) a learner, i.e. pupil:- disciple, a learner (from manthano), to learn, from a root "math" - indicating thought accompanied by endeavor - in contrast to didaskalos, "a teacher"; hence it denotes "one who follows one's teaching, as the "disciples" of John, (Mat. 9: 14), of the pharisees, (Mat. 22: 16) of Moses, (John 9:28).

A disciple was not only a pupil, but an adherent (same as glue - to stick to); hence they are spoken of a imitators of their teacher; (John 8:31; 15:8)

3100 - matheteuo (math-ayt-yoo-o) the verb usage: the sense of being the "disciple" of a person. Been made a disciple (Mat. 13: 52), it is used in the transitive sense in the active voice in (Mat. 28: 19 and Acts 14:21)

During Jesus' earthly ministry, and during the days of the early church, the term that was used most frequently to designate one of Jesus' followers was "disciple" (mathetes)(262 times). Its different in the OT and in the rest of the NT. There is a scarcity of words for "disciple" in the OT, and mathetes does not occur at all in the Epistles and Revelation. However, other terms and expressions point to theological concepts of discipleship everywhere in Scripture when Jesus walked with his disciples during his early ministry. Yet OT prepares for that relationship, and the Epistles and Revelation describe how that relationship was carried out after Jesus' ascension.

The idea of discipleship in the OT is the covenant relationship between Israel and God.

1. God and Israel
2. Jesus and His Disciples
3. Following God (Israel walking in the ways of God)
4. Personal commitment to Jesus
5. The Church follows the Risen Christ
6. The goals of Discipleship
7. Toward others: Servanthood
8. Toward the world

Jesus concludes the Great Commision with the crucial element of discipleship: "I am with you always, to the very end of the age" (Matt. 28:20)

As disciples become salt and light in this world, walking the narrow path, loving and providing hope to the world, they become living examples for others to follow. Such as Paul has said "Follow my example, as I follow the example of Christ" (I Cor. 11:1)

THE DIVIDED KINGDOM

The two political states of Judah and Israel that came into existence shortly after the death of Solomon and survived together until the fall of Israel in 722 B.C. The Northern Kingdom (Israel), and The Southern Kingdom (Judah), were operated as separate countries from approx. 924 B.C. until 722 B.C. At times the two countries were at war with each other. At other times they were friendly towards each other. The Northern Kingdom came to an end in 722 when the Assyrians destroyed the capital city, Samaria. The Southern Kingdom fell to the Babylonians in 587 B.C. (it was reborn under the leadership of men like

Zerubbabel, Joshua, Haggai, Zechariah, Ezra, and Nehemiah, beginning in 538 with the return from exile, but did not become an independent state except briefly under the Maccabeans.) The events that led to the division can be traced to the reign of Solomon. From a Religious perspective, Judah and Israel continued the apostate practices of Solomon. The beginning of the Divided Kingdom marked the beginning of the end for the nations of Judah and Israel as influential entities in Palestine. The Southern Kingdom included the city of Jerusalem and the temple. Levites and Priests from the Northern Kingdom came to Judah, as well as Israelites who set their hearts to seek the Lord. In the providence and purposes of God, Judah was separated from Israel in order to preserve the integrity of the worship of Yahweh (2 Chron. 13:9-11). The majority of Judah's Kings were godly, while Israel did not have one King that was faithful to Jehovah.

*1 Kings 11:9 -33; 2 Chron. 10:1-11; I Sam. 11:8; 2 Sam. 20:1; I Kings 12:16

DROPSY
Greek:
5203 - hudropikos (hoo-dro-pik-os) from a compound of (5204 - hudor - water), and (3700 - as looking watery); dropsical, suffering from dropsy —Luke 14:2

English:
Edema is a condition of abnormally large volulme in the circulatory system or in tissues between the body's cells (interstitial spaces). Normally the body maintains a balance of fluid in tissues by ensuring that the same amount of water entering the body also leaves it. In edema, either too much fluid moves from the blood vessels into the tissues, or not enough fluid moves from the tissues back into the blood vessels. This fluid imbalance can cause mild to severe swelling in one or more parts of the body. Endema is a sign of an underlying problem, rather than a disease unto itself. Treatment: reducing sodium intake; maintaining proper weight; exercise; elevation of the legs; use of support stockings; massage; and travel breaks;

DRUNK WITH WINE ... EXCESS
Greek:
Asotia - (as-o-tee'-ah), unsavedness, i.e. (by impl.) profigacy:- excess, riot.
Debauchery - indulgence in sensuality, orgies; seduction from virtue or duty.
　　The original sense is "incurable", then we have the ideas of dissipation, gluttony, volutuousness, and indiscipline. The only OT instances are - Prov. 7:11 and 28:7. The reference in Luke 15:7 is to the prodical's life of dissipation, and in Ephesians 5:18 (drunk with wine, wherein is excess; but be filled with the spirit), KJV.

ESV - drunk with wine which is debauchery.
Titus 1:6; I Peter 4:4 to a disorderly life (rather than voluptuousness)

DUMB

Hebrew:

481—alam (aw~lam'), to tie fast; hence (of the mouth) to be tongue-tied:- bind, be dumb, put to silence—Ps. 39:2

483 - 'illem (ii-lame'), from 481; speechless' - dumb (man)—Ex. 4:11 ; Hab. 2:18

1748 - duwmam (doo-mawm'), from 1826; still; adverb—silently: dumb, silent, quietly wait—Hab. 2:19

Greek:

216—alalos (al'-al-os), mute:- dumb—Mk, 7:37

880—aphonos (af-o~nos), voiceless, i.e. mute (by nature or choice); fig. unmeaning:- dumb, without signification—Acts 8:32; Peter 2:16

2974 - kophos (ko-fos'), blunted, i.e. (fig.) of hearing (deaf) or speech (dumb):—deaf, dumb, speechless—Luke 11:14

4623 - siopao (see-o-pah'-o), (silence, i.e. a hush; prop. mutenes, i.e. involuntary stillness, or inability to speak; and thus differing from 4602, which is rather a voluntary refusal or indisposition to speak, although the terms are often used synonymously); to be dumb (but not deaf also, like 2974), to be calm (as quiet water):- dumb (hold) peace—Luke 1 :20

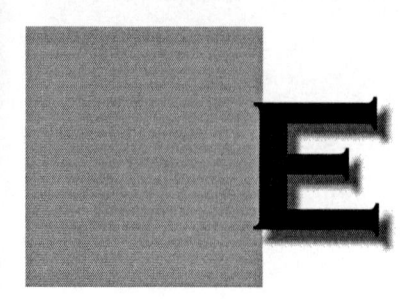

EARTH

Hebrew:

127 - adamah (ad-aw-maw) (a) ground (as general, tilled, yielding sustenance) (b) piece of ground, a specific plot of land; (c) earth substance (for building or constructing); (d) ground as earth's visible surface; (e) land, territory, country; (f) whole inhabited earth; (g) city in Napthtali

King James Usage - Total: 225 times

(lands - 125/ earth - 53/ ground - 43/ country -1/ husbandman - 2/ husbandry - example: Genesis 3:17; Genesis 3:19; Genesis 5:29

776 - erets (eh-rets) 1. land, earth (a) earth -1. whole earth (as opposed to a part); 2. earth (as opposed to heaven); 3. earth (inhabitants)

(b) land - 1. country, territory; district, region, tribal territory, piece of ground; land of Canaan, Israel; inhabitants of land; Sheol, land without return, (under) world; city (state) (c) ground, surface of the earth - ground; soil

(d) (in phrases) - people of the land; space or distance of country (in measurements of distance); level or plain country; land of the living; end (s) of the earth;

(e) (almost wholly late in usage) - lands, countries;

(f) often in contrast to Canaan

King James Usage - Total: 2504 times

(land - 1543/ earth - 712/ country - 140/ ground - 98/ world - 4/ way - 3/ common - 1/ field - 1/ nations -1/ wilderness & 4057 - 1)

example: Genesis 1:26

EASTER

3957 - pasch-a (pas-khah), from (6453) which means pecach (peh-sakh), passover, sacrifice of passover, animal victim of the passover.

In most languages of Christian societies, other than English, German & some Slavic languages, the holiday name is derived from Pesach, the Hebrew name of Passover a Jewish holiday to which the Christian Easter is intimately linked. Easter depends on Passover, not only for its symbolic meaning, but also for its position in the calendar; The paschal sacrifice (which was accustomed to be offered for the people's deliverance of old from Egypt). The paschal lamb, i.e. the lamb the Israelites were accustomed to slay and eat on the 14th day of the month of Nisan (the first month of their year) in memory of the day on which their Fathers preparing to depart from Egypt, were bidden by God to slay and eat a lamb, and sprinkle their door posts with its blood, that the destroying angel, seeing the blood might passover their dwellings; Christ crucified is likened to the slain paschal lamb, the pascha supper, the paschal feast, the feast of the Passover, extending from the 14th to the 20th day of the month - Nisan. The English name "Easter", and the German, "ostern", derive from the name of Germanic Goddess of the Dawn (thus, of Spring, as the dawn of the year) - called aster, astre, and ostre, in various dialects of Old English. In England, the Annual Festive time in her honor was in the "month of Easter" or ostumonath equivalent to April.

EASTER in the Early Church

The observance of any non-Jewish special holiday throughout the Christian year is believed by some to be an innovation post dating the Early Church. The ecclesiastical historian Socrates Scholasticus (b. 380), attributes the observance of Easter by the church to the perpetuation of local custom, "just as many other customs have been established," stating that neither Jesus nor his disciples enjoined in keeping of this or any other festival. However, when read in context, this is not a rejection or denigration of the celebration, but is merely part of a defense of the diverse methods for computing its date. Although he describes the details of the Easter celebration as deriving from local custom, he insists the feast itself is universally observed.

Latin - (pascha or Festa Paschalia) Greek - (pascha)
Hebrew - (pascha)

EFFECTUAL—Adjective (describe a noun)

Greek:

1756 - energes - active, powerful in action — energy, (work comes from same root word)

VERBS (action)

1753 - energeia (en-erg-iah) efficiency (energy), operation, strong, (effectual), working

1754 - energeo - to put forth power, be operative, to work (the ususal meaning is rendered by the verb to work effectually)

James 5:16 would translate - the supplication or prayer of a righteous man availeth or is capable of producing results much in its working

EFFEMINATE
Greek:
- 3120 - malakos (mal-ak-os'), soft" i.e. fine (clothing); fig. a catamite:- effeminate; "soft to the touch" (Lat., mollis, Eng., "mollify," "emollient," etc.), is used (a) of raiment, Matthew 11:8 (twice); Luke 7:25; (b) metaphorically, in a bad sense, I Cor. 6:9, "effeminate," not simply of a male who practices forms of lewdness, but persons in general, who are guilty of addiction to sins of the flesh, voluptuous.
- *note - catamite is a noun for a boy kept by a pederast. [Latin catamitus, from Catamitus, Ganymede from Etruscan Catmite, from Greek Ganumedes, GANYMEDE (cupbearer of the gods).]
- * pederast is a noun for a man who practices pederasty. [Greek paiderstes, "lover of boys": paid-, PEDO + erastes, lover, from erasthai, to love, akin to eros, love, Eros.]

EFFULGENCE
Greek:
- 541 - apaugasma (ap-ow'-gas-mah), "radiance, effulgence," is used of light shining from a luminous body
- (apo, "from," and auge, "brightness"). The word is found in Heb. 1:3, where it is used of the Son of God as "being the effulgence of His glory.' The word "effulgence" exactly corresponds (in its Latin form) to apaugasma. The "glory" of God expresses all that He is in His nature and His actings and their manifestation. The Son, being one with the Father in Godhood, is in Himself, and ever was, the shining forth of the "glory," manifesting in Himself all that God is and does, all, for instance, that is involved in His being "the very image of His substance," and in His creative acts, His sustaining power, and in His making purification of sins, with all that pertains thereto and issues from it.

ELI ELI LAMA SABACHTHANI "ELOI ELOI"
- 2241 - eli (ay-lee), my God: - eli
- My God, My God why has thou forsaken me
- The forms of the first word translated vary in the two narratives, being Eli (Matt.) & Eloi (Mark). With some perversions of form probably from Psalm 22:1 ('Eli 'Eli lama 'azabhtani). A statement uttered by Jesus on the cross just before His death, translated, "My God My God why has thou forsaken me? There is an interesting but difficult problem in connection with interpretation of this passage. There is a mixture of Aramaic & Hebrew. The various readings and translations of the latter word, sabachthani, only add confusion to an effort at explanation of the real statement. Certainly the Aramaic played a great part in

the translation and transmission of the original. The Spirit revealed by Jesus in His utterance seems to be very much like that displayed in the Garden when He cried out to have the cup removed from Him.

EMMANUEL - IMMANUEL - IMMANUW'EL

Hebrew:

6005 - immanuel or immanuw'el (im-maw-noo-ale) God with us, God [is] with us, or with us is God

(1) symbolic and prophetic name of the Messiah, the Christ, prophesying that he would be born of a virgin and would be "God with us"

From the root - 5973 - im (eem) = with, against, beside, toward, as long as, in spite of and 410 - el (ale) = strength, strong, mighty, majesty, power, God, Jehovah *it is also the name of Isaiah's son

Greek:

1694 - emmanuel (em-man-oo-ale) God with us, the title applied to the Messiah

According to "Bible Questions and Answers" Bible question: what does Immanuel mean?

Bible answer: The word Immanuel appears 3 times in the Bible.

The Sign - the word Immanuel occurs 2 times in the OT. The first time is at the announcement that Jesus would be virgin born. Therefore the Lord Himself will give you a sign: Behold a virgin will be with child and bear a son and shall call his name Immanuel (NASB) Is. 7:14. Then it will sweep on into Judah, it will overflow and pass through, it will reach even to the neck; and the spread of its wings will fill the breath or your land, 0 Immanuel (NASB) Is. 8:8. Some have said that the Hebrew word for "virgin" should be simply, young woman. But that is not exactly correct since the word means young unmarried woman. God is giving us a sign, a virgin gives birth to a child. Is it a sign when a married woman gives birth? If all God is saying is that a sexually active woman gives birth, we must ask, "what kind of sign is that?" The conclusion is obvious. The passage is referring to a virgin is giving birth. That is the sign of Immanuel- Jesus! The next time Immanuel occurs in the Bible is in the next chapter of Isaiah. Here it says that God - Immanuel, owns the land of Israel. This means that Immanuel lived before He became a human baby.

The Meaning - what is the meaning of Immanuel? The Apostle Matthew explains in the Gospel of Matthew.

BEHOLD, THE VIRGIN SHALL BE WITH CHILD, AND SHALL BEAR A SON, AND THEY SHALL CALL HIS NAME IMMANUEL, "which translated means" "GOD WITH US" (NASB) Matthew 1 :23

Conclusion: Immanuel means "God with us." That is who Jesus is - our God!

EMULATIONS
Greek:

3863 - parazeloo (par-ad-zay-lo-o) "to provoke to jealousy" (para, "beside," used intensively, and zeloo), is found in Rom. 10:19 and 11:11, of God's dealings with Israel through his merciful dealings with Gentiles with a view to stirring his fellow nationals to a sense of their need and responsibilities regarding the gospel; in I Cor. 10:22, of the provocation of God on the part of believers who compromise their divine relationship by partaking of the table of demons; in Gal 5:20, of the works of the flesh

ENEMIES

6862 - tsar (tsar) adjective—from root word meaning to bind, tie up, shut up, suffer distress, to press hard upon, to show hostility toward, to vex; 1. narrow, tight; 2. straits, distress; 3. adversary, foe, enemy, oppressor; 4. hard pebble, flint (enemy 37, adversary 26, trouble 17, distress 5, affliction 3, foes 2, narrow 2, strait 2, flint 1 sorrow 1)

English definition (as noun)

1. one who feels hatred toward, intends injury to, or opposes another; a foe; 2 a. a hostile power or force, such as a nation; b. a member or unit of such a force; 3. a group of foes or hostile forces; 4. something destructive or injurious in its effects

(as adjective) of, relating to, or being a hostile power or force

ENOCH

Hebrew:

2585 - henoch -chanowk (khan-oke); initiated; a patriach; Enoch

1. son of Cain (Gen. 4:17) after whom a city was named
2. son of Jared and father of Methuselah (Gen. 5:18, 21). Enoch was a man of outstanding sanctity who enjoyed close fellowhip with God (Gen. 5:22,24: for the expression 'walked with God', cf Gen. 6:9; Mi. 6:8; Mal. 2:6). Like Elijah (2 Ki. 2:11), he was received into the presence of God without dying (Gen. 5:24).

It is probable that the language of Psalm 49:15; 73:24 reflects the story of Enoch.

In that case the example of Enoch's assumption played a part in the origin of Jewish hope for life with God beyond death. (In the Apocrypha, Wisdom 4:10-14 also treats Enoch as the outstanding example of the righteous man's hope of eternal life.)

Greek:

1802 - enok (en-oke')

In the NT Hebrews 11:5 attributes Enoch's assumption to his faith; the expression 'pleased God' is the Greek Setuagint translation of 'walked with God' (Gen. 5:24). Jude 14 quotes a prophecy attibuted to Enoch.

ERR
Greek:
- 635 - apop1anao (ap-op-1an-ah'-o), "to cause to wander away from, to lead astray from" (apo, "from" and planao, "to cause to wander." Is used metaphoric all of leading into error, Mark 1322, KN, "seduce," RV, "lead astray"; I Tim. 6:10, in the passive voice, KN, "have erred," RV, "have been led astray."
- 795 - astocheo (as-tokh-eh'o), " to miss the mark, fail" (a, negative, stochos, "a mark"), is used only in the Pastoral Epistles, I Tim11:6, "having swerved"; 6:21 and 2 Tim. 2:18, "have erred."
- 4105 - planao (plan-ah-o), in the active voice, signifies "to cause to wander, lead astray, deceive" (plane, "a wandering"; cf. Eng., "planet"); in the passive voice, "to be led astray, to err." It is translated "err," in Matt. 22:29; Mark 12:24,27; Heb. 3:10; James 1:16 (KN, "do not err," RV, "be not deceived"); 5:19.

THE ETHIOPIAN EUNUCH
This Prime Minister was sent to Jerusalem under the authority of Queen Candace of Ethiopia. His main task was to seek knowledge concerning the new religion that revolutionized Israel, and then to return to his own land. (Ethiopians then were under Judaism, while at the same period Europe was worshiping idols). He journeyed over a thousand miles across Africa before reaching his destination. While there, he gathered Biblical material regarding Christ and His divine will. When his visit to Jerusalem came to an end, the eunuch mounted his chariot and traveled toward Gaza with a roll, which contained the fifty-third chapter of Isaiah. It was this chapter he was reading when Philip the Evangelist approached his chariot, questioning him about his understanding of the Scriptures. He informed Philip that he obtained no values in what he had read and asked him to explain the material to him (since he only knew Judaism). So, the Evangelist did accordingly, and when they saw water, the Ethiopian received baptism (Acts 8:26 - 39). This eunuch left Ethiopia as a queen's treasurer, but it is almost certain that he became a more important figure when he returned to his land. Today Ethiopia still upholds the Christian faith which was instituted by this Prime Minister nearly two thousand years ago.

The British writer C.F. Rey in his book, "Unconquered Abysinnia" (Ethiopia), declares that Ethiopia was a great nation when the first book of the Bible was written, and was practicing Christianity while Europe was still worshiping Thor and Odin (Acts 17:23; I Thess. 1:9.)

EXCESS
Greek:
192 - akraisia (ak-ras-ee-a) denotes "want of strength" (a negative, kratos, "stength"), hence, "want of self control, incontinence," Matt. 23:25, "excess"; I Cor. 7:5, "incontinency.

401 - anachusis (an-akh—oo-sis) " pouring out, overflowing" (akin to anacheo, "to pour out"), is used metaphorically in I Pet. 4.4, "excess" said of the riotous conduct described in verse 3.

810 - asotia (as-otee-ah) unsavedness, "prodigality, profligacy, riot" (from a, negative, and sozo, "to save"); it is translated "riot" in Eph. 5:18, RV, for KJV, "excess"; in Titus 1:6 and I Pet. 4:4, "riot" in KJV and RV. A synonymous noun is aselgeia, "lasciviousness, outrageous conduct, wanton violence.

3632 - oinophlugia (oy-nof-loog-ee-ah) an overflow (or surplus) of wine, i.e. vinolency (drunkenness):"excess of wine"

EXEGESIS
From a Greek word meaning 'to lead out'; involves an extensive and critical interpretation of the authoritative text, especially of a holy scripture, such as the Old and New Testaments of the Bible, the Talmud, the Midreash, the Qur'an, etc. Exegesis also is used to describe the elucidation (to make clear or plain; clarify) of philosophical and legal texts. An exegete is a practitioner of this art, and the adjectival form is exegetic. The plural of the word exegesis is exegeses.

The word exegesis can mean explanation, but as a technical term it means "to draw the meaning out of" a given text.

Exegesis may be contrasted with eisegesis, which means to read one's own interpretation into a given text. In general, exegesis presumes an attempt to view the text objectively, while eisegesis implies more subjectivity.

An exegesis is the interpretation and understanding of a text on the basis of the text itself. A hermenueutic is a practical application of a certain method or theory of interpretation, often revolving around the contemporary relevance of the text in question. Traditional exegesis requires the following: analysis of significant words in the text in regard to translation; examination of the general historical and cultural context, confirmation of the limits of the passage, and lastly, examination of the context within the text. According to some forms of christianity, two different forms of exegesis exist: revealed and rational.

* Revealed exegesis considers that the Holy Ghost inspired the authors of the scriptural texts, and so the words of those texts convey a divine revelation.

* Rational exegesis bases its operation on the idea that the authors have their own inspiration, so their works result from human intelligence.

A common published form of a biblical exegesis is known as a 'bible commentary'.

EXPRESS IMAGE (HEBREWS 1:3)

5481- charakter (khar-ak-tare), a graver (the tool or the person), i.e. (by impl.) engraving ([character] the figure stamped, i.e. an exact copy or [fig.] representation):- express image.

Representation, express image (English, character). Occurs only in Hebrews 1:3, where it is translated "express image," referring to the person of Jesus Christ. Distinguished from charagma (5480), graven mark. See (1504) eikon, to be like, or resemble. The Greek Lexicon.

"A tool for engraving" (from charasso, "to cut into, to engross"; "character," "characteristic"); then, "a stamp" or "impress," as on a coin or a seal, in which case the seal or die which makes an impression bears the "image" produced by it, and vice versa, all the features of the "image" correspond respectively with those of the instrument producing it. In the NT it is used metaphorically in Hebrews 1:3 of the Son of God as "the very image (marg. 'the impress') of His substance." the prase expresses the fact that the Son "is both personally distinct from, and yet literally equal to, Him of whose essence He is the adequate imprint." The Son of God is not merely his "image" (His charakter), He is the "image" or impress of His substance, or essence. The Vine's Complete Expository Dictionary.

F

FACE
Hebrew:

6440 - paniym (paw-neem'), "face" (as the part that turns). This noun appears in biblical Hebrew about 2,100 times and in all periods except when it occurs with the names of persons and places, it always appears in the plural. It is also attested in Ugaritic, Akkadian, Phoenician, Moabite, and Ethiopic.

In its most basic meaning, this noun refers to the "face" of something. First it refers to the face of a human being (Abram fell on his face).

A look on someones face or one's "countenance" (Cain's countenance fell) To pay something to someone's "face" (to pay them personally),

The surface or visible side of a thing, (the Spirit of God moved upon the face of the waters),

The Bible speaks of God as though He had a "face" "... For therefore I have seen thy face, as though I had seen the face of God" (Gen. 33:10).

The word paniym is used to identify the bread that was kept in the holy place. The KJV translates it as "the showbread," while the NASB renders "the bread of the presence" (Num. 4:7). This bread was always kept in the presence of God.

FAITH
Hebrew - only used 2 times

529 - emuwn (ay-moon) established, i.e. trusty; also - trustworthiness: - faith (ful); trust

530 - emunah (em-oo-naw)—certainty; steady;

Greek:

4102 - pistis ((pis-tis) from 3982: persuasion; conviction (of religious truth, or the truthfulness of Gold or a religious teacher), expecially reliance upon Christ for salvation; the system of religious (gospel) truth itself: - assurance, belief, believe, faith, fidelity

Used always in the NT of "faith in Fad or Christ, or things spiritual"

THE WORD WINDOW

FAITHFULNESS

Hebrew:

Noun-

530 - emunah - (em-oo-naw) firmness, security, steady, truly, truth, verily

In the Hebrew O.T. it occurs 49 times as a noun, mainly in Ps. (22 times). The first time its used, is in relation to Moses hands (Exodus 17:12). He was sat on the stone- "and his hands were "steady" until the going down of the sun".
The basic meaning of emunah is "certainty" and faithfulness. Man shows himself faithful in relations with his fellow man (I Sam. 26:23), but generally, the person to whom one is faithful is the Lord Himself, (II Chron. 19:9). All His works reveal His "faithfulness" (Ps. 33:4). His commandments are an expression of His "faithfulness" (Ps. 119:86).

The word "emunah" is synonymous with "sedeg" (righteousness- Isa. 11:5), with hesed (lovingkindness - Ps. 98:3), and with mispat (justice - Jer. 5:1). The relationship between God and Israel is best described by the word hesed (love), but as a synonym emunah fits well. Man's acts (Prov. 12:22) and speech (Prov. 12:17), must reflect his favored status with God. As in the marriage relationship, "faithfulness" is not optional. For the relation to be established the two parties are required to respond to each other in "faithfulness". In Jesus "faithfulness" was established when people witness in Him God's grace (hesed), and truth (emunah): John puts them side by side in John 1:18.

The Greek Septuagint translations are: "aletheia" -225- (truthfulness; dependability; uprightness; truth; reality) and "pistos" -4103 - (trustworthy; faithfulness; reliability; confidence; faith)

King James Version translates: faithfulness; truth; set office; faithfully; faithful

Verb -

—539 - aman - to be certain; enduring; to build up or support; to trust; believe; to foster as a parent or nurse; to render (or be) firm or faithful; steadfast;
found 100 times in the O.T.

Three words are derived from this verb: "aman" (amen) "emet" (true) "emunah" (faithfulness)

FAMILIAR

Hebrew:

3045 - yada (yaw-dah) know; to know; learn to know; perceive and see; perceive; find out and discern; desire; admit; acknowledge; confess; to recognize; to know by experience; to make known; be acquainted with; to reveal; be revealed; to make oneself known; to be instructed; declare; reveal oneself —Job 19:14 (know 645, known 105, knowledge 19, perceive 18, shew 17, tell 8, wist 7, understand 7, certainly 7, acknowledge 6, acquaintence 6, consider 6, declare 6, teach 5, misc. 85)

7965 - shalown (shaw-lome) completeness, soundness, welfare, peace

(a) completeness (in number); (b) safety, soundness (in body); (c) welfare, health, prosperity; (d) peace, quiet, tranquility, contentment; (e) peace, friendship - 1. of human relationships - 2. with God, especially in covenant relationship; (f) peace (from war); (g) peace (as adjective) —Psalm 41:9

(peace 175, well 14, peaceably 9, welfare 5, salute 4, prosperity 4, did 3, safe 3, health 2, peaceable 2, misc.15)

Familiar spirits - consulting of, forbidden — Lev 19:31; 20:6, 27; Deut. 18:10, 11 vain - Isaiah 8:19; 19:3

those who consulted, to be cut off — Lev. 20:6, 27 instances of those who consulted—

Saul—I Samuel 28:3-25; I Chronicles 10:13

We're not provided with a definition for familiar spirits. It seems that all references related to familiar spirits are tied to the two definitions used 3045 - the knowing or getting to know, the revealing, etc ... and 7965 - that deals with relationships).

FAVOR/FAVORED

Hebrew:

7522 - ratsown (raw-tsone) "favor; goodwill; acceptance; will; desire; pleasure." Used 56 times in OT

Represents a concrete reaction of the superior to an inferior. When used of God, ratsown may represent that which is shown in His blessings: "And for the precious things of the earth and fullness thereof, and for the good will of him that dwelt in the bush"

(Deut. 33:16). This word represents the position one enjoys before a superior who is favorably disposed toward him. Also signifies a voluntary or arbitrary decision.

7521 - ratsah (raw-tsaw) Verb - to be pleased with or favorable to, be delighted with, be pleased to make friends with; be graciously received; make oneself favored." Occurs 50 times (O.T.)

Greek:

5485 - charis (khar-ece) denotes (a) objectively, "grace in a person, graciousness," (b) subjectively, 1. "grace on the part of a giver, favor, kindness,"

2. "a sense of favor received, thanks," It is rendered "favor in Lk. 1:30; From chairo (5463), to rejoice, or chara (5479), joy, favor, acceptance, a kindness granted or desired, a benefit, thanks, gratitude, grace. A favor of the loving-

kindness of God finding its only motive in the bounty and freeheartedness of the Giver; unearned and unmerited favor, Charis stands in direct antithesis to erga (2041), works, the two being mutually exclusive. God's grace affects man's sinfulness and not only forgives the repentant sinner, but brings joy and thankfulness to him. In contrast to charis stands eleos (1656), mercy, which is concerned not with sin itself, as does charis, but with the misery brought upon the sinner as a consequence of that sin.

5487 - charitoo (khar-ee-to-o) Verb - to endow with charis, primarily signified "to make graceful or gracious," and came to denote, in Hellenistic Greek, "to cause to find favor" Luke 1:28 It does not here mean to endue with grace. Grace implies more than favor; grace is a free gift, favor may be deserved or gained.

FEEL, FEELING, FELT

Hebrew:

995 - biyn (bene) to separate mentally (or distinguish), understand: - consider attend, be cunning, diligently, direct, discern, eloquent, feel, know, look well to, perceive, view

3045 - yada (yaw-dah) to know (to ascertain by seeing) - used many ways: observation, care, recognition. acknowledge, aquaintance, instruct, kinsmen (cause to, let, make), familiar, friend

4184 - muwsh (moosh) to touch: - feel, handle

4959 - mash ash (maw-shash) to feel, to grope, feel

Greek:

524 - apalgeo (ap-alg-eh-o) to bear troubles with greater equanimity, to cease to feel pain for, past feeling

1097 - ginosko (ghin-oce-ko) to learn to know, get a knowledge, to become known, to know, perceive

3958 - pascho (pas-kho) to experience a sensation or impression (usually painful), feel, passion, suffer, vex

4834 - sumpatheo (soom-path-eh-o) to have a fellow- feeling for or with = touched with the feeling of (have compassion)

5426 - phroneo (fron-eh-o) to think, to be minded (I understand), to excercise the mind, to have an opinion

5584 - pselaphao (psay-laf-ah-o) to handle, touch, feel, to seek after tokens of a person or a thing

examples:
Hebrew - 995 - ps 58:9
3045 - Job 20:20

4184 - Gen 27:21
4959 - Gen 27:12

Greek - 524 - Eph. 4:19
1097 - Mk. 5:29
3958 - Acts 28: 5
5584 - Acts 17:27

FELLOWSHIP

Hebrew:

2266 - chabar (khaw-bar) to unite, join, bind together, be joined, coupled, be in league, heap up, have fellowship with, be compact, be a charmer

a. 1. to unite, be joined
    2. to tie magic charm, charm
b. to unite with, make an ally of; join, ally; to be allied with, be united, to be joined together
c. to join together, pile up (words)
d. to join oneself to, make an alliance, league together—Lev. 6:2

8667 - tesuwmeth (tes-oo-meth) pledge:- fellowship, security, deposit—Psalm 94:20

Greek:

2842 - koinonia (koy-nohn-ee-ah) fellowship, association, community, communion, joint participation, intimacy, intercourse, the right hand as a sign and pledge of Fellowship (in fulfilling the Apostolic office)—Acts 2:42; I Cor. 1:9; etc ... (fellowship 12, communion 4, communication 1, distribution 1, contribution 1, to communicate 1)

2844 - koinonos (koy-no-nos) a partner, associate, comrade, companion, sharer
a. of the altar in Jerusalem which the sacrifices are offered
1. sharing in worship of the Jews
    b. partakers of (or with) demons
1. brought to fellowship with them because they are authors of heathen worship—I Cor. 10:20

3352 - metoche (met-okh-ay) a sharing, communion, fellowship—II Cor. 6:14

4790 - sukoinoneo (soong-koy-no-neh-o) to become a partaker together with others, or to have fellowship with a thing—Eph. 5:11

FERVENT/FERVENTLY
Greek:
2204 - zeo (dzeh-o) 1. to boil with heat, be hot
a. used of water
b. metaph.
1. used of boiling anger, love, zeal, for what is good or bad
2. fervent in spirit, said of zeal for what is good KJ usage - be fervent 1, fervent 1
2205 - zeolos (dzay-los) 1. excitement of mind, ardour, fervour of spirit
a. zeal, ardour in embracing, pursuing, or defending anything (1) zeal in behalf, for a person or thing (2) the fierceness of indignation, punitive zeal; b. an envious and contentious rivalry, jealousy
KJ - zeal 6, indignation 2, envy 1, envying 5, fervent mind 1, jealous 1, emulation 1
1754 - energeo (en-erg-eh-o) 1. to be operative, be at work, put forth power; to work for one, aid one; 2. to effect; 3. to display one's activity, show one's self operative. KJ usage - work 12, showforth (one's) self 2, wrought 1, be effectual 1, effectually work 1, effectual fervent 1, work effectually in 1, be might in 1, to do 1
1618 - ektenenes (ek-ten-ace) 1. stretched out; 2. metaph. - intent, earnestly, assiduosly. KJ usage - without ceasing 1, fervent 1
1619 - agonizomai (ag-o-nid-zom-ahee) 1. to enter a contest: contend in the gymnastic games; 2. to contend with adversaries, fight; 3. metaph. - to contend, struggle, with difficult and danger; 4. to endeavor with strenuous zeal, strive to obtain something. King James usage - strive 3, fight 3, labor fervently 1

Examples: 2204 - Acts 18:25; 2205 - II Cor. 7:7
1754 - Mat. 14:2; Mark 6:14; I Cor. 12:6, 11; Eph 1:11; 1618 - I Peter 4:8
1619 - Col. 4:12; I Peter 1:22

FINISHER
Greek:
5051 - teleiotes (tel-i-o-tace'), from teleios (5046), what achieves its goal. A completer, perfecter, one who brings something through to the goal so as to win and receive the prize, a consummater: - finisher—Hebrews 12:2
Looking unto Jesus the author and finisher of our faith, who for the joy that was set before him endured the cross, despising the shame, and is set down at the right hand of the throne of God.

FIRST FRUIT(S)

Hebrew:

1061 - bikkuwr (bik-koor) first fruits, (a) first of crops and fruit that ripened, was gathered and offered to God according to the ritual of Pentecost

(b) the bread made of the new grain offered at Pentecost

(c) the day of the First Fruits (Pentecost)—Numbers 28:26.

*also spelled bikkurim, and as a noun appears 16 times. The "first grain and fruit" harvested was to be offered to God (Num.28:26) in recognition of God's ownership of the land and His sovereignty over nature. Bread of the "first fruits" was bread made of the first harvest grain, presented to God at Pentecost (Lev. 23:20).

(first fruit 14, first ripe 2, first ripe figs 1, hasty fruit 1)

7225 - re'shith (ray-sheeth) first, beginning, best, chief, choice part. It means the first (in place, time, order, or rank), first of its kind (e.g., with regard to time), firstfruits (Gen. 49:3, cf., Rev 3:14 where Jesus Christ is the Source of creation); the beginning of a fixed period of time (Gen. 1:1; Deut. 11:12), commencement, origin (Gen. 10:10; Jer. 28:1); former state (Job 42:12), former times (Is.46:10); the best, the choicest, firstling. Re'shith forms part of the first word in the Bible. Some modernistic translators have attempted to translate this first phrase as: "When God began to create ..... " Both the Sept. translation of Gen. 1:1 and the Gr. construction of John 1:1 properly translate the text. They leave no doubt that Gen. 1:1 was the initial act of creation.

Re'shith refers to the initiation of a series of historical events (Gen. 10:10); Jer. 26:1) as well as a foundation (Ps. 111:10; Prov. 1:7). It is the start, not the end (Job 8:7; 42:12). Quite often it is used of the firstfruits which were offered in the tabernacle (Lev. 2:12; 23:10; Deut. 18:4; 26:10; Neh. 12:44) and the choicest "fruits" were so distinguished (Num. 18:12)

(beginning 18, first fruit 11, first 9, chief 8, misc. 5)

Greek:

536 - aparche (ap-ar-khay) denotes, primarily, "an offering of firstruits" (akin to aparchomai, "to make a beginning"; in sacrifices, "to offer firstfruits"). Though the English word is plural in each of its occurrences except Romans 11:16, the Greek word is always singular. Two Hebrew words are thus translated, one meaning the "chief' or "principal part," e.g., Num. 18:12; Prov. 3:9; there other, "the earliest ripe of the crop or of the tree," e.g., Exod. 23:16; Neh. 10:35; they are found together, e.g. in Exodus 23:19, "the first of the firstfruits."

The term applied in things spiritual, (a) to the presence of the Holy Spirit with the believer as the firstfruits of the full harvest of the Cross, Rom. 8:23;

(b) to Christ Himself in resurrection in relation to all believers who have fallen

asleep, I Cor.15:20, 23; (c) to the earliest believers in a country in relation to those of their countrymen subsequently converted, Rom. 16:5; I Cor. 1:15; (d) to the believers of this age in relation to the whole of the redeemed,
II Thess. 2:13, (see Note below) and James 1:18.

*Note: 1. In James 1:15 the qualifying phrase, "a kind of," may suggest a certain falling short, on the part of those mentioned, of what they might be.

2. In II Thess. 2:13, instead of aparches, "from the beginning," there is an alternative reading, well supported, - aparchen- "(God chose you) as firstfruits;" (first fruit~8)

FOES

341 - oyeb (o-yabe') noun, from 340 - to hate (as one of an opposite tribe or party) hence to be hostile. Hating, an adversary, enemy (personal or nation) (enemy 280, foes 2) Note the difference between enemies and foes as used here and bear in mind that an adjective describes a noun

TO FORGIVE

Hebrew:

5545 - salah or calach (saw-lakh) "to forgive." This verb appears 46 times in the OT. The meaning "to forgive is limited to biblical and rabbinic Hebrew; in Akkadian, the word means "to sprinkle,"and in Aramaic and Syriac signifies "to pour out." The meaning of salah in Ugaritic is debatable.

The first biblical occurrence is in Moses' prayer of intercession on behalf of the Israelites: " … It is a stiffnecked people; and forgive our iniquity and our sin, and take us for thine inheritance": (Ex. 34:9). The basic meaning undergoes no change throughout the OT. God is always the subject of "forgiveness." No other OT verb means "to forgive," although several verbs include "forgiveness" in the range of meanings given a particular context (e.g. nasa and awon in Ex. 16:63).

Most occurrences of salah are in the sacrificial laws of Leviticus and Numbers. In the typology of the OT, sacrifices foreshadowed the accomplished work of Jesus Christ, and the OT believer was assured of "forgiveness" based on sacrifice: "And the priest shall make an atonement [for him in regard to his sin]" (Numbers 15:25, 28), "And it shall be forgiven him"
(Lev. 4:26). The mediators of the atonement were the priests who offered the sacrifice. The sacrifice was ordained by God to promise ultimate "forgiveness" in God's sacrifice of His own Son. Moreover, sacrifice was appropriately connected to atonement, as there is no forgiveness without the shedding of blood (Lev. 4:20; cf. Heb 9:22).

Out of His grace, God alone "forgives" sin.

THE WORD WINDOW

Greek:

In the Septuagint, salah is most frequently translated by hileos einai (to be gracious; be merciful), hilaskesthai ("to propitiate, expiate") and apievai ("to forgive, pardon, leave, cancel").

The translation "to forgive" is found in most English versions (KJV, RSV, NASB, NIV and at times also "to pardon" (KJV, RSV)

FORSAKE

Hebrew:

488 - alman (al-mawn) widowed, forsaken, (forsaken as a widow)—Jer. 51:5

2308 - chadal (khawdal) desist, be lacking or idle, cease, end, fail, forsake, leave (off), let alone, unoccupied—Judges 9:11

5203 - natash (naw-tash) to leave, permit, forsake, cast off or away, reject, suffer, join, spread out or abroad, be loosed, cease, abandon, quit, hang loose, cast down, lie fallow, let fall, forgo, draw—Prov. 6:20 (forsake 15, leave 12, spread 3, spread abroad 1, drawn 1, fall 1, lie 1, loosed 1, cast off 1)

5800 - azab (aw-zab) about 215 times - to leave, forsake, abandon, leave behind, to be left over, to let go, to depart from something (Gen. 2:24), to leave entirely - finality or completeness (Isa 7:16), something to remain while one leaves the scene (Gen 39:12) ; to put distance between - in a spiritual or intellectual sense (Ps. 37:8), to let go or allow to leave (Ps. 49:10)

7503 - rapha (raw-faw) to sink down, drop, to sink, relax, abate, withdraw, to let drop, abandon, refrain, let alone —Deut. 4:31; Ps. 138:8 (feeble 6, fail 4, weaken 4, go 4, alone 4, idle 3, stay 3, slack 3, faint 2, forsake 2, abated 1, cease 1)

Greek:

646 - apostasia (ap-os-tas-see-ah) a falling away, defection, apostasy—Acts 21:21

657 - apostassomai (ap-ot-as-som-ahee) to set apart, separate, to separate to one's self, withdraw one's self from anyone (bid farewell) —Luke 14:33

2641 - kataleipo (kat-al-i-po) to leave behind, to depart from, leave, to reserve, to cause to be left over, like our "leave behind", it is used of one who on being called away cannot take another with him, like our "leave" leave alone, disregard (of those who sail pass a place without stopping)—II Peter 2:15

FRANKINCENSE

Greek:

3030 -libanos (lib'an-os), from a Semitic verb signifying "to be white," a vegetable resin, bitter and glittering, obtained by incisions in the bark of the arbor thuris, "lithe incense tree," and especially imported through Arabia; it was used for fumigation at sacrifices, Exod. 30:7, etc., or for perfume, Song of Solomon 3:6. The Indian variety is called looban. It was among the offerings brought by the wise men, Matt. 2:11. In Rev. 18:13 it is listed among the commodities of Babylon. The "incense" of Rev. 8:3 should be "frankincense."

FULLERS SOAP

- 3526 - kabac (kaw-bas'), to trample; hence to wash (prop. by stamping with the feet), whether lit. or fig. (including the fulling process or fig. :- fuller - wash (ing)
- Full - to increase the weight and the bulk (of cloth) by shrinking and beating (pressing)
- Fuller - worker who shrinks and thickens cloth fibers through wetting and beating the material
- borith mekabbeshim, i.e. "alkali of those treading cloth". mention is made (Prov. 25:20; Jer. 2:22), of nitre and also (Mal. 3:2) of soap (Hebrew - borith) used by the fuller in his operations.
- It does not appear that the Hebrews were acquainted with what is now called "soap," which is a compound of alkaline carbonates with oleaginous matter. The word purely is lit. "as with bor" used in Isaiah 1:25
- (RV thoroughly, "as with lye"). This word means "cleanness," and hence that which make clear, or pure, alkali. The ancients made use of alkali mingled with oil, instead of soap (Job 9:30) and also in smelting metals, to make them melt and flow more readily and purely.
- **Malachi 3:2 - the refiner's fire purifies, and fullers' (laundry men's) soap cleanses

G

GAP THEORY
The theory that there is a time gap of aeons -eon- (an indefinitely long period of time; an age; eternity), between Gen. 1:2 and 1:3. According to this theory, the scenario is as follows: (1:1) God created the universe; (1:2) then the earth became formless and void (a time gap); (1:3) then the earth was remade. In this gap, according to the theory, geological time must have developed.

GENESIS
Greek, having the meanings of "birth", "creation", "cause", "beginning", "source", and "origin", also called The First Book of Moses, is the first book of the Torah (five books of Moses), The Tanakh, and the Old Testatent. In Hebrew it is called B'reshit, after the first word of the Hebrew (meaning "in the beginning"). This is in line with the pattern of naming the other four books of the Pentateuch.

GENTILE/GENTILES
Hebrew:
1471 - gowy - ghoy (go-ee) a. nation, people
1. usually non-Hebrew people; 2. of descendants of Abraham; 3. of Israel
b. of swarm of locust, other animals (fig.) c. Goyim or Ghoyim = Nations

It originates from 1465. It means person, inhabitant, populace, people, tribe, nation; the non-Israeli or heathen peoples. It is a general word used to refer to nations at large. Scholars now believe that the basic idea of "ghoy" is a defined group of people or a large segment of a given body which is defined by context. The plural form (ghoyim) is often used to refer to the pagan nations which surrounded Israel. They were defined politically, ethnically, and territorially (Gen. 10:5). In its general sense the term could even be applied to the descendants of Abraham (Gen. 12:2; 17:20; 21:18). Moses called Israel by that word (Ex.33:13). "Ghoyim" wicked (Deut. 9:4,5), abominable (Deut. 18:9), and idolatrous (II Kings 17:29). God, through Moses and the prophets, warned the Israelites not to imitate the other nations (Deut. 32:28). God planned to save them through the Messiah (Is. 2:2; 11:10; 42:6; 60:10) ("Nations" used 374x, "Heathen" used 143x, "Gentiles" used 30x and "People" used 11x)

Greek:
1483 - ethnikos (eth-nee-koce) like the gentiles—Gal. 2:14
1484 - ethnos (eth-nos) 1. a multitude (whether of men or beasts) associated or living together; a. a company, troop, swarm
2. multitude of individuals of the same nature or genus
a. the human family
3. tribe, nation, people, group
4. in the OT, foreign nations not worshipping the true God, pagans, "gentiles"
5. Paul uses the term for "Gentile Christians"
("Gentiles" used 93x, "Nation" used 64x, "Heathen" used 5x, "People" used 2x)
Gentile—Mat. 12:21
Nations—Mat. 28:19
1672 - hellen - (hel-lane) 1. a Greek either by nationality, whether a native of the main land or of the Greek islands or colonies
2. in a wider sense it embraces all nations not Jews that made the language, customs and learning of the Greeks their own, the primary reference is to a difference of religion and worship
Gentile—Romans 2:9, 10
Greek—Galatians 3:28

GENTLENESS

Greek (emphasis on Gal. 5:22)
5544 - crestotes (khray-stot'-ace) benignity, kindness. It is joined to philanthropia (5363), philanthropy, anoche (463), forbearance (Rom. 2:4), and opposite apotomia (663), severity or cutting something short and quickly (Rom. 3:12), "kindness" (II Cor. 6:6; Eph. 2:7; Col 3:12; Titus 3:4); "gentleness" (Galatians 5:22). It is the grace which pervades the whole nature, mellowing all which would have been harsh and austere. Thus, wine is chrestos (5543), mellowed with age (Luke 5:39); Christ's yoke is chrestos, as having nothing harsh or galling about it (Matt. 11:30). Contrast agathousune (19), it pertains to character without the necessary altrustic externalization found in agathousune, active benignity. Chrestotes has only the harmlessness of the dove, not the wisdom of the serpent, which agathosune may have indicated in sharpness and rebuke.
Related words: chrestos, kind or good in oneself, mellow.

GIANT(S)

English - (noun) a person or thing of extraordinary size or importance: Greek Mythology - one of a race of man like beings of enormous strength and stature who warred with the Olympians, by whom they were finally destroyed; any similar being in folklore or myth; (adjective) of immense size; gigantic; huge.

Vulgar Latin: gangante (unattested)

Latin: gigas

Hebrew: 1368 - gibbor (ghib-bore) powerful; warrior, tyrant: - champion, chief, giant, man, mighty man (from 1397 which means a valiant man or warrior; generally a person)

King James usage: valiant, upright, champion, chief mightiest, strongest

5303 - nephiyl (nef-eel) a feller; i.e. a bully or tyrant: - giant

(from 5307) naphal which means to fall; to fall (of violent death); to fall prostrate, prostrate oneself; to fall upon; attack; desert; fall in the hand of; to fall short; fail; result; to settle; waste away; be inferior to cause to fall, fell throw down; knock out; overthrow

7497 - rapha (raw-faw) a giant: - giant; (from 7495 in the sense of invigorating - which means to cure or mend; to heal; physician; repair; make whole)

example:

1368 - Num. 13:33 - sons of Anak, which come of the giants (5303) - Num. 13:33 - And there we saw the giants

Gen. 6:4 - There were giants in the earth

7497 - II Sam. 21:16 - which was of the sons of the giants

(7495) - Ex. 15:26 - for I am the Lord that "healeth" thee —-(JEHOVAH RAPHA)

GLUTTON

Greek:

1064 - gaster (gas-tare) denotes "a belly"; it is used in Titus 1:12, with the adjective argos, "idle" metaphorically, to signify a glutton, RV, "(idle) gulttons" [KJV "(slow) bellies"]; elsewhere, Luke 1:31. See womb.

GLUTTONOUS

5314 - phagos (fag-os) a glutton, akin to phago, "to eat," a form used for the aorist or past tense of esthio, denotes "a glutton," Matthew 11:19; Luke 7:34

GNASH

Hebrew:

2786 - charaq (khaw-rak') to grate the teeth: - gnash

Greek:
1030 - brugmos (broog-mos'), from 1031; a grating (of the teeth):- gnashing
1031 - brucho (a primary verb; to grate the teeth (in pain or rage):- gnash; Bruco primarily "to bite or eat greedily" and denotes "to grind or gnash with the teeth,: —— Acts 7:54

GODHEAD
Greek:
  2304 - theios (thi'-os) god-like (divinity):- divine (2x); Godhead (lx)
  Means (divine) and is used (la) of the power of God (II Pet. 1:3), and (lb) of His nature (II Pet. 1:4), both of which proceed from Himself. (2) In Acts 17:29 it is used as a noun with the definite article, to denote the Godhead, the Deity, the one true God.
  2305- theiotes (thi-ot'-ace) (Godhead (lx). derived from theios (2304), and is to be distinguished from theotes (2320 - Col. 2:9). In Rom. 1:20 the apostle is declaring how much of God may be known from the revelation of Himself which He has made in the creation, from those vestiges of Himself which men may everywhere trace in the world around them. Yet it is not the personal God whom any man may learn to know by these aids; He can be known only by the revelation of Himself in His Son. Theotes (indicates the divine essence of Godhood, the personality of God; theiotes (2305), the attributes of God, His divine nature and properties.
  2320- theotes (theh-ot'-ace) Godhead (lx). This word stresses deity, the state of being God [see 2305] —-Col. 2:9

GODLY
Hebrew:
  430 - elohiym (el-o-heem), plural of gods in the ordinary sense; but specifically used of the supreme God; occasionally applied by way of deference to magistrates; and sometimes as a superlative:angels, God (gods) (dess, -ly)— Mal. 2:15
  2623 - chaciyd (khaw-seed), from 2616; prop. kind, i.e. (religiously) pious (a saint):- godly (man), good, holy, (one), merciful, saint, [un-] godly—Ps.4:3; PS.12:1

Greek:
  2152 - eusebes (yoo-seb-ace), from 2095 and 4576; well-reverent, i.e. pious:- devout, godly—2 Peter 2:9 2153 - eusebos (yoo-seb-oce'), adv. from 2152; piously: - godly—2 Tim. 3:12

2316 - the os (theh'os), a deity, especially (with 3588) the supreme Divinity; fig. a magistrate; by Heb. very:—x exceeding, God, god [-ly, -ward]—2 Cor. 1:12

GOODNESS

Greek (emphasis on Gal. 5:22)

19 - agathosune (ag-ath-o-soo'nay); active goodness. In Galatians 5:22, referred to as goodness; but the English word is inclusive of particular graces whereas Paul must refer to a particular grace. It is more than chrestotes (5544), a mellowing of character. It is character energized expressing itself in agathon (18), active good. Thus chrestotes in action is agathosune. A person may display his agathosune, his zeal for goodness and truth in rebuking, correcting, chastising. Christ's righteous indignation in the temple (Matt. 21:13) showed His agathosune, but not His chrestotes, mellowness.

Agathosune does not spare sharpness and rebuke to cause good, agathon in others, whereas chrestotes demonstrates only its softness and benignity (a kindly or gracious act).

GREAT WHITE THRONE

2362 - throne - This "Judgment seat" is to be distinguished from the premillennial, earthly throne of Christ, (Mat. 25:31) and the postmillennial "Great White Throne" at which only the "dead" will appear—Rev. 20:11 "And I saw a great white throne, and him that sat on it, from whose face the earth and the heaven fled away; and there was found no place (12) And I saw the dead, small and great, stand before God; and the books were opened, which is the book of life: and the dead were judged out of those things which were written in the books, according to their works."

GREEK ALPHABET

1. the letters of a language, arranged in the order fixed by custom. 2. A system of characters or symbols representing sounds or things. The basic or elementary principles; rudiments.

THE ENGLISH WORD ALPHABET COMES FROM THE FIRST 2 LETTERS OF THE GREEK ALPHABET—-alpha & beta

Our interest lies in Hellenistic Greek which identifies the kind of Greek used roughly in number of years as the number of the Antichrist and split equally between AD and BC. The vernacular Hellenistic, the popular "street" Greek, the "lingua franca" of the period is called Koine Greek.

This is a guide to transliteration - from Greek to English with Hellenistic Greek pronunciation:

Name	Transliteration	Phonetic sound	Example
alpha	(ahl-fah)	a	a as in father
beta	(bay-tah)	b	b as in ball
gamma	(gahm-ma)	g	g as in gone
delta	(dell-tah)	d	d as in dog
epsilon	(ep-sih-lawn)	e	e as in met
zeta	(dzay-tah)	z	z as in adze
eta	(ay-tah)	e	e as in they
theta	(thay-tah)	th	th as in thin
iota	(ee-oh-tah)	i	i as in fit or machine
kappa	(cap-ah)	k	k as in kill (soft accent)
lambda	(lahm-dah)	l	l as in land
mu	(moo)	m	m as in mother
nu	(new)	n	n as in now
xi	(ksee) x	x	as in wax, likes, asks
omicron	(au-mih-crawn)	o	o as in log
pi	(pea, pie)	p	p as in pea
rho	(hrow)	r	r (rh) as in her, courage
sigma	(sig-mah)	s	s as in sit, sign
tau	(rhyme with "how")	t	t as in tell (soft accent)
upsilon	(oop-sih-lawn)	u	u as in new (German "u")
phi	(fee)	ph	ph as in phone, graphic
chi, khi	(key)	ch	kh as in ach, or Bach
psi	(psee)	ps	ps as in ships, or lips
omega	(oh-may-gah)	o	o as in only, obey

THE WORD WINDOW

GROSS (TO WAX)

Hebrew:

6205 - araphel (ar-aw-fel), gloom (as a lowering sky):- (gloss, thick) dark (cloud) —- IS. 60:2; Jer. 13:16

Greek:

3975 - pachuno (pakh-oo'-no), from pachus, "thick," signifies "to thicken, fatten"; in the passive voice, "to grow fat"; metaphorically said of the heart, to wax gross or dull —- Matt. 13:15; Acts 28:27

H

HALLOWED

Hebrew:

6942 - qadash (kaw-dash) to consecrate, sanctify, prepare, dedicate, be hallowed, be holy, be sanctified, be separate; to show oneself sacred or majestic; to be honoured, be treated as sacred; to set apart as sacred, to observe as holy, keep sacred, hallow; to be consecrated, to devote to regard or treat as sacred or hallow, to keep oneself apart or separate; to cause himself to be hallowed (of God) to be observed as holy, to consecrate oneself

Greek:

37 - hagiazo (hag-ee-ad-zo) to make holy, to purify, hallow, sanctify, be holy

To withdraw from fellowship with the world by first gaining fellowship with God.
Hagiazo is a verb and means to render holy, separated from sin in general and in particular as abstaining from fornication
Matthew 6:9 "hallowed be thy name" (to be set apart as holy, sanctified, consecrated)

HAM

Hebrew:

2526 - cham (khawm) ot: - hot or warm (from the tropical habitat), son of Noah father of Cush (Ethiopia), Mizraim (Egypt), Phut (Libya), and Canaan (Palestine) grandfather of many, however, included in his lineage is "Jebus" son of Canaan. "Jebus" is the father of the Jebusite race (Jerusalem)—Josh. 18:28; Judg. 1:21

A curse was put on Ham's son Canaan for looking at his naked father (Noah), the curse was not on Ham. Ham the patriarch was not cursed dark but created (born) dark. He is considered the paternal ancestor of Ethiopia, Egypt, Libya, Carthage, and many African tribes, Northern an Southern Arabia, Crete, Cyprus, Asia Minor (Hittite), a portion of Israel, and the black Americans. These progenies are called Hamites.

The Israelites, before possessing sovereignty over the black Canaanites, experienced an earlier slaver themselves, in "Negro-Egypt", an occurrence which fulfilled the prophecy "servant of servants" (Ex. 1:8-14; 3:7-22; Gen. 9:25). The children of the Hebrew race (nation) were born on the continent of Africa, and much of their social, natural and applied sciences, customs, etc., were borrowed from the African Negroes.

Gen. 10:6, 9:22-25; Deut. 7:1; 11:23; Nahum 3:9; Hab. 3:7; I Chron. 4:40; Ps. 78:51; Ps. 105:23 -27; 106:22

HAM'S DESCENDANTS

Cush	Mizraim	Phut	Canaan
Ethiopia	Egypt	Libya or Cyrenacia Phoenicians	Canaanites and

KEYWORDS

Name	Definition	Origin
Amorite	Highlanders	Descendants of Canaan
Canaan	Humble	Fourth Son of Ham
Cush	Black	First Son of Ham
Cushan	Blackness	Derived from Cush
Cushi	Ethiopia	Derived from Cush
Cushite	Ethiopia	Derived from Cush
Heth	Hittite	Second son of Canaan
Hittite		Descendants of Heth
Hivite	Villagers	Descendants of Canaan
Jebus	Jerusalem	Third son of Canaan
Mizraim	Egypt	Second Son of Ham
Phut	Libya	Third son of Ham
Sidon or Zidon	Fishing	First son of Canaan

The black sons of Ham and their offspring are characterized throughout the Bible and their nations are the first to be mentioned therein (Gen. 2:10-13). Within the past 150 years, archaeological and anthropological research in the ruins of Ethiopia, Egypt, and Canaan (Palestine), has produced overwhelming evidence that the children of Ham had developed nations and civilizations as old as Man's history.

HARDENED (IN DEALING WITH PHARAOH)
Hebrew:

2388 - chazaq (khaw-zak'), to be bound fast, be attached, to make firm, strengthen, support; to preserve; to be firm, be strong, be courageous, be valiant, be helpful; to conquer; to seize, retain, hold fast, lean, play the man, become (wax) mighty, prevail, be recovered, behave self valiantly, withstand, keep; to gird; to encourage; to harden, to be obdurate (I Kings 2:2; Ezra 10:4; Haggai 2:4). It is a word frequently used to describe battle scenes. Twelve times in the Book of Exodus chazaq is used in describing the condition of Pharaoh's heart. Pharaoh was an obstinate sinner who reacted negatively to God's decree. Since the Hebrews thought of God as being in control of everything, this included Pharaoh. Pharaoh had the choice of compliance with God's will, but he refused. Compare Acts 4:25-28. The term was also frequently used for construction. — Exodus 7:13

*strong 48x, repair 47x, hold 37x, strengthened 28 x

3513 - kabad (kaw-bad) or kabed (kaw-bade'), to be heavy, be weighty; to be grievious, be severe; to be numerous; to be honored; be renowned; be honored; be esteemed; be glorious; to be dull; to show great or mighty; to be wealthy; to be rich; to make heavy; make hard; to make dull; to oppress; to get renown (Gen. 13:2; Is. 6:10; Nah. 3:15). The main idea is "to be heavy," which then becomes wealthy (heavy with goods, property, money), sinful (heavy handed), great (large, heavy), noteworthy (impressive, heavy), honored (carries a lot of weight), glory (heavy, awesome). See doxa (1391) in the NT Lexical Aids. That glory was ultimately revealed in Jesus (John 1:14; 17:1-5). — Exodus 8:15

*honour 34x, glorify 14x, honourable 14x, heavy 13x, harden 7x, glorious 5x, sore 3x, made heavy 3x, chargeable 2x, great 2x, many 2x, heavier 2x, promote 2x

HEALING
Hebrew:

4832 - marpe (mar-pay), healing, cure - Jer. 8:15

health, profit, sound (mind) - Prov. 4:22, 6:15 healing, incurable (with negative) - 2 Chron. 21:18

7495 - rapha - (raw-faw) to heal

1. of God - Gen. 20:17, 50:2; 2. healer; physician- Jer. 8:22; 3. of hurts of nations; to be healed; to heal in order to get healed

8585 - ta-alah - (teh-aw-law)

1. conduit, water course, trench

1. healing (of new flesh & skin forming over wound) a. bandage, plaster (for healing of wound)

THE WORD WINDOW

I kings 18:32, Job 38:25, Isa.36:2, Jer. 8:15, 30:13, 46:11, Ek. 31:14
724 - aruwkah (ar-oo-kaw) health, restoration

Greek:
 2386 - iama (ee-am-ah) - a means of healing, remedy, medicine - I Cor.12:9, 12:28, 12:30
 2323 - therapeuo (ther-ap-yoo-o) - to serve, do service, to heal, cure, restore to health
 2322 - therapeia - (ther-ap-i-ah) - service rendered by one to another, medical service, caring, household service, attendant - I Cor. 12:28

HEARING

akoe (ak-o-ay)—the sense of hearing; the organ of hearing, the ear; the thing heard; a. instruct, namely oral, b. of preaching the gospel, c. hearsay, report or rumor

HEBREW ALPHABET

Translitered as	NAME	Pronounce as
’	’aleph	(silent)
b (bh 12	beth	ball
g (gh or g)	gimel	gone
d (dh or d)	daleth	dog
h	he	hat
w or v	vav	very
z	zayin	zeal
ḥ or ch	heth	bach (the composer)
ṭ	teth	ten
y	yodh	yet
k (kh or k)	kaph	king
l	lamedh	long
m	mem	men
n	nun	new
s	samech	sign
‘	‘ayin	(silent)
p (ph or P)	pe	pea (phone)

THE WORD WINDOW

HEBREW ALPHABET (CONTINUED)

Transliterated as	NAME	Pronounce as
s(. under s) or ts	tsadhe	hits
q	qoph	unique
r	resh	run
ś	sin	so
š or sh	shin	ship
t (th or t)	tav	toe (then)

HEIR–JOINT HEIR

Hebrew:

3423 - yarash (yaw-rash) to occupy (by driving out previous tenants and possessing in their place); to seize, to rob, to inherit; also to expel, to impoverish, to ruin; cast out, consume, destroy, disinherit, dispossess—Gen 15:3; Jer. 49:2

Greek:

2816 - kleronomeo (klay-rom-om-eh-o) to be an heir to, inherit—Heb. 1:14

2818 - kleronomos (klay-ron-om-os) denotes one who obtains a lot or portion, a sharer by lot

a. the person to whom property is to pass on the death of the owner, (Matt.21:38)

b. one to whom something has been assigned by God, on possession of which however, he as not yet entered, as Abraham, Rom. 4:13, 14; Heb. 6:17; Christ, Heb. 1:12; the poor saints, James 2:5;

c. believers, inasmuch as they share in the new order of things to be ushered in at the return of Christ, Romans 8:17; Gal. 3:29; 4:7; Titus 3:7;

d. one who receives something other than by merit, as Noah, Heb. 11:7

4789 - sunkleronomos (soong-klay-ron-om-os) from sun (4862), together, and kleronomos (2818), an heir, one who has a lot or who is allotted something. One who participates in the same lot, a joint heir (Rom. 8:17). Refers to a personal equality based on an equality of possession. In Hebrews 11:9 it speaks of Isaac and Jacob in their relation to Abraham; in I Peter 3:7 of women in relation to their husbands being joint heirs of the grace of life; in Ephesians 3:6 of the Gentiles being joint heirs with Israel (see also Eph. 1:11)

THE WORD WINDOW

HERESY

Greek:

139 - hairesis (hah-ee-res-is) (a) "a choosing, choice" (from haireomai, "to choose"); then, "that which is chosen," and hence, "an opinion," especially a self-willed opinion, which is substituted for submission to the power of truth, and leads to division and the formation of sects, Gal. 5:20; such erroneous opinons are frequently the outcome of personal preference or the prospect of advantage; see II Pet. 2:1, where "destructive" (RV) signifies leading to ruin; some assign even this to (b); in the papyri the prevalent meaning is "choice", (b) "a sect"; this secondary meaning, resulting from (a), is the dominating significance in the NT—Acts 5:17; 15:5, 14; 26:5; 28:22; "heresies" in I Cor. 11:19

Dissensions arising from diversity of opinions and aims

Heresy from haireo or haireomai (138) to choose, select. A form of religious worship, discipline or opinion (Acts 5:17; 24:14; Gal. 5:20). In contrast to schisma (4978), schism, it is only theoretical. One can hold different views than the majority and remain in the same body but he is a heretic, But when he tears himself away, schizo (4977) then he is schismatic. Heresy is theoretically schismatic; schismaticalness is practical heresy.

INDIGNATION

Hebrew:

2194 - za'am (zaw-am), to denounce, express indignation, be indignant, be defiant, show anger—Dan. 11:30

2195 -za'am (zah-am), from 2194, anger, indignation—Is. 66:14

2534 - chemah (khay-maw), heat, rage, hot displeasure, indignation, anger, wrath, poison, bottles, fever, venom, burning anger—Esther 5:9

3707 - ka'ac (kaw-as), to be angry, be vexed, be indignant, be wroth, be grieved, provoke to anger & wrath—Neh. 4:11

7110 - qetseph - (keh-tsef), wrath, anger of God, of man, splinter, twig, broken twig, meaning dubious—Deut. 29:28

Greek:

23 - aganakteo (ag-an-ak-teh'-o), "to be indignant, be moved with indignation" (from agan, "much," achomai, "to grieve"), is translated "were moved with indignation" of the ten disciples against James & John, Matt. 20:24; in Mark 10:41, RV (KJV, "they began to be much displeased"). To be greatly afflicted.

24 - aganaktesis (ag-an-ak'-tay-sis), from 23; indignation;

*Note: (1) orge, "wrath," is translated "indignation" in Rev. 14:10, KJV; RV, "angeL" (2) thumos, see anger, (3) In Acts 5:17, the KJV translated zelos by "indignation" (RV "jealousy"); in Heb. 10:27, KJV, "indignation" (RV, "fierceness")

INFIRMITY—INFIRMITIES

Hebrew:

1738 - davah (daw-veh) to be sick (as if in menstruation): - infirmity—Lev. 12:2

2470 - chalah (khaw-law) to be rubbed or worn; hence (fig) to be weak, sick, afflicted; or to grieve, make sick; also to stroke (in flattering), entreat:- beseech, be diseased, (put to) grief, be grieved, (be grievous, infirmity, intreat, lay to, put to pain, make prayer, sick sore, be sorry, make suit, woman in travail, be (become) weak, be wounded—Ps. 77:10

4245 - macaleh (makh-al-eh) or machalah (makk-al-aw) from 2470; sickness:- disease, infirmity, sickness—Prov. 18:14

Greek:
- 769 - astheneia (as-then-i-ah) from a, without, and strenos, strength. Weakness, sickness; (John 5:5; Gal. 4:13). In the NT this word and related words, astenes (772), weak, sick, and astheneo (770), to be of sickness or weakness, are the most common expressions for sickness and are used in the comprehensive sense of the whole man; but it can also refer to a special form of bodily weakness or sickness. 771 - asthenema (as-then-ay-mah) from astheneo (770), to be weak or powerless. The suffix ma indicates the result of being weak (Romans 15:1, cf. II Cor. 11:29)
- 3554 - nosos (nos-os) the regular word for disease, sickness. It is a disease of a grievous kind. It is joined to malakia (Mat. 4:23, 24) denoting a slighter infirmity. From nosos comes the English "nosology," the classification of diseases. Deriv. "noseo" (3552), to be sick in body but also to rave like a person in the delirium of a fever (I Tim. 6:4); nosema (3553), the result of nosos, disease (John 5:4 TR).
- Synonym: astheneia (769), sickness, weakness; malakia (3119) ailment, softness; arrhostia, although only the adj. or adj. noun arrhostos ([732], sick, ill) is found in the NT.

INIQUITY

Hebrew:
- 5753 - avah (aw-vaw) to crook, to pervert, do wrong, "to do iniquity." Verb appearing in the Bible 17 times. In Arabic it appears with the meaning "to bend" or "to deviate from the way." It is often used as a synonym of hata, "to sin," as in Psalm 106:6
- 5771 - avon (aw-vone), perversity, (moral evil), mischief, "iniquity; guilt; punishment." Noun appearing 231 times in the OT. limited to Hebrew and biblical Aramaic. The prophetic and poetic books employ avon with frequency. The Pentateuch as a whole employs the word about 50 times. The first use comes from Cain and takes the meaning of "punishment" (Gen. 4:13).
- Iniquity as an offense to God's holiness is punishable. As serious as "iniquity" is in the covenantal relationship between the Lord and His people, the people are reminded that He is a living God who willingly forgives "iniquity" (Exod. 34:7).
- Isaiah 53 teaches that God put upon Jesus Christ our "iniquities" (v. 5. 6, 11)
- 205 - aven (aw-ven) strictly nothingness, trouble, wickedness, "iniquity; misfortune." Noun meaning to be strong. Found only in the Northwest Semitic languages. Occurs about 80 times and almost exclusively in poeticprophetic language. The first occurence is in Num. 23:21.

Aven in a deeper sense characterizes the way of life of those who are without God.

The Septuagint has several translations: anomia (lawlessness"); kopos (work; labor; toil"); mataios ("empty; fruitless; useless; powerless"); and adikia ("unrighteousness; wickedness; injustice"). The KJV has these translations: "iniquity; vanity; wickness."

INTEGRITY

Hebrew:

8537 - tom (tome), completeness; fig. prosperity; usually (mor.) innocence:- full, integrity, perfect, upright,
Gen. 20:5, 6; I King 9:4; Ps. 7:8; Ps. 25:21; Ps. 26:1; Ps. 26:11; Ps. 41:12; Ps. 78:72; Prov. 19:1; Prov. 20:7
8538- tummah (toom-maw), fem. of 8537; innocence:- integrity
Job 2:3,9; Job 27:5; Job 31:6; Prov.11:3

English:
Steadfast adherence to a strict moral or ethical code - (incorruptibility). The state of being unimpaired; soundness
The quality or condition of being whole or undivided; completeness
The synonym — Honesty

INTERCESSION/INTERCESSIONS

Greek: noun

1783- enteuxis - (ent-yook-sis) primarily denotes "a lighting upon, meeting with"; then; "a conversation"; hence, "a petition," a meaning frequent in the papyri; it is a technical term for approaching a king, and so for approaching God in "intercession"; it is rendered "prayer" in I Tim. 4:5; in the plural in 2:1 (i.e., seeking the presence and hearing of God on behalf of others). For synonymous words, proseuche, deesis, see PRAYER.

verbs

1793 - entunchano - (en-toong-khan-o) primarily "to fall in with, meet with in order to converse" then, "to make petition," especially "to make intercession, plead with a person," either for or against others; (a) against, Acts 25:24, "made suit to (me)," RV [KJV "have dealt with (me)], i.e. against Paul; in Rom. 11:2, of Elijah in "pleading" with God, RV (KJV, "maketh intercession to"), against Israel; (b) for, in Rom. 8:27, of the intercessory work of the Holy Spirit for the saints; v. 34, of the similar intercessory work of Christ; Heb. 7:25
See: DEAL WITH, PLEAD, SUIT

5241 - huperentunchano (hoop-er-en-toong-khan-o) "to make a petition" or "intercede on behalf of another" (huper, "on behalf of," and enteuxis), is used in Romans 8:26 of the work of the Holy Spirit in making "intercession" (see enteuxis, verse 27)

Praying or pleading on someone else's behalf (Isa. 53:12). An intercessor serves as a go between. Jesus and the Holy Spirit intercede for Christians (Rom. 8:26-27, 34).

Christians are to intercede for one another (I Tim. 2:1)

INTERPRET/INTERPRETATION/INTERPRETER

Greek: verbs

2059 - hermeneuo (her-mayn-yoo-o) (cf. Hermes, the Greek name of the pagan god Mercury, who was regarded as the messenger of the gods), denotes "to explain, interpret" (Eng. "hermeneutics"), and is used of explaining the meaning of words in a different language, John 1:38.

1329 - diermeneuo (dee-er-main-yoo-o) a strenghtened form of (dia, "through") signifies "to interpret fully, to explain." In Luke 24:27, it is used of Christ in interpreting to two on the way to Emmaus "in all the Scriptures the things concerning Himself," RV, "interpreted" (KJV, "expounded"); in Acts 9:36, it is rendered "is by interpretation," lit. "being interpreted" (of Tabitha, as meaning Dorcas); in I Cor. 12:30 and 14:5,13,27, it is used with reference to the temporary gift of tongues in the churches; this gift was less inferior in character to that of prophesying unless he who spoke in a "tongue" interpreted his words, 14:5; he was, indeed, to pray that he might interpret, v. 13; only two, or at the most three, were to use the gift in a gathering, and that "in turn" (RV); one was to interpret, in the absence of an interpreter, the gift was not to be exercised, v. 27.

3177 - methermeneuo (meth-er-mane-yoo-o) "to change or translate from one language to another (meta, implying change, and No.1), "to interpret," is always used in a passive voice in the NT, "being interpreted," of interpreting the names, Immanuel, Matt. 1:23; Golgotha, Mark 15:22; Barnabas, Acts 4:36; in Acts 13:8, of Elymas, the verb is rendered "is ... by interpretation," lit. "is interpreted" it is used of interpreting or translating sentences in Mark 5:41; 15:34.

nouns

2058 - hermeneia (her-may-ni-ah) "translation"; is used in I Cor. 12:10; 14:26

1955 - epilusis (ep-i1-oo-sis) from epiluo, "to loose, solve, explain," denotes "a solution, explanation," lit., "a release: (epi, "up," luo, "to loose"), II Peter 1:20, "(of private) interpretation"; i.e., the writers of Scripture did not put their own construction upon the "God breathed" words they wrote.

ISHMAEL
Hebrew:

3458 - ishmael (ish'ma-el), 1. Abraham's eldest son, by Hagar the Egyptian hand maiden (Gen. 16:15; 17:23).

God promises Abraham a son (Gen. 15:4; 17:16–21 with emphasis on verse 21)

Abraham's wife Sarah, had given Hagar to Abraham because she despaired of ever becoming a mother. But later, Sarah bore Abraham a son, Isaac, and God said that he (as originally instructed), instead of Ishmael, should be Abraham's real heir. An Angel foretells' his name and character (Gen. 16:11 - 16); "and he shall be a wild man, his hand will be against every man, and every man's hand against him; and he shall dwell in the presence of all his brethren."

He was born at Mamre, when Abraham was eighty-six years of age, eleven years after his arrival in Canaan. At the age of thirteen he was circumcised. He grew up a true child of the desert, wild and wayward. On the occasion of the weaning of Isaac his rude and wayward spirit of insult and mockery (21:9, 10); and Sarah, discovering this, said to Abraham, "Expel this slave and her son." Sadly, Abraham put them out. He settled in the land of Paran, a region lying between Canaan and the mountains of Sinai; and God was with him (Gen. 21: 9-21). He came together with his brother Isaac to bury their father. He had 12 sons, who became the founders of so many Arab tribes or colonies, the Ishmaelites, who spread over the wide desert spaces of Northern Arabia from the Red Sea to the Euphrates (Gen. 37:25, 27, 28; 39:1), "their hand against every man, and every man's hand against them." He died at the age of 137. According the the Quran he is the father of Islam (the founder Muhammad as his descendant); however, much has been written to disprove Muhammad as a direct descendant.

*there are 5 other Ismael's listed in the Bible

ISSUE (OF BLOOD)
Hebrew:

2100 - zuwb (zoo b) to flow freely (as water), i.e. (spec) to have a (sexual) flux; fig. to waste away; also to overflow:- flow—Lev 15:25

2101 - zowb (zobe) from 2100; a seminal or menstrual flux: issue—Lev 15:2

2231 - zirmah (zir-maw) a gushing of fluid (semen):- issue—Eze. 23:20

3318 - yatsa (yaw-tsaw) to go (bring) out, in a great variety of applications, lit. and fig., direct and proxim: after, appear, assuredly, bear out, begotten, break out bring out, exact, fall, fall (out) draw forth, issue out, send with commandment, shoot forth, spread, spring out, stand out—Is. 39:7

4138 - mowledeth (mo-leh-deth) from 3205; nativity (plur. birth-place); by impl. lineage, native country; also offspring "family": begotten, born, issue, kindred, native—Gen 48:6

4726 - maqowr or maqor (maw-kore) something dug, i.e. (gen) source (of water, even when naturally flowing; also of tears, blood [by euphem. of the female pudenda]; fig. of happiness, wisdom, progeny): fountain, issue, spring, well (spring)—Lev. 12:7

6849 - tsephiah (tsef-ee-aw) an outcast thing: issue—Is. 22:24

Greek:

131 - haimorrheo (hahee-mor-hreh'-o) from 129 and 4482; to flow blood, i.e. have hemorrhage: diseased with an issue of blood—Matt: 9:20

4511 - rhutis (hroo-tece) from 4506 in the sense of its congener 4482; a flux (of blood):- issue—Mark 5:25

4690 - sperma (sper'-ma) from 4687; something sown, i.e. seed (including, the male "sperm"); by impl. offspring; spec. a remnant (fig. as if kept over for planting): - issue, seed—Matt. 22:25

JEBUS

Jebus was the third son of Canaan and father of the Jebusite race. During the breakup at Babylon, Jebus followed his father and two brothers, Sidon and Heth, to the Land of Canaan. (Later on it was called Israel). While living in the land, he founded a city west of Jordan and named it Jerusalem (Josh. 18:28; Judg. 1:21; 19:10; I Chron. 11:4–5). His offspring had occupied that city long before the Hebrews left Egypt as slaves (Ex. 3:17; 23:23; 33:1–2; 34:11; Joshua 3:10). But forty years after the Exodus, many Jebusites were driven out of Jerusalem by Joshua (Gen. 15:18–21; Neh. 9:8. When Joshua invaded Jereusalem, the city was very old). Their territory was assigned to the children of Benjamin; however, they were permitted to remain in Jerusalem where there occurred much false worshipping and intermarrying between the two races (Judg. 1:21; 3:5-6).

In 1190 B.C., the Jebusites rebelled against Israel to retain strategic grounds; their stronghold was "Zion", which remained hostile to Israel for two hundred years (Josh. 15:63). Thereafter, the Jebusites were constantly harassed by David until their fall in 988 B.C. Their defensive city Zion became the capital of Israel's empire and is often called the city of David following its captivity (II Sam. 5:7; I Chron. 11: 5- 8). During Solomon's era, the Jebusites were used as bond servants and keepers of the "Great Temple" which was built in Zion. Finally, Jebus' offspring as a race lost their identity through mixed breeding among the Hebrews.

Gen. 10:6, 15 -16; I Kings 9:20 -21; II Chron. 8:7

JEHOVAH (WRITTEN AS YHWH)

3068 - (ye-ho-vaw) Jewish national name of God:- the Lord. Compare with 3050 - Jah, the Lord, most vehement.

An artificial form for the personal name of God. The consonants "J" and "Y" represent yodh and "v" is waw. The consonant "H" is the Hebrew letter he. The vowels are from another Hebrew word for "master". Strictly speaking, the name is not "Jehovah", but YAHWEH or YAHWAH. Most versions translate these four letters as "the Lord".

Yahweh - a recreation of the Tetragrammaton (Gr. meaning 4 letter word), (the 4 Hebrew letters usually transliterated as YHWH or JHVH, used as a biblical & holy name for God) which was never pronounced aloud in the reading of the Torah from the late Second Temple period. Its pronunciation was lost by medieval Judaism. Through modern linguistics the pronunciation Yahweh was no longer based primarily on traditions preserved in late patristic sources. Both the vocalization yahwe and yahu (a shortened form used chiefly in personal names) were confirmed by a variety of ancient Near Eastern inscriptional materials from the 1st and 2nd millennia B.C.

The newly derived name which now appears to fit into the typical patterns of formation of divine names of ancient Near East, and at the same time conform to the linguistic laws of old (pre-biblical) Hebrew, was first suggested in the 18th century and later developed in modern form. This view holds that yahweh was originally a finite "hiphil" verb derived from a Northwest Semitic root hwy "to come into being" or "to exist". The divine name would thus go back to a verbal form meaning "he causes to come into existence" or in effect "he creates". The English transliteration Jehovah was dropped by most biblical translators of the 20th century. Masoretic scribes in medieval copies had developed the practice of pointing (marking- long or short) the vowels yehowah (accent "O" and the "a") instead of yahowah (accent first "a" and "O") to avoid breaking the taboo of using the holy name for God. This practice was misunderstood by English bible translators.

JEHOVAH - "the existing one". "The self existent or eternal" 1. The proper name of the one true God

a. unpronounced except with the vowel pointings of 0136
0136 - Adonay (ad-o-noy) 1. my Lord, lord a. of men
b. of God 2. Lord - title, spoken in place of Yahweh in Jewish display of reverence
1933 - awh - hava' (haw-vaw)
1961 - hyh - hayah (haw-yaw)
0183 - hwa - 'avah (aw-vaw)
(Lord 6510x, God 4x, Jehovah 4x)
    Ex. 6:3, Ps. 83: 18, Is. 12:2, Is. 26:4
Examples: Jehovah-Jireh. (Yahweh sees & provides)—Gen. 22:14
Jehovah-nissi (Yahweh is my banner)—Ex. 17:15
Jehovah-shalom (Yahweh is peace)—Judges 6:24
Jehovah-Ro'iy (Yahweh is my Shepherd)—Ps. 23:1
Jehovah-Shammah (Yahweh is there)—Eze. 48:35
Jehovah-Tsidkenu (Yahweh is our righteousness)—Jer. 23:6; 33:16

JESUS

Greek:

2424- iesous (ee-ay-sooce) Jehoshua , Jehovah is salvation
1. Jesus, the Son of God, the Saviour of mankind, God incarnate
2. Jesus Barabbas was the captive robber whom the Jews begged Pilate to release instead of Christ
3. Joshua was the famous captain of the Israelites, Moses successor (Acts 7:45; Heb. 4)
4. Jesus, son of Eliezer, one of the Ancestors of Christ (Luke 3)
5. Jesus, surnamed Justus, a Jewish Christian, associate of Paul in the preaching the gospel (Col.4)

Jesus 972, Jesus (Joshua) 2, Jesus (Justus) 1in the New Testatment

Names for JESUS (number 1)
The Way (John 14:6)
The Truth (John 14:6)
The Life (John 14:6)
Good Shepherd (John 10:11)
The Light (John 1:7)
Bread of Life (John 6:35)
Immanuel (Isa. 7:14)
Savior (II Peter 3:18)
Wonderful Counselor (Isa. 9:6)
Mighty God (Isa. 9:6)
Everlasting Father (Isa. 9:6)
Prince of Peace (Isa. 9:6)
The Word (John 1:1)
The Resurrection (John 11:25)
Lord (Matthew 8:8)
Son of Man (Mark 2:28)
Son of God (I John 4:15)
God (John 20:28)

JOT

iota- (ee-o-tah) from the Hebrew yod - , the smallest Hebrew letter, is mentioned by the Lord in Matt. 5:18, to express the fact that not a single item of the Law will pass away or remain unfulfilled.

JOUDHOUR (ROOTS) OF HAM

The name Ham has been Scripturally used to describe people and places; besides its original meaning (black), the name has also adopted other definitions, such as dark, ebony, sunburned, chocolate and brown.

Scholars throughout the ages have agreed that Ham and his offspring belong to the Negro family of nations. Ham and his children are recorded in Genesis 10:6 - 20.

"A forgotten people, while others were uncivilized, discovered science and art. A race which is modernly rejected because of their woolly hair and dark skin, are the founders of the laws of nature, religious and civil systems which still control the universe" ..... Count C. F. Volney, Ruins of Empires, pp. 16-17;

Oeuvers, Vol. 2, pp. 65-68. 1803.

"Back in the ages which are barely historic, where history renders only faint hintings, are evidence of a broad ancient civilization, raw, unripe, flashy, barbaric, yet all at the same period, controlled the world from its headquarters of power in the Euphrates, the valley of the Ganges, and the Nile, and it was of the Negro race! The Babylonians and Egyptians seem to have been Negroes, who built eminent empires long before the Semites, Mongols or Aryans. Deep-down in the mud and mire of the beginnings .... , rest the contribution of the Negroes to the superstructure of modern civilization." J. P. Widney. Race life of the Aryans, Vol. 2, pp. 238 - 39, 241. N.Y.

"Modern cannons, flying missiles, ship propellers, automatic hammers, gas motors, meat cleavers, and even the upholstery tack hammers ... were developed in Africa's early use of power." John W. Weatherwax, The African Contribution.

JUDGMENT SEAT

Greek

968 bema - (bay-ma) where believers are to be made manifest, that each may receive the things done in (or through) the body, according to what he/she has done, whether it be good or bad. There they (we) will receive rewards for faithfulness to the Lord. —

The Judgment Seat of Christ—(Rom. 14:10) (II Cor. 5:10)

A step, pace, the space which covers a foot-breath; a raised place mounted by steps

a. platform, tribune

1. of the official seat of a Judge
2. of the "Judgement Seat of Christ"—Romans 14:10
3. Herod built a structure resembling a throne at Caesarea, from which he viewed the games and made speeches to the people

KEEPER
Hebrew:
8104 -shamar (shaw-mar'), to keep, guard (a garden, Gen. 2:15; 3:24; a flock, Gen 30:31; a house, Eccl. 12:3); to keep safe, preserve (I Sam. 26:15; Job12:7); to watch (as a watchman of cattle or sheep, I Sam. 17:20; as a prophet, Is. 21:11; 62:6); to hedge around something (as with thorns); to retain (Gen. 37:11; 41:35); to abstain from something (Deut. 4:9); to observe (a covenant, Gen 17:9,10); the commandments of God, I Kings 11:10; the Sabbath, Is. 56:2, 6; a promise I Kings 3:6), to regard; to attend; to be kept, be guarded; to take heed, beware; to revere (Psalm 31:6).

The first occurrence of shamar is Gen 2:15 which has the sense of tending or exercising great care over the garden. In the same way Harhas kept the priest's garments (2 Kings 22:14). God was the "Keeper of Israel" (Psalm 121:4). It has the sense of watching over someone in I Sam. 2615 and besieging a city in 2 Sam. 11:16. In a religious vein, shamar expresses the careful attention which was paid to the obligations of a covenant, to laws or to statutes. Abraham gave orders to his children to keep the way of the Lord (Gen. 18:19). Also, the word can refer to a narrow watching (i.e. lying in wait for someone to ambush him, Job 13:27. The Cherubim guarded against intruders (Gen. 3:24). Cain asked, "Am I my brothers "keeper"? (Gen. 4:9). Satan was warned not to touch Job's life (Job 2:6).

LASCIVIOUSNESS
Greek:

766 - aselgeia (as-elg-'-i-a), licentiousness (sometimes incl. other vices): - lasciviousness (6x); wantoness (2), filthy (1x) aselgeia is best described as wanton, lawless insolence; a disposition of the soul not having or bearing a struggle with remorse; no restraints and is translated "filthy (conversation)," in II Peter 2:7
—Mk.7:22; II Cor. 12:21; Gal. 5:19; Eph. 4:19; I Pet 4:3; Jude 4

LEARN
Hebrew:

502 - alph or alaph (aw-lof) to learn; to teach—Proverbs 22:25

3925 - lamad (law-mad) to learn; teach; exercise; to be taught, be trained—Is. 2:4, Mic. 4:3 (teach 56, learn 22, instruct 3, diligently 1, expert 1, skillful 1, teaches 1)

Greek:

198 - akriboo (ak-ree-bo-o) to learn carefully, translated in Matt. 2:7 as "diligently enquired"

1097- ginosko (ghin-oce-ko) "to know by observation and experience" is translated "to learn" in the RV of Mark 15:45; John 12:9

3129 - manthano (man-than-o) denotes (a) "to learn" (akin to mathetes, a disciple), "to increase one's knowledge," or "be increased in knowledge," frequently "to learn by inquiry" or observation (Matt. 9:13; 11:29). Said of "learning" Christ, Eph. 4:20, not simply the doctrine of Christ, but Christ Himself, a process not merely of getting to know the person but of so applying the knowledge as to walk differently from the rest of the Gentiles (Matt. 11:29)

3453 - mueo (moo-eh-o) "to initiate into mysteries" is translated "I have learned the secret" in Phil. 4:12, RV (KJV, "I am instructed")

3811 - paideuo (pahee-dyoo-o) to educate or discipline; to instruct, train, is translated "instructed" in Acts 7:22, RV (KJV, "learned"); in I Timothy 1:20, "(that) they might be taught," KJV, "that they might learn"

LEAVEN

Hebrew:

2557 - chametz (khaw-mates'), ferment, (fig.) extortion:- leaven, leavened (bread); from 2256 (which means to be pungent; i.e. in taste [sour], dyed—Lev.2:11 (the Lord shall be made with leaven); Ex. 34:25

7603 - se'or (seh-ore'), barm or yeast-cake (as swelling with fermentation):- leaven; from 7604 (which means (to swell up; redundant-leave, remain—Ex. 12:15; Lev. 2:11 (for ye shall burn no leaven)

Greek:

2219 - zume (dzoo-may), "leaven, sour dough, in a high state of fermentation," used in general in making bread.

2220 - zumoo (dzoo-mo-o), "to leaven, to act as leaven," passive voice in Matt. 13:33 and Luke 13:21; active voice in I Cor. 5:6 and Gal. 5:9.

It required time to fulfill the process. Hence, when food was required at short notice, unleavened cakes were used, e.g., Gen. 18:6; Ex. 12:8. The Israelites were forbidden to use "leaven" for 7 days at the time of Passover, that they might be reminded that the Lord brought them out of Egypt "in haste," Deut. 16:3, with Ex. 12:11; the unleavened bread, insipid in taste, reminding them, too, of their afflictions, and of the need of self-judgement, is called "the bread of affliction." "Leaven" was forbidden in all offerings to the Lord by fire Lev. 2: 11; 6:17. Being bred of corruption and spreading through the mass of that in which it is mixed, and therefore symbolizing the pervasive character of evil, "leaven" was utterly inconsistent in offerings which typified the propitiatory sacrifice of Christ.

In the OT "leaven" is not used in a metaphorical sense. In the NT it is used (a) metaphorically (1) of corrupt doctrine, Matt. 13:33 and Luke 13:21, or error as mixed with the truth; Matt. 16:6, 11; that the kingdom of heaven is likened to "leaven," does not mean that the kingdom is "leaven." The same statement, as made in other parables, shows that it is the whole parable which constitutes the similitude of the kingdom; the history of Christendom confirms the fact that the pure meal of the doctrine of Christ has been adulterated with error; (2) of corrupt practices, Mark 8:15 (2nd part), the reference to the Herodians being especially applied to their irreligion; I Cor. 5:7,8; (b) literally, in Matt. 16:12, and in the general statements in I Cor. 5:6 and Gal. 5:9, where the implied applications are to corrupt practice and corrupt doctrine respectively.

LEVITICUS

The English title of this book, derived from the Greek translation of the OT (the Septuagint), means "pertaining to the Levites." Though the book is a manual for the priests (who were from the tribe of Levi), many of its laws concern all the Israelites. The Hebrew title ("and He called," from the first word of the book) emphasizes the theme of God's call to holiness (cf. 11:45).

About 56 times within the book it is said that the Lord spoke these words to Moses, who either wrote them down himself or had them written down (cf. 4:1; 6:1; 8:1; 11:1; 12:1). Jesus Christ also attested to the bks. Mosaic authorship (Mark 1:44; cf. Lev. 13:49).

The language of sacrifice pervades the book, with the word "sacrifice" occuring 42 times. "Priest" is found 189 times, "blood" 86 times, "holy" 87 times, and "atonement" 45 times. The regulations emphasize holiness of body as well as of spirit. The NT refers to Leviticus about 90 times. The book may be viewed in three complementary ways. It is a book about the holiness of God and His requirements for fellowship with Himself. Thus, it is also a book that reveals the sinfulness of man. And it may be viewed as a book about atonement, the provision of access to God for sinful man. God required the sacrifice of innocent animals for the covering of man's sin. These sacrifices were symbolic of the ultimate sacrifice which would take away the sin of the whole world (John 1:29).

LINQUA FRANCA

1. medium of communication between peoples of different languages. 2. a mixture of Italian with Provencal, French, Spanish, Arabic, Greek, and Turkish, formerly spoken on the eastern Mediterranean coast. Linqua - language + franklish (that is European).

1. Proto- first in time; earliest. 2. First formed; primitive; original. 3. Being a form of a language that is the ancestor of a language or group or related languages.

ARAMAIC/PROTO-HEBREW ALPHABET

The early Aramaic or Proto-Hebrew alphabet was developed sometime during the the 10th or early 9th century BC and replaced Assyrian cuneiform as the main writing system of the Assyrian empire. This alphabet is thought to be the ancestor of a number of Semitic alphabets. At the end of the 6th century BC the Early Aramaic alphabet was replaced by the Hebrew square script which is also known as the Aramaic alphabet.

THIS IS A CONSONANT ALPHABET WITH NO VOWEL INDICATION WRITTEN FROM RIGHT TO LEFT IN HORIZONTAL LINES

Aramaic, a language which was the lingua franca of much of the near East from about 7th century BC until the 7th century AD, when it was largely replaced by Arabic. Classical or Imperial Aramaic was the main language of the Persian, Babylonian and Assyrian empires and spread as far as Greece and the Indus valley.

Aramaic was once the main language of the Jews and appears in some of the Dead Sea Scrolls. It is still used as a liturgical language by Christian communities in Syria, Lebanon and Iraq, and is still spoken by small numbers of people in Iraq, Turkey, Iran, Armenia Georgia and Syria.

The oldest written parts of the Bible found were transcribed in three languages. What scholars call the Hebrew Bible (the same books Jews call the Tanakh or Written Torah and Christians call the Old Testament) was first written in Hebrew with a few chapters of the books of Ezra and Daniel recorded in Aramaic.

"MANY PEOPLE BELIEVE THAT JESUS AND HIS APOSTLES SPOKE IN ARAMAIC"

Aramaic alphabet (left to right - 'aleph to taw)
kaf (k) yod (y) tet (t) het (h) zayin (z) waw (w) he (h) dalet (d) gimel (g) beyt (b) 'alef (')
taw (t) sin (s) res (r) qop (q) sade (s) pe (p) 'ayin (,) samek (s) nun (n) mem (m) lamed (l)

John 1:1,2,12-14) In the beginning (of creation) there was the manifestation, and that manifestation was with God and God was (the embodiment of) that manifestation. 2 this was in the beginning with God.

12 But all those who did receive him, He assigned them to be children of God, (to them) who believe in his name; 13 they who (did not become so) through blood, nor through the desire of the flesh and neither through a man's will power, except they became born (so) from God.

14 And the manifestation became flesh and made his dwelling amongst us and we saw his glory, glory as (that) uniquely (of the nature) of the Creator, full of grace and blessing.

Peter in Aramaic -2786 - Keepa - Kepha Kepha (Kay-fas), the rock; Cephas (i.e. Kepha) surname of Peter

THE WORD WINDOW

LIST
Greek:

2309 - thelo (thel'-o), there is a distinction betwen thelo and boulomai (1014, to design, to decree. Thelo indicates not only willing something, but also pressing on to action. Boulomai is deciding, but not pressing on to execute that which is decided. Thelo in the NT denotes elective inclination, love. It occurs frequently biblical Greek with the ace. of the objective, which is rare with boulomai. Nevertheless, boulamai may be use for thelo, and thelo, though far more rarely, for boulomai. Thelo, therefore, means to will as the equivalent of to purpose, to be decided upon seeing ones desire to its execution.Thelo also means to be inclined (Acts 26:5); to have a mind to; to wish or desire (John 3:8). to list —Matthew 17:12; Mark 9:13

1014 - boulomai (boo'iom-ahee), "to will", be minded; —listeth—James 3:4

LONGSUFFERING
Greek:

3115 makrothumia (mak-roth-oo-mee-ah), from adj. makrothumos, which doesn't occur in the NT. Patience; a self-restraint of the mind before it gives room to action or passion; forbearance, long-suffering. The person who has power to avenge himself, yet refrains from the exercise of this power. It is patience with respect to persons while hupomone' (5281), endurance, is patience toward things or circumstances. Makrothumia and hupomone are often found together (II Cor. 6:4, 6; II Tim. 3:10). Makrothumia is associated with mercy (eleos [1656] and is used of God (Rom. 2:4; I Pet. 3:20).

From the same as 3116; longanimity, i.e. (obj) forbearance or (subj) fortitude:- longsuffering, patience.

  3316 - makrothumos (mak-roth-oo-mace); adv. of a compo. of 3317 and 2372; with long (enduring) temper, i.e. leniently:- patiently

LUCIUS OF CYRENE
Chosen man of God who was a teacher and prophet of an Antioch church located in Syria, about three hundred miles of Jerusalem. Lucius was from Cyrene, which is in the northern part of Africa. He like Simon the Cyrenian, supported the black Church established in Jerusalam. Simeon the Niger was also from Africa, but from a different region called Niger. He with Simeon, ordained Barnabas and Saul by the demand of the Holy Gost. Acts 13:1

MAJESTY

Hebrew:

1347 - ga'own (gaw-ohn'), arrogance or majesty; excellency, pomp, pride, swelling—Micah 5:4

1420 - geduwlah (ghed-oo-law'), greatness; mighty acts:- dignity, great things, majesty—Est. 1:4

1926 - hadar (haw-dawr), magnificence, i.e. ornament or splendor:- beauty, comeliness, excellency, glorious, glory, goodly, honour, majesty—Ps. 21:5

1935 - howd (hode), grandeur (imposing from and appearance):-beauty, comeliness, excellency, glorious, glory, goodly, honour, majesty

Greek:

3168 - megaleiotes (meg-al-i-ot'-ace), denotes "splendor, magnificence" (from megaleios) the goddess Diana. In Luke 9:43, (KJV, "mighty power"); in 2 Peter 1:16, "majesty." In the papyri writings it is frequent as a ceremonial title.

3172 - megalosune (meg-al-o-soo'-nay, from megas, "great," denotes "greatness, majesty"; it is used of God the Father, signifying His greatness and dignity in Heb. 1:3, "the Majesty (on high)," and 8:1, "the Majesty (in the Heavens)" and in an ascription of praise acknowledging the attributes of God in Jude 25.

MALEFACTOR(S)

Greek:

2555 - kakopoios (kak-op-oy-os), to do evil. Evil-doer. Used as an adj. noun, meaning pernicious, injurious; an evil-doer or a malefactor, behaving in a bad way. Used in John 18:30 and I Peter 2:12, 14; 3:16 in a moral sense corresponding to behaving in an evil way or doing evil. Only in I Peter 4:15 does it appear in the sense of generally injurious, denoting one who is injurious to the community.

2557 - kakourgos - (kak-oor'-gos), from kakos (2556), bad, and ergon (2401), work. An evil-doer, malefactor (Luke 23:32,33,39; 2 Tim. 2:9). In the Greek writers the word is joined with "thieves," as also in Luke 23:32. There are some who suggest the deriviation of the word is from kakos, bad, and orge (3709), anger. In this sense it would stress the malicious, cunning, and treacherous character of an evil-doer.

2556 - kakos (kak-os), from the verb chazo or chazomai, to give back, recede, retire, retreat in battle. Evil, wicked. One that is evil and as such gets others into trouble (Mark 7:21; Rom. 1:30). From this is derived kakia (2549), wickedness, iniquity, evil, affliction. Syn. poneros (4190), malicious, indicating willful harm to others, an element not necessarily found in kakos. The kakos may be content to perish in his own corruption, but the poneros (a name also attributed to Satan, Matt. 6:13; Eph. 6:16) is not content unless he is corrupting others as well and drawing them in the same destruction with himself.

MANSION

Greek:

3438 - mone (mon-ay) from meno (3306 - to remain, dwell, abide), a mansion, habitation, abode, a staying, i.e. residence (the act or the place)

A dwelling place, room, or place to live (John 14:2, 23 KJV). The NIV renders it "rooms"

MARANATHA

Greek:

3134 - maranatha (mar'-an-ath'-a), of Chaldean origin (mean. our Lord has come); maranatha, i.e. an exclamation of the approaching divine judgment:- maran-atha.

An expression used in I Cor. 16:22, is the Greek spelling for two Aramaic words, formerly supposed by some to be an imprecatory utterance or "a curse reinforced by a prayer," an idea contrary to the intimations conveyed by its use in early Christian documents, e.g. "The teaching of the Apostles," a document of the beginning of the 2nd cen., and in the "Apostolic Constitutions" (vii. 26), where it is used as follows: "Gather us all together into Thy Kingdom which Thou has prepared. Maranatha, Hosanna to the Son of David; blessed is He that cometh, etc."

"At first the title Marana or Maran, used in speaking to and of Christ was no more than the respectful designation of the Teacher on the part of the disciples." After His resurrection they used the title of or to Him as applied to God, "but it must here be remembered that the Aramaic-speaking Jews did not, save exceptionally, designate God as 'Lord'; so that in the 'Hebraist' section of the Jewish Christians the expression 'our Lord' (Marana) was used in reference to Christ only" (Dalman, The Words of Jesus).

THE WORD WINDOW

MARK = GOAL IN NIV

(specific focus on Philippians 3:14 KJV = mark) **4649 - skopos (skop-os) noun, from skopeo (4648),

("scope") a watch (sentry or scout); to look to toward a goal, give heed. Used as a "mark' at the goal or end of a race. (Phil. 3:14, cf. II Cor. 4:18) also see II Timothy 4:7,8.

4648 - skopeo (skop-eh-o) to look towards an object, to contemplate, give attention to; literally, to spy out (Phil. 3:17)

*As he who runs a race never takes up short of the end, but is still making movements forward as fast as he can, so those who have heaven in their eye must still be pressing forward to it in holy desires and hopes, and constant endeavors and preparations.

Heaven is called the "mark" here, because it is that which every good Christian has in his eye; as the archer has his eye fixed upon the "mark" he designs to hit. Heaven is the prize we fight for, and run for, and wrestle for, what we aim at in all we do, and what will reward all our pains. Eternal life is the gift of God (Rom. 6:23), but it is in Christ Jesus; through his hand it must come to us, as it is procured for us by him. There is no getting to heaven as our home but by Christ.

MATRIX

Hebrew:

7358 - rechem (rekh-em) from 7355 which means to fondle; by implication to love, especially to compassionate: -have compassion, mercy (-iful, on upon), (have) pity and 7356 which means the womb (as cherishing the fetus) by implication a maiden: bowels, tender love, (great tender), mercy, pity

rechem - the womb:- matrix, womb—Ex. 13:12; Ex. 34:19; Numbers 3:12 womb 21x, matrix 5x

MEEK & MEEKNESS

Hebrew:

6035 - anav (aw-nawv) or anayv (aw-nawv), depressed (fig.), in the mind (gentle) or circumstances (needy, especially saintly): - humble, lowly, meek, poor— Num. 12:3

6037 - anvah (an-vaw), mildness (royal); also oppressed:- gentleness, meekness —Ps. 45:4

6038 - anavah (an-aw-vaw) condescension, human and subj. (modesty), or divine and obj. (clemency): gentleness, humility, meekness—Zeph. 2:3

Greek: adjective

4239 - praus (prah-ooce') denotes "gentle, mild, meek"; Christ uses it of His own disposition, Matt. 11:29; He gives it in the Beatitudes Matt. 5:5, cf. epios, "gentle," of a soothing disposition noun

4240 - prautes (prah-oo'-tace), from 4239; mildness, i.e. (by impl.) humility: - meekness. In its use in Scripture, in which it has a fuller, deeper significance than in nonscriptural Greek writings, it consists not in a person's "outward behavior only; nor yet in his relations to his fellow-men; as little in his mere natural disposition. Rather it is an inwrought grace of the soul; and the exercises of it are first and chiefly towards God. It is that temper of spirit in which we accept His dealings with us as good, and therefore without disputing or resisting; it is closely linked with the word tapeinophrosune (humility), and follows directly upon it, Eph. 4:2; Col. 3:12 - cf. Zeph. 3:12, "meek and lowly" ... it is only the humble heart which is also the meek, and which, as such does not fight against God and more or less struggle and contend with Him. The meaning of prautes "is not readily expressed in English, for the terms meekness, mildness, commonly used, suggest weakness and pusillanimity to a greater or less extent, whereas prautes does nothing of the kind. Prautes describes a condition of mind and heart, and as 'gentleness' is appropriate rather to actions, this word is no better than that used in both English Versions. It must be clearly understood, therefore, that the meekness manifested by the Lord and commended to the believer is the fruit of power.

MELCHIZEDEC -

Greek form - MELCHIZEDEK (mel-kis-e-dek) (my king is Zedek)

A king of Salem and priest of the Most High God. Abraham paid tithes to him and was blessed in turn by Melchizedek. There was also a priestly order of Melchizedek which was long before the Aaronic priesthood (Gen. 14:18-20); (Ps. 110:4).

This priest was also a king, which was not the case with the Aaronic priesthood. All other reference to this man and to his priesthood are in the Book of Hebrews. Here we are told that he was a high priest and that his ancestry is shrouded in mystery since it is not known. He was king of Salem, i.e., king of peace, and the translation of his name is "king of righteousness" (Heb. 7:14). Salem is usually identified as Jerusalem (Ps. 76:2). The thrust of the NT reference all in the one book is that Christ is superior to all creatures and men, and specifically in this Melchizedek connection, that Christ's royal priesthood is of a kind that precedes the Aaronic and that continues after it even forever (Heb 7:23-10:18).

MEMORIAL DAY

A day to honor fallen heroes, observed on the last Monday in May. Originally called Decoration Day, observance for those who have died in our

Nations Service. There are many stories as to its actual beginnings with over 2 dozen cities and towns laying claim to being the birth place of Memorial Day. While Waterloo, NY was officially declared the birthplace by Pres. Lyndon Johnson in May 1966, its difficult to prove conclusively the origins of the day. Its about reconciliation; it is about coming together to honor those who gave their all. It was officially proclaimed on May 5, 1868, by General John Logan, Nat. Commander of the Grand Army of the Republic, and was first observed on May 30, 1868. The first state to to officially recognize the holiday was New York in 1873. By 1890 it was recog. by all the Northern States, the South refused to acknowledge the day, honoring their dead on a separate day, until after World War I. Traditional observance has diminished over the years. Most people no longer remember the proper flag etiquette for the day. While there are still some towns and cities that still hold parades, most have not in decades. Some people think the day is for honoring any and all dead, and not just those fallen in service to our country. Many feel that when Congress made the day into a 3 day weekend with the National Holiday Act of 1971, it made it all the easier for people to be distracted from the spirit and meaning of the day. On Jan. 19, 1999, a bill was introduced in the Senate which proposed to restore the traditional day of observance ot Memorial Day back to May 30 instead of "the last Monday in May." On April 19, 1999, it was introduced to the House. To date there has been no further developments on the bill.

MERCY -

Hebrew - 2617 - checed (kheh-sed) - kindness, favor, loving-kindness, mercy, pity. From the word chacad (khaw-sad) - to be kind, show self merciful.

7355 - racham (raw-kham) - to fondle, to love, compassionate, have compassion.

2603 - chanan (khaw-nan) - to bend or stoop in kindness to an inferior; to favor.

Greek: Noun

1656 - eleos (el-eh-os) - compassion (human or divine, expec. active), tender mercy, the outward manisfestation of pity - it assumes need on the part of him who receives it, and resources adequate to meet the need on the part of him who shows it. It is used of God, who is rich in mercy - Ep. 2:4 - and has provided for all men. Mercy is the act of God, peace is the resulting experience in the heart of man. Grace describes God's attitude toward the lawbreaker and the rebel: mercy is the atitude toward those who are in distress.

3628 - oiktirmos - (oyk-tir-mos) - pity, mercy, compassion for the ills of others Heb. 10:28, II Cor. 1:3. God the Father of Mercies

THE WORD WINDOW

4698 - splagehnon - (splangkh-non) - figuratively: pity or sympathy, bowels, inward affection + tender mercy, the heart, feelings of kindness.

Verbs

1653 - eleeo (el-eh—eh-o) - to compassionate (by word or deed, spec. by divine grace) have compassion, to feel sympathy with the misery of another, to have pity or mercy on, to show mercy

2433 - hilaskomai - (hil-as-kom-ahee) - to atone, to make reconciliation for, to the Greek meant - to cause the gods to be reconciled; their good will was not regarded as their natural condition, but as something to be earned. The heathen believed their gods to be naturally alienated in feeling from man.

448 - anileos- "(an-ee-leh-oce) - without mercy - James 2:13 Adjectives

1655- eleemon (el-eh-ay-mone) - merciful

2436 - hileos (hil-eh-oce) - propitious, merciful - Luke 6:36; was used in profane Greek just as in the case of the verb (which see). There is nothing of this in the use of the word in Scripture. The quality expressed by it there essentially appertains to God, though man is undeserving of it.

It is used only of God, Heb.8:12; Matt. 16:22.

MINISTER/MINISTERED/MINISTERS/MINISTRY

Hebrew:

1777 - diyn (deen) to judge (as empire); to strive or contend for, minister—Ps. 9:8

3027 - yad - see serve

5656 - abodah (ab-o-daw) work (any kind); bondservant, labor, ministering—Num.4:47

6399 - pelach (pel-akh) to serve, or worship:- minister—Ezra 7:24

8120 - shemash (shem-ash) from 8121 (to be brilliant) through the idea of activity implied to serve, minister—Dan. 7:10

8334 - sharath - serve (see serve)—Ex. 24:13

Greek:

1247 - diakoneo (dee-ak-on-eh-o) serve, minister, use the office of deacon—Mt. 4:11

1248 - diakonia (dee-ak-on-ee-ah) attendance, aid, service (official)—Rom. 12:7

1249 - diakonos (dee-ak-on-os) waiter; deacon (ess)—I Cor. 3:5

1325 - didomi (did-o-mee) to give, bestow—Eph.4:29

2023 - epichoregeo (ep-ee-khor-ayg-eh-o) to fully supply; to aid or cont.—II Pet. 1:11

2418 - hierourgeo (hee-er-oorg-eh-o) officiate (as a priest)—Rom. 15:16

2038 - erazomai (er-gad-zom-ahee) to be engaged in or with, commit, labor for, minister about—I Cor. 9:13

3008 - leitourgeo (li-toorg-eh-o) to perform rel. or charitable functions—Heb. 10:11
3009 - leiktourgia (li-toorg-ee-ah) public function (as preist)—Luke 1:23
3010 - leitourgikos (li-toorg-ik-os) engage in holy service—Hebrews 1:14
3011 - leitourgos (li-toorg—os) functioning in the Temple or Gospel—Rom. 13:6
3930 - parecho (par-ekh-o) to hold near, i.e. to present—I Tim. 1:4
5256 - hupereteo (hoop-ay-ret-eh-o) to be a subordinate—Acts 24:23
5524 - choregeo (khor-ayg-eh-o) to furnish, supply, provide—II Cor. 9:10

MIRY

Hebrew:

1207· bitstsah (bits-tsaw'), from 1206 (mire - mud); a swamp:- mire(ry place) • • Eze.47:11

2917 - tiyn (teen), interchan. for a word corresponding to 2916; clay:-miry···Dan. 2:41

3121 - yaven (yaw-ven), from the same as 3196 (intoxication; wine; banqueting); prop. dregs (as effervesing); hence mud: mire, miry.—Ps.40:2

MIZRAIM

Hebrew:

4714 - Mitsrayim (mits-rah-yim) Egypt, Egyptians, Mizraim

Mizraim was the son of Ham (an African by blood) and the father of Ludim, Anamim, Lehabim, Naphtuhim, Pathrusim, Casluhim (from whom came the Philistines) and Caphtorim. During the desertion of Babel, Mizraim followed his two brothers Cush and Phut to Africa. There he dwelt, populating an area known as Lower Egypt which was once named Mizraim. Mizraim is still the alternate name for Egypt and is revealed several times as the Land of Ham in Ps. 78:51; 105:23 - 27; 106: 19 - 23. The Egyptians were ruled by great Pharaohs such as Menes, Ahmose I (Amos), Zoser, Khufu, Amenophis or Amenhotep III (an Ethiopian), and Ramesses II. Several of these pharaohs reigned in Egypt during Israel's oppression.

Egypt has a vast army that protected its borders, and its high culture marked it as a superior nation. The Egyptians, like the Ethiopians, were masters of architecture, astronomy, medicine, science, art, agriculture, and military technique. That knowledge they primarily borrowed while under the Ethiopian Dynasty. A native priest named Manetho, writing in about 300 B.C. divided the history of his nation into thirty dynasties, a system that is still employed. There is also a predynastic period, extending from 4500 to 3000 B.C., with the dual kingdoms of upper Egypt to the South and Lower Egypt, the Nile delta to the North. They united under Menes. Years later after Egypt's last (XXXth) Dyn. had been succeeded by the Macedonians and then the Romans, the baby Jesus

and his family found refuge from Herod in this ancient land (Mt. 2:14, 19-21).
Gen. 10:6, 13-14; I Chron. 1:8, 11; Jer. 37:4 -7; Amos 9:7

MODEST

MODEST (focus on I Timothy 2:9)

Greek:

2287 - kosmios - (kos'mee-os), order. Orderly, decent, i.e. decorous:- of good behavior, modest. (I Timothy 2:9; 3:2). Plato presented a kosmios as the citizen who is quiet in the land, who fulfills the duties which are incumbent on him as such and is not disorderly. He as well as Paul, associated such persons with sophron (4998), sensible, self-controlled, one who voluntarily places limitations on his freedom. The virtue of the kosmios, however, is not only the propriety of his dress and demeanor, but of his inner life, unerring and expressing itself in the outward conversation. Contrast with semnos (4586), venerable, one who has a grace and dignity not obtained from earth only. While one who is kosmios behaves himself well in his earthly citizenship and is an asset, the semnos owes his quality to that higher citizenship which is also his. Semnos inspires not only respect but reverence and worship.

Syn. hieroprepes (2412), one who acts like a sacred person.

NATURAL/NATURALLY
adjectives

5446 - phusikos (foo-see-kos) originally signifying "produce by nature, in born," from phusis, "nature" English - physical, physics, etc., denotes (a) according to nature Rom. 1:26, 27; (b) "governed by mere natural instincts," II Peter 2:12, RV, "(born) mere animals," KJV and RV marg., "natural (brute beasts)."

5591 - psuchikos (psoo-khee-kos) "belonging to the psuche, soul" (as the lower part of the immaterial in man), "natural, physical," describes the man in Adam and what pertains to him (set in contrast to pneumatikos, "spiritual"), I Cor. 2:14; 15:44 (twice), 46 (in the latter used as a noun); James. 3:15, "sensual" (RV "natural" or "animal"), here relating perhaps more especially to the mind, a wisdom in accordance with, or springing from the corrupt desires and affections; so in Jude 19.

nouns

1078 -genesis (ghen-es-is) "birth," is used in James 1:23, of the "natural face," lit., "the face of his birth," "what God made him to be", generation, nature

*note: in Romans 11:21,24 the preposition kata, "according to," with the noun phusis, "nature," is translated "natural," of branches, metaphorically describing members of the nation of Israel.

adverb

5447 - phusikos (foo-see-koce) "naturally, by nature" (akin to 5446), is used in Jude 10. *note: in Phil. 2:20, KJV, "gnesios", "sincerely, "true, sincere, genuine"; is translated "naturally" (RV, "truly," "genuinely")

NETHINIMS
Hebrew:

5411 - nathiyn (naw-theen) or nathuwn (Ezra 8:17) (naw-thoon'), one given, i.e. (in the plural only) the Nethinim, or Temple servants (as given up to that duty):- Nethinims. 18 occurrences; AV translates as Nethinims ... 18 times. 1. Nethinims. 1 a. temple slaves assigned to the Levites and priests for service in the Sanctuary. The appointed; appointed; the given ones.

Ezra 8:15-20 I. ... found there none of the sons of Levi - that is, the ordinary Levites, notwithstanding the privilege of exemption from all taxes granted. 16 - then sent I for Eliezer ... with commandment unto Iddo the chief... Ezra sent this deputation either by virtue of authority which by his priestly character he had over the Levites, or the royal commission with which he was invested. The deputation was dispatched to Iddo, who was a prince or chief of the Nethinims—- for the Persian government allowed the Hebrews during their exile to retain their ecclesiastical government by their own chiefs, as well as to enjoy the privilege of free worship. Iddo's influence procured and brought to the camp at Ahava 38 Levites, and 220 Nethinims, the descendants of the Gibeonites, who performed the servile duties of the temple.

NIGER

Greek:

3526 - niger (neeg'-er) of Latin origin; black;

also called Simeon (Acts 13:1). Leader of the church at Antioch and prophet.

*From the word Niger derived the European words Negrum, Negre, Negrillo, Nigrito, Negrus, Negro, nigger, etc. The Ethiopian royal-title "Negus," which means King, is a synonym of the Portuguese word Nego, meaning Negro. The derogative word nigger, is linked to the words Negro, Nego, Niger and Negus, meaning King; see the following sources: Oxford English Dictionary, p. 306, Portuguese-English Dictionary, by Taylor, pi 440, Grande Dizionario Della Lingua Italiana, p. 322, Origins Etymology Dictionary, pp. 431- 432, and Kleins Comprehensive Etymological Dictionary of the English Language, p. 1037.

NIMROD

5248 - Nimrod (nim-rode), son of Cush and grandson of Ham. "The mighty hunter". Was the first man to try to build his way to heaven. With his fertility of invention, he managed to draw and start a gigantic tower, so that he and his fellow servants could see heaven as well as earth. This tower was built in a city called Babel, which was the beginning of his empire. Nimrod sought help from Japheth and Shem's family, and they made and hauled baked bricks under his supervision.

God was not pleased with their eagerness to reach His heaven, so He paid them a visit that caused confusion in their speech. This chaos of tongues caused them to scatter abroad leaving Nimrod's dream unfinished. In Micah 5:5-6, Babylon is noted as being the region of Nimrod; and for centuries, prior to and after "Micah," Babylon was constructed, inhabited and governed by the seed of Ham.

The original Babylonians were Negroes, through Nimrod (Gen. 10:8-10). Rawlinson says the Babylonians were Ethiopians by blood, and the Chaldeans should be viewed as Negroes, not Semites or Aramaeans ... Rawlinson's remarks are found in the following source: "Seven Great Monarchies," Vol. 1, pp. 29, 34. Jastrow, in his book, "Hebrew and Babylonian Traditions," states that the Babylonians called themselves "black-head people."
Gen. 10: 8-10; 11:3-9; I Chron. 1:10; Micah 5:6

OF LIKE PASSIONS (AS USED IN ACTS 14:15)

verse 11 - and when the people saw what Paul had done, they lifted up their voices, saying in the speech of Lycaonia, The gods are come down to us in the likeness of men.

12 - and they called Barnabas, Jupiter; and Paul, Mercurius because he was the chief speaker. 13 - Then the priest of Jupiter, ... brought oxen and would have done sacrifice with the people.

14- Which when the apostles, Barnabas and Paul, heard of, they rent (tore off) their clothes, and ran in among the people, crying out,

15-And saying, Sirs, why do ye these things? We also are men of like passions with you ..... We too are only men, human like you. We too have the same nature as you   .

OG

Hebrew:

5747 - Og (ogue), long necked

King Og was an Amorite ruler of strategic city Bashan, which was well-fortified with high walls and a ready army. Og never dreamed such an insufficient force as Israel could annihilate him, so he prepared for battle and met them at his chief city Edrei. There he fought, expecting a major victory, but instead experienced the agony of defeat. His territories, like Sihon's, were separated among the tribes of Israel. King Og was one of the last remnant giantlike kings. His bedstead amazed Moses: its dimensions were thirteen feet by six feet, and it was made of iron (Deut. 3:11). He had an enormous build!

Og, like Sihon, was a black, a great descendant of Ham, through Canaan (Gen. 10:6, 15-16).

The Hebrew guerilla warfare of Canaan triggered great resentment, causing hundreds of thousands of Negro Canaanites to exile to Africa. The only modern tribe, like the Negro Biblical Rephaim (Gen. 15:18-20, a tall tribe of Negro giants), known to be of giant stature is the Negro "Watusi" now living in east-central Africa. The average height of these people is over seven feet and six inches. There are no other races on earth which grow to such heights.

Since the Land of Canaan (now called Palestine) was territorially adjoined to Africa, many black giantlike Canaanites fled the land during Israel's intrusion. They migrated south and settled in central Africa where they gradually decreased in height, due to crossbreeding with people of smaller stature.

ONE (FOCUS ON JOHN 10:30)

Greek:

1520 - heis (hice), mia (fem.); hen (neut.) One. In the masculine heis must be distinguished from the neut. hen. Heis means one numerically while hen means one in essence, as in John 10:30; "I and my Father are one (hen)" (i.e., one in essence although two different personalities). Had it said heis, it would have meant one person, meaning hen (neuter form) is proper.

ONE HUNDRED FORTY FOUR THOUSAND

12,000 from each of the 12 tribes of the "children" of Israel

Doesn't mean that only 144,000 Israelites will be saved, but that 12,000 chosen in each tribe will be protected from the wrath of Satan and the Antichrist.

The great multitude that will be saved are described as "they which came out of the great tribulation, and have washed their robes, and made them white in the blood of the Lamb" (Rev. 7:14)

ONLY BEGOTTEN

3439 - monogenes - (mon-og- en-ace) from root word "mono" which means sole, single or only -and the word "ginomai" which means to cause to be (generate) or become (come into being), be divided, be finished, be found, be fulfilled, be ordained to.

It means only-born, for example sole: - only (begotten, child) not verbatim -from "Vine's Complete Expository Dictionary"

Its used 5 times in reference to Christ as the Son of God - all in the books of John. Its translated "only begotten" in17 of the relationship; of Isaac to Abraham.

John 1:14 indicated that as the Son of God, He was the sole representative of the being and character of the one who sent Him. John's purpose is to demonstrate what sort of glory it was that he and his fellow apostles had seen. That he is not merely making a comparison with earthly relationships is indicated by "from".

The glory was that of a UNIQUE relationship and the word begotten does not imply a beginning of His Sonship. It suggest relationship, but not the same as how it applies to man (generational). Christ did not become (as in an event in time used like in begetting), but His coming was irrespective of time. He didn't become because He always was and eternally is. He is not after the Father - He is the Father.

The word also suggests the thought of the deepest affection, as in the case of the Old Testament word "yachid" which means "only one", Gen 22:12, "only son", Jer. 6:26; Amos 8:10; Zech. 12:10; "only beloved", Prov. 4:3, and darling", Ps 22:20; 35:17.

In John 1:18 where it says "the only begotten son, which is in the bosom of the Father", expresses both His eternal union with the Father in the Godhead and the indescribable intimacy and love between them, the Son sharing all the Father's counsels and enjoying all His affections. Another reading is - "monogenes Theos" - God only-begotten. In John 3:16 "God sent His only begotten Son" the value and the greatness of the gift lay in the Sonship of Him who was given. His Sonship was not the effect of His being given. In I John 4:9 the statement "God hath sent His only begotten son into the world" does not mean that God sent out into the world one who at His birth in Bethlehem had become His Son. - the cross reference and parallel statement, "God sent forth the Spirit of His Son" Galatians 4:6, which could not mean that God sent forth One who became His Spirit when He sent Him.

"ONLY BEGOTTEN"

For even a better understanding, please note that in the Greek, this is only one word - the Greek word is monogenes. It is not to be broken down into 2 (two) words. Many people want to separate the words to use "only as sole and begotten as born. Don't do this!

PARABLE

Greek:

3850 - parabole (par-ab-ol-ay) comparison, figure, parable, proverb

The following meanings are to be distinguished 1. a comparison, similitude, or simile in which one thing is compared with another (Luke 4:23)

2. It is by some interpreted to mean merely a special doctrine or a weighty, memorable speech (Matt. 22:1)

3. A visible type of emblem representing something different from and beyond itself (Heb. 9:9)

3942 - paroimia (par-oy-mee-ah) a wayside saying, a by-word. The word is sometimes spoken of as a "parable" (John 10:6). Two dangers are to be avoided in seeking to interpret the "parables" in Scripture, that of ignoring the important features, and that of trying to make all the details mean something. The Mosaic tabernacle with its services was a parable, a type, emblem, or figurative representation of the good things of Christianity.

PASSETH

Hebrew:

1980 - halak (haw-lak'), to walk (in a great variety of applications, lit. and fig.):- along, apace, behave (self), come, (on), continually, depart, enter, exercise (self), forward, get, go, move (self), on, out, up, needs, pass (away), be at the point—Ps. 78:39

2498 - chalaph (khaw-laf), to slide by, i.e. (by impl.) to hasten away, pass on, spring up, pierce or change: abolish, alter, change, cut-off, go on forward, grow up, be over, renew—Job 9:11

5674 - abar (aw-bar'), to cross over; used very widely of any transition (lit. or fig.), alienate, alter, beyond, bring (over, through) carry over, convey over, current, deliver, do way, enter, escape, fall, get in, on, over, through, have away, pass (-age, along, away, beyond, by, enger, on, out, over through)—Ex. 30:13; Job 30:15

THE WORD WINDOW

Greek:
3855 - parago (par-ag'-o), to lead near, i.e. (reflex. or intrans.) to go go along or away:-depart, pass (away, by, forth)—I Jn. 2:17
3928 - pearerchomai (par-er'-khom-ahee), to come near or aside, i.e. to approach (arrive), go by (or away), (fig.) persish or neglect. (caus) avert: come (forth), go, pass (away, by, over), past, transgress—Lk. 18:37
5235 - huperballo (hoop-er-bal'-lo), to throw beyond the usual mark, i.e. (fig.) to surpass (only act. part. supereminent):-exceeding, excel, pass—Eph. 3:19
5242 huperecho (hoop-er-ekh'-o), to hold oneself above, i.e. (fig.) to excel; part. (as adj., or neut. as noun) superior, superiority:-better, excellency, higher, pass, supreme—Phil. 4:7

PATIENCE/PATIENT/PATIENTLY

Hebrew:
750 - arek (aw-rake) long (pinions) patient, slow to anger—Ecc. 7:8
2342 - chuwl (khool) to twist, whirl, dance, writhe, fear trimble, travail, be in anguish, be pained, bring forth, to wait, anxiously, to be brought forth, suffering torture, to wait longingly, to be distessed "patiently"—Psalm 37:7
6960 - qavah (kaw-vaw) 1.to wait, look for, hope, expect, linger for. 2. to collect, bind together, to be collected, "patiently"—Psalm 40:1

Greek:
420 - anexikakos (an-ex-ik-ak-os) patient of ills and wrongs, forbearing—II Tim. 2:24
1933 - epiekes (ep-ee-i-kace) 1.seemly, suitable, 2. equitable, fair, mild, gentle, "patient", (gentle 3x, patient 1 x, moderation 1 x)— I Timothy 3:3
3114 - makrothumeo (mak-roth-oo-meh-o) to be of a long spirit not to lose heart,

a. to perservere patiently & bravely in enduring misfortunes and troubles
b. to be patient in bearing the offenses and injuries of others
1. to be mild and slow in avenging
2. to be long suffering, slow to anger, slow to punish (be patient, have patience, have long patience, bear long, be long suffering; patiently endure)—James 5:7; I Thes. 5:14
3115 - makrothumia (mak-roth-oo-mee-a) patience, endurance, consistancy, steadfastness, perserverance 2. forebearance, longsuffering, slowness in avenging wrongs —James 5:10
5278 - hupomeno (hoop-om-en-o) to remain (a) to tarry behind 2. to remain i.e. abide, not recede or flee
a. to preserve: under misfortunes and trials to hold fast to one's faith in Christ

THE WORD WINDOW

b. to endure, bear bravely and calmly: ill treatments (endure, take patiently, tarry behind, abide, patient, suffer)
   5281 - hupomone (hoop-om-on-ay) steadfast, constancy, endurance—James 1:3 a. in the NT the characteristic of a man who is not swerved from his deliberate purpose & loyalty to faith & peity by even the greatest trials and sufferings
 b. be patiently and steadfastly
 2. a patient, steadfast waiting for
 3. a patient, enduring, sustaining, perseverence

PERADVENTURE
  Hebrew:
   194 'ulay (oo-lah'ee), peradventure; perhaps; suppose; if; less." The 43 occurrences of this word appear in every period of biblical Hebrew. This word meaning "peradventure or perhaps" usually expresses hope. 'Ulay also expresses fear or doubt: Peradventure the woman will not be willing to follow me unto this land; must I needs bring thy son again unto the land from whence thou camest: (Gen. 24:5). Hence perhaps: - if so be, may be, peradventure, unless.
   3863 -luw' (100) or lu (100), if; by implication (as a wish) would that 1:- if (haply), peradventure, I pray thee, though, I would, would God (that)—Gen. 50:15
   6435 - pen (pane), removal; used only as conj. lest: peradventure, that not—Gen. 31:31

  Greek:
   3379 - mepote (may'-pot-eh), not ever; also if (or lest) ever or perhaps:- if peradventure, lest (at any time, haply), not at all, whether or not—2 Tim. 2:25
   5029 - tacha (takh'-ah), as if neut., shortly, i.e. (fig.) possibly:- peradventure (-haps)—Romans 5:7

PERFECT
  Hebrew:
   1585 - gamar (ghem-ar) to complete, perfect—Ezra 7:12
   4357- miklah (mik-law) completeness, perfection—II Chron. 4:21
   7999 - shalam (shaw-lam) to be in covenant of peace, be at peace to cause to be at peace, to live in peace, complete, sound, uninjured, reward, make safe, to make whole, restore—Is. 42:19
   8003 - shalem (shaw-lame) complete, safe, perfect, whole, full, at peace, finished, unharmed, peace of mind—I Chron. 12:38

THE WORD WINDOW

8535 - tam (tawm) perfect, complete, one who lacks nothing in physical strength, beauty, etc. sound, wholesome, an ordinary quiet sort of person; morally innocent, having integrity, one who is morally & ethically pure—Job 1:1

8549 - tamiym (taw-meem) complete, whole, entire, sound, entire (of time), healthful, unimpaired, innocent, having integrity, what is complete or entirely in accord with truth and fact —- Gen. 6:9

8552 - tamam (taw-mam) to be complete, be finished, be at an end; to be upright, to be consumed, to cease doing, to make sound, make perfect, whole — Is. 18:5

Greek:

195 - akribeia (ak-ree-bi-ah) exactness, exactest care, in accordance with the strictness of the Mosaic Law —Acts 22:3

197 - akribesteron (ak-ree-bes-ter-on) more exactly, more perfect — Acts 24:22

199 - akribos (ak-ree-boce) exactly, accurately, diligently, circumspectly, perfect, perfectly — Luke 1:3

2005 - epeteleo (ep-ee-tel-eh-o) to bring to an end, accomplish, perfect, execute, complete; to leave off, to impose upon—Gal. 3:3

2675 - katatizo (kat-ar-tid-zo) to render, i.e. to fit, sound complete, to mend (what has been broken or rent), to repair; to equip, put in order ethically: to strengthen; perfect, complete, make one what he ought to be—II Cor. 13:11

3647 holokleria (hol-ok-lay-ree-ah) of an unimpaired condition of the body in which all its members are healthy and fit for use; good health—Acts 3:16

4137 - pleroo (play-ro-o) to make full, to fill up, to cause to abound, to render full, to make complete in every particular, to render perfect; to carry into effect; to bring realization of matters of duty: to perform, execute, of sayings, promises, prophecies, ratify, accomplish, to receive fulfillment—Rev. 3:2

5046 - teleios (tel-i-os) brought to an end, finished, wanting nothing to completeness, perfect, that which is perfect, full grown adult, mature—Matt. 5:48; James 1:4

5048 - teleioo (tel-i-o-o) to make perfect, complete, to carry through completely and what is yet wanting in order to render a thing full; to be found perfect; to bring to an end, to accomplish—I John 4:17

PHARAOH'S DAUGHTER

A black princess (according to the Jewish historian Josephus, her name was "Thermuthis") and daughter of Pharaoh Seti I, while Israel underwent slavery, saved the life of a Hebrew infant while bathing in a river, accompanied by maids. The princess insisted that they bring the child to her, and as she heard him cry, became compassionate toward him, saying: "This is one of the Hebrews' children." She named the child Moses and reared him in the

Pharaoh's palace. It was this Moses who led the Exodus of the slaves from Egypt under Ramses II. The Greek historian Herodotus (484-425 B.C.), who is styled as the father of history, clearly stated the the Egyptians of his day possessed black skins and woolly hair.
Ex. 2:5; 3:7, 11-12.

PHARISEES

Greek

5330- pharisaios (far-is-ah-yos) from an Aramaic word peras (found in Dan 5:28), signifying "to separate," owing to a different manner of life from that of the general public. The "Pharisees" and Sadducees appear as distinct parties in the latter half of the 2nd century B.C., though they represent tendencies traceable much earlier in Jewish history, tendencies which became pronounced after the return from Babylon (537), B. C.. The immediate progenitors of the two parties were, respectively, the Hasidaeans and the Hellinizers; the latter, the antecedents of the Sadducees, aimed at removing Judaism from its narrowness and sharing in the advantages of Greek life and culture. The Hasidaeans, a transcription of the Hebrew chasidim, i.e., "pious ones," were a society of men zealous for religion, who acted under the guidance of the scribes, in opposition to the godless Hellinizing party; they scrupled to oppose the legitimate high priest even when he was on the Greek side. Thus the Hellenizers were a political sect, while the Hasidaeans, whose fundamental principle was complete separation from non Jewish elements, were the strictly legal party among the Jews, and were ultimately the more popular and influential party. In their zeal for the Law they almost defied it and their attitude became merely external, formal, and mechanical. They laid stress, not upon the righteousness of an action, but upon its formal correctness. Consequently their opposition to Christ was inevitable; His manner of life and teaching was essentially a condemnation to theirs; hence His denunciation of them, e.g., Matthew 6:2,5,16; 15:7 and chapter 23.

While the Jews continued to be divided into these two parties, the spread of the testimony of the gospel must have produced what in the public eye seemed to be a new sect, and in the extensive development which took place at Antioch, Acts 11:19 - 26, the name "Christians" seems to have become a popular term applied to the disciples as a sect, the primary cause, however, being their witness to Christ. The opposition of both "Pharisees" and Sadducees (still mutually antagonistic, Acts 23:6-10) against the new "sect" continued unabated during apostolic times.

PHUT

Phut was Ham's third son; the Scriptures do not mention any of his sons by name, but it is certain that he had sons from whom the Libyans or Cyrenians are descended. These people were located on the upper northern part of Africa and their principal city was Cyrene. They played a vital and fatal role during and after the Crucifixion. It was Simon the Cyrenian who helped Christ carry his cross to Golgotha (Mark 15:21-22). We even find the Cyrenians during the Pentecostal period listening to Peter's instructions.

When Stephen attempted to preach salvation in Jerusalem, a few Cyrenians and other groups had him stoned. There were, however, some Cyrenians who did not approve of his execution and continued to preach Christ's word. These Cyrenians (Phutites) were black people of the Jewish faith, and it was they who helped spread Christianity to the Greeks (Acts 11:20).

The Jewish historian, Flavius Josephus, states that Phut was the founder of Libya, and that he called the inhabitants Phutites after himself. The Greek Septuagint and the Latin Vulgate on four occasions identify Phut as "Libyans" or "Libya." Gen. 10:6; Jer. 46:9; Ezek. 27:10; 30:5; Nahum 3:9; Acts 2:10; 6:9.

PICNIC

Began life as a 17th century French word. A 1692 edition of Origines de la Francoise de Menage, mentions "Picquenique" as being of recent origin marks the first appearance of the word in print. The first documented appearance of the term outside the French Language, occured 1748, but it was 1800 or thereabouts before anyone can prove it made it into the English Language. Even then it still wasn't America - it was in England.

Upon receiving many inquiries about the chain letter connecting the starting of picnic with slavery and hangings, the Smithsonian Institution was contacted. Dr. Alonzo Smith, a research fellow in African-American Studies at the Smithsonian, spoke out against the e-mail joke.

POSSESS

Hebrew:

3423- yarash (yaw-rash') or yaresh (yaw-raysh'), to seize, take possession of, possess; to inherit; to occupy; to drive away, expel; to take away; to be an heir, to disinherit, to dispossess; to become poor, make poor, to devour. It has the legal sense of becoming an heir (Jer. 32:8) and the military sense of invasion for the purpose of settling in the territory. Both meanings are prominant with regard to God's covenant with Israel. God told Abraham that the land of Canaan would belong to his descendants but, after leaving Egypt, they had to take possession of the Promised Land, Yarash occurs frequently in Deut. Because the people needed to be reminded of their legacy after forty years of wandering in the wilderness. The time was just prior to Joshua's military campaign. A new generation had arisen; they believed that God would make them victorious if they had the proper faith.

Gen. 15:16, coupled, with Lev. 18:24-30, teaches that a nation cannot occupy a land for long if they are in rebellion against God. God is righteous in punishing them (Deut. 9:1-5; 18:12). Therefore, God used other nations to drive them out (Neh. 9:26-31). However, they repented of their sin and God allowed them to return under the Persians (Ezra 9:10-15).

Compare one of Jesus' beatitudes (Matt. 5:5). This concept carries over into the NT in several passages. The believer's inheritance is in heaven, but Satan must be defeated before we obtain it.

PRAISE

Hebrew:

1288 - barak (baw-rak) to kneel; to bless God (as an act of adoration), and (vice versa) man (as a benefit); praise, salute—Judges 5:2,3

1974 - hilluwl (hil-lool) (in the sense of rejoicing) a celebration of thanksgiving for harvest: merry, praise—Lev. 19:24

1984 - halal (haw-lal) to be bright, to shine; to be splendid, to boast; to praise, to celebrate, glorify; to be praised, to be famous; to cause to shine, to make bright, to give light; to deserve praise. At the heart of the word is the idea of radiance. From this came the connotation of the ebuillience of rejoicing and praising God. From this comes the "praise" "hallelujah", called for giving glory to God. There are instances where applied to human beings (ex. Gen. 12:15; II Sam. 14:25)

2167 - zamar (zaw-mar) idea of striking with the fingers; to touch the strings or parts of a musical instrument; to make music, accompanied by the voice; hence to celebrate in song and music:- give praise, sing forth praises, psalms—Ps. 57:7

3034 - yadah (yaw-daw) to throw, cast, to speak out, confess; to praise; to sing; to give thanks. Essentially, it is the acknowledgement of sin, man's character, or the nature and work of God. "halal" emphasizes pride in an object, while "yada" stresses recognition and declaration of a fact, whether it is good or bad. The secondary meaning of this verb is the expression of thanks to God by way of "praising". In these contexts, "bless" would be a good translation. Praise leads to thanksgiving.

4110 - mahalal (mah-hal-awl) from "1984"; fame:- praise—Prov. 27:21

7623 - shabach (shaw-bakh) also "shavach" to address in a loud tone, be loud; to glorify or praise God (I Chr. 16:35; Ps. 117:1), to boast (Ps. 106:47); to triumph; to pacify through words, to calm anger, to still waves, to soothe with praises (Ps. 63:3). The idea in Ps. 65:7 is similar to what occured in Mat.

THE WORD WINDOW

8:23-27 where Jesus calmed the violent waves.

7624 - shebach (sheb-akh) also "shevach" this word corresponds to "shabach". It means to adore, to adulate, to praise. It only occurs five times in Daniel (Dan. 2:23; 4:34, 37; 5:4, 23)

8416 - tehillah (teh-hil-law) comes from "1984". The meaning is laudation, a hymn (Ps. 22:3), a song of praise - a technical musical term for a song which exults God, Psalm 145's title and Neh. 12:46), a psalm (the title to the entire Book of Psalms is in the plural form), glory, praiseworthiness (i.e. a quality describing God), deeds which are worthy of praise (Ex. 15: 11)

8426 - towdah (to-daw) source from "3034". It means an extension of the hand, a confession (Joshua 7:19), a vow; thanks, thanksgiving (Ps. 26:7), a sacrifice of thanksgiving, a type of peace offering (Lev. 7:12); offering praise to God for a sacrifice (Ps. 50:14,23), a thanksgiving choir or procession who gave thanks in praising God (Neh. 12:31, 38, 40)

Greek:
133 ainesis (ah-ee-nes-is) a praising (the act)—Heb. 13:15
134 - aineo (ahee-neh-o) to praise (God)—Rom 15:11
703 - arete (ar-et-ay) praise, virtue—I Pet. 2:9
1391 - doxa (dox-ah) glory (as very apparent): dignity, glory (ious), honor, praise, worship —John 9:24
1867 - epaineo (ep-ahee-neh-o) to applaud:- commend, laud, praise—I Cor. 11:17
1868 - epainos (ep-ahee-nos) laudation, a commendable thing: praise—I Pet. 2:14
2127 - eulogeo (yoo-log-eh-o) to speak well of, to bless (thank or invoke a benediction upon, prosper): - bless, praise—Luke 1:64
5214 - humneo (hoom-neh-o) from word meaning to hymn, i.e.. sing a religious ode; by implication to celebrate (God) in song: - sing an hymn (praise unto)—Heb. 2:12

PRAY/PRAYER

Hebrew:
577 - anna (awn-naw) form 164 and 4994: oh now!: - I (me) beseech (pray) thee. O. I ask you.
2470 - chalah (khaw-law) to be rubbed or worn; to be weak, sick, afflicted; to grieve, lay to, put to pain, make prayer, woman in travail, be wounded
2603 - chanan - see supplication (to plead for grace)
3863 - luw (100) if, peradventure, I pray thee, though, I would, would God (that)
4994 - na (naw) a particle of entreaty or exhortation. It means I pray you! Now!

THE WORD WINDOW

O! It was used in submissive and modest requests (Gen. 18:21) when speaking to superiors. See Psalm 118:25, a cry at the time of the triumphal entry (cf. Mat. 21:9), Hosanna is the transliteration of the Hebrew phrase "0 save us!" Jesus approved of this enthusiastic outburst (Luke 19:40).

6279 - athar (aw-thar) to burn incense in worship, i.e. intercede (listen to prayer), to supplicate. This word for prayer depicts an imploring, beseeching, spontaneous petition of God who is waiting to listen.

6293 - paga (paw-gah) to impinge; to meet with, encounter (Gen.28:11), to push against; to strike, hit, attack, rush at someone with hostility (Ruth 2:22; I Sam. 10:5) to kill (Judges 8:21), to entreat; intercede for help (Isa. 53:12), to reach to, reach something, to border upon; to cause to fall on, lay upon; to make a pact (Isa. 47:3), to make peace, a peace treaty

6419 - palal - see supplication

6739 - tsela (tsel-law) bowing, pray

7592 - shaal (shaw-ale) to inquire, to request, to demand: - ask, beg, borrow, lay to charge, consult, demand, desire, pray, wish

Greek:

1189 - deomai (deh-om-ahee) to beg (as binding oneself), petition, beseech, pray (to) make a request

2065 - erotao (er-o-tah-o) to request, ask, beseech, desire, entreat, pray

2171 - euche (yoo-khay) a prayer, vow (Acts 18:18)

4335 - proseuche - see supplication - prayer (to God), the most frequent term.

1162 - deesis - see supplication

Note: Prayer is properly addressed to God the Father - Mat. 6:6; John 16:23, and the Son - Acts 7: 59; II Cor. 12:8; but in no instance in the NT is prayer addressed to the Holy Spirit distinctively, for whereas the Father is in Heaven, Mat. 6:9, and the Son is at His right hand, Romans 8:34, the Holy Spirit is in and with the believers, John 14:16, 17. In its most simple form prayer is conversation and intercession with God. One may address a prayer, a request or petition, to a man or men, but here we are concerned with prayers to Deity. These may be the recitation or reading of liturgical prayers or they may be spontaneous creations of the heart and mind. Prayer can include petition and intercession, thanks and praise, adoration, and meditation. The Bible does not lay down laws relative to the time and place for prayer, nor does it require any particular attitude or position to be assumed by the one who is praying.

PRECEPT

Hebrew:

4687 - mitsvah (mits-vaw); from 6680; a command, whether human or divine (collect. the Law):- (which was) commanded (ment), law, ordinance, precept.

The Law (of Moses when used collectively), an ordinance; the due. It was the terms of the contract in a deed of purchase for a plot of land (Jer. 32:11). Sometimes it was the instruction of a teacher to his pupil (Prov. 2:1, 3:1). Once it was used for the Ten Commandments (Ex. 24:12). Mitsvah was used much more often to describe the particular conditions of God's covenant with Israel. There were clear-cut directives which were revealed by inspiration and in effect until the cross of Christ (Col. 2:14).

6673 - tsav (tsawv); from 6680; an injunction:- commandment, precept

Greek:

1785 - entole (en-tol-ay'); injunction, i.e. an authoritative prescription:- commandment, precept.

Commandment, whether from God or man (Matt. 15:3; I John 2:3). Related to entellomai (1781), from en (1722), in, upon, and tello, to charge, command (Matt. 4:6; Mark 13:34; John 15:17; Acts 13:47). Entole is the most common of the words meaning commandment. See diatagma, edict, decree; diatage (1296), disposition; entalma (1778), a religious commandment; epitage (2003), commanding authority, order, command; paraggelia (3852), charge, Entole stresses the authority of the one commanding, while entalma (1778) stresses the thing commanded.

1778 - entalma (en-tal-mah); an injunction, i.e., religious precept:- commandment, but emphasizing the thing commanded, a commission (Matt. 15:9; Mark 7:7; Col. 2:22). Derived entellomai (1781), from en (1722), in, and tello, to charge, command, emphasizing the thing commanded; entole (1785) commandment, which stresses the authority of the one commanding.

PRECIOUS

Hebrew:

3368 - yaqar (yaw-kawr), Adjective -"precious; rare; excellent; weighty; noble." None of the 35 biblical appearances of this word occurs before I Sam., but they are scattered throughout the rest of the Bible.

First, yaqar means "precious" in the sense of being rare and valuable: "And he took their king's crown from off his head, the weight whereof was a talent of gold with the precious stones: and it was set on David's head" (II Sam. 12:30). The emphasis is on the nuance "rare" in I Sam. 3:1: "And the word of the Lord was precious in those days; there was no open vision." Second, the word can focus on the value of a thing; "How excellent is thy loving-kindness, O God!" (Ps. 36:7) Third, this word means "weighty" or "noble": "A little foolishness is weightier than wisdom and honor" (Eccl. 10:1 NASB); like dead flies which make perfume stink, so a little foolishness spoils wisdom and honor- it is worth more in a negative sense (cf. Lam. 4:2)

Verb

3365 - yaqar , "to be difficult, be valued from, be valued or honored, be precious." This verb occurs 11 times in biblical Hebrew. The word means "to be precious" in I Sam. 26:21: "Then said Saul, I have sinned: return, my son David: for I will no more do these harm, because my soul was precious in thine eyes this day …"

Noun

3366 - yaqar "precious thing; value; price; splendor; honor." This noun, appears 16 times in biblical Hebrew. The word signifies "value or price: (Zech. 11:13), "splendor" (Esth. 1:4), and "honor" (Esth. 8:16).

In Jer. 20:5 the word refers to "precious things": "Moreover I will deliver all the strength of this city, and all the labors thereof, and all the precious things thereof …"

PREDESTINATE

Greek:

4309 - proorizo (pro-or-id'-zo), This verb is to be distinguished from proginosko, "to foreknow"; the latter has special reference to the persons foreknown by God; proorizo has special reference to that to which the subjects of His foreknowledge are "predestinated."

PRESUMPTION & PRESUMPTUOUS

English

presumption (pri-zump'-shen), behavior or language that is boldly arrogant or offensive; effrontery.

The act of presuming or accepting as true. Acceptance or belief based on reasonable evidence; an assumption or supposition. A condition or basis for accepting or presuming. Law. An inference as to the truth of an allegation or proposition, based on probable reasoning, in the absence of, or prior to, actural proof or disproof. [Middle English presumpcion, from Old French, from Late Latin praesumptio, audacity, from Latin, a taking for granted, assumption, from praesimere, PRESUME]

Hebrew:

2086 - zed (zade), an adj. comes from 2101 (a seminal or menstrual flux: issue). It has the meaning of proud, insolent, wanton, wicked. Since its root means "to seethe," it has the flavor of inflated pride, swelling up. In Psalm 19:13, it is correctly translated "presumptuous (sins)."

Greek:

5113 - tolmetes (tol-may-tace'), from [5111 boldness, through the idea of extreme conduct, to venture]

A daring (audacious) man: - presumptuous. Daring, shameless and irreverent daring—II Peter 2:10

PRIEST & PRIESTHOOD

Hebrew:

3548 - kohen (ko-hane'), This word is found 741 times in the OT. More than one-third of the references are found in the Pentateuch. Leviticus, which has about 185 references, is called the "manual of the priests." The term was used to refer not only to the Hebrew priesthood but to Egyptian, Philistine, Dagon, Baal, Chemosh, and of the Baalim and Asherim.

A "priest" is an authorized minister of deity who officiates at the altar and in other cultic rites. A "priest" performs sacrificial, ritualistic, and mediatorial duties; he represents the people before God. By contrast a "prophet" is an intermediary between God and the people. The priesthood constituted one of the central characteristics of OT religion. A passage showing the importance of the priesthood is Num. 16:5-7: "And he spake unto Korah and unto all his company, saying, even tomorrow the Lord will show who are his, and who is holy; and will cause him to come near unto him: even him whom he hath chosen will he cause to come near unto him .... the man whom the Lord doth choose, he shall be holy ... " The "priests" were to act as teachers of the Law, a duty they did not always carry out.

Greek:

2409 - hiereus (hee-er-yooce) "one who offers sacrifice and has the charge of things pertaining thereto,". The NT knows nothing of a sacerdotal class in contrast to the laity; all believers are commanded to offer the sacrifices mention in Rom. 12:1; Phil. 2:17.

749 - archiereus (ar-khee-er-yuce) designates (a) the high "priests" of the Levitical order, frequently called the chief priests in the NT. The divine institution of the priesthood culminated in the "high priest," it being duty to represent the whole people, e.g., Lev. 4:15, 16. Christ is the high priest, the great high priest, etc.

2406 - hierateuma (hee-er-at-yoo-mah), "a priesthood", a body of priests," consisting of all believers, the whole church (not a special order from among them), called "a holy priesthood," I Pet. 2:5; "a royal priesthood," v. 9; the former term is associated with offering spiritual sacrifices, the latter with the royal dignity of showing forth the Lord's excellences.

2420 - hiersoune (hee-er-o-soo'-nay) "a priesthood," signifies the office, quality, rank & ministry of "a priest," Hebrews 7:11,12,24, where the contrasts between the Levitical "priesthood" and that of Christ are set forth.

2405 - hierateia (hee-er-at-i'-ah), "a priesthood," denotes the priests office, Luke 1:9; Heb. 7:5, RV 2407 - hierateuo (hee-er-at-yoo'-o), signifies "to officiate as a priest," Lk. 1:8, "he executed the priest's office"

PROPHECY/PROPHESY/PROPHESYING

Hebrew:
4853 - massa (mas-saw) burden, utterance—Pro. 30:1
5016 - nebuwah (neb-oo-aw) prediction—II Chron. 9:29
5030 - nabiy (naw-bee) prophet, inspired man—Gen. 20:7
5012 - naba (naw-baw) to speak as a prophet—Num. 11:25
5013 - neba (neb-aw) to speak as a prophet—Ezra 5:1
2372 - chazah (khaw-zaw) to gaze at; have a vision—Isa. 30:10
5197 - nataph (naw-taf) to speak by inspiration—Micah 2:6
5029 - nebiy (neb-ee) prophet—Ezra 6:14
5031 - nebiyah (neb-ee-yaw) prophetess—Ex. 15:20
2374 - chozeh (khaz-o) beholder in vision—Isa. 30:10

Greek:
4394 - propheteia (prof-ay-ti-ah) prediction—I Cor. 14:22
4396 - prophetes (prof-ay-ace) forteller—Acts 13:20
4397 - prophetikos (prof-ay-tik-os) prophetic—Romans 16:26
4395 - propheteuo (prof-ate-yoo-o) to foretell events, divine—John 11:51
5578 - pseudoprophetes (psyoo-dop-rof-ay-tace) pretended forteller–Mat. 24:11

Two basic concepts underlie the words Prophet/Prophetess/Prophecy: forthtelling and foretelling. The first is the more basic and frequent. It means that one person becomes the "mouthpiece" for another, often consoling or correcting. See "nabiy" - Ex. 7:1. Prior to the time of Samuel, a prophet wss called a "seer" in Israel. Later there were schools (i.e. a membr of a class, order, or guild) of "prophets". The "Prophetess" may be only the wife of a "prophet" or she may be an actual prophet (Ex. 15:20; II King 22:14; Isa. 8:3; Luke 2:36). According to the Vine's Complete Expository Dictionary: "With the completion of the canon of Scripture prophecy apparently passed away, I Cor. 13: 8, 9. In his measure the teacher has taken the place of the prophet, cf. the significant change in II Peter 2:1. The difference is that, whereas the message of the prophet was a direct revelation of the mind of God for the occasion, the message of the teacher is gathered from the completed revelation contained in the Scriptures"

QUEEN CANDACE "QUEEN"

Candace was a queen of Ethiopia around the time of Christ. Her name is royal, as she is descended from a long line of Candaces. She is credited for bringing Christianity to her country by sending her high treasurer, the eunuch, to Jerusalem to seek information concerning the new religion of Christ. According to Reisner, all Candaces, like the Pharohs of Egypt, were buried in pyramids. The Candaces were the first women ever to rule a country without any interruption for seven hundred years. One of the most remarkable Candaces of Ethiopia reigned during the era of Alexander the Great. Other than carrying the title of Queen, she also commanded Ethiopia's army, and several times led her country into decisive battles, even against Alexander in 332 B.C. During that campaign, the Queen was able to stop the conqueror, forcing him to return to Egypt. To protect his fame, he made no other attempt to conquer the children of Cush. Candace is a title not a name; Acts 8:27

QUEEN OF SHEBA

The Queen of Sheba was a black woman who resided in Africa and Arabia. She was an Ethiopian by blood, land, and culture, an admirable descendant of Ham's first son, Cush, same as Ehiopia (Gen. 10:7). The Jewish historian Josephus mentioned her as Queen of Ethiopia and Egypt. The Bible addresses her as "Queen of Sheba" in honor of an Arabian country (Sheba), in which Ethiopia dominated during her reign. When talk of Solomon's wisdom spread abroad, this queen, being a woman of respect, did not accept such outrageous news" She felt that Solomon's reputation was over exaggerated, and thus, for assurance, made a triumphant trip to commune with him. The king welcomed her with honor, granting her full rights to survey his riches. But the queen doubted Solomon and began questioning him to see if he could measure up to his reputation. He answered all of her questions and she became satisfied. They exchanged gifts and she returned to her own land (Axum, the capital of Ethiopia's empire). The queen is noted for this famous remark: "The half was not told me." She was remembered by the Savior during his teaching. He called her the "Queen of the South."

The land "Sheba" (modernly known as Yemen) of southern Arabia was a colony of Ethiopia during the Queen of Sheba's reign. Though her royal palace existed in Ethiopia, the queen ruled her kingdom from both territories. The nation Ethiopia and the Land of Sheba were under one monarchal rule. This single government was probably constituted in respect of kinship, since both countries were of the same ethnic background, "Ethiopians." During the scattering of Babal, some of Ham's children journeyed north and south of Arabia; three of them were Raamah, Sheba and Dedan, descendants of Cush (Gen: 10:7; II Ghron. 21 :16.) It was Sheba who populated the southern peninsula and later built the wealthy country called "Sheba" (Isa. 60:6; Ezek. 27:2-23), which remained popular during Solomon's empire.

The Arabian writer Hamdani, who lived during the 10th century, states in his manuscript that the Queen of Sheba's mother was an Ethiopian (Black) named Ekeye. According to Hamdani, the queen lived in Africa and Arabia, but mostly in Africa. Gen. 10:7; I Kings 10:1; II Chron. 9:1-12; Matt. 12:42

QUICKEN

Hebrew:

2421 - chayah (khaw-yaw), to live, whether lit. or fig.; to revive:- keep (leave, make) alive, nourish up, preserve (alive), quicken, recover, repair, restore (to life), revive, (X God) save (alive, life), be whole—Ps. 71 :20; PS.143:11

Greek:

2227 - zoopoieo (dzo-op—oy-eh'-o), vitalize (lit. or fig.): -make alive, give life, quicken; from zoos (alive), and poi eo (4160) to make. vivify (John 6:63; I Cor. 15:45). Used primarily in the NT of raising the dead to life (John 5:21; Rom. 4: 17; 8: 11; I Cor. 15:22; 36; I Peter 3: 18). Generally used in reference to salvation, answering to the Pauline connection between righteousness and life (Gal. 3:21).

4806 - suzoopoieo (sood-zo-op-oy-eh'-o), to reanimate conjointly with (fig.):- quicken together with; used in Eph. 2:5; Col. 2:13, of the spiritual life with Christ, imparted to believers at their conversion.

R

RACA
Greek:
4469 - rhaka (rhak-ah), O empty one, i.e. thou worthless (as a term of utter villification): - raca, its and Aramaic word akin to the Heb. req, "empty," the first a being due to a Galilean change. In the KJV of 1611 it was spelled racha; in the edition of 1638, raca. It was a word of utter contempt, signifiying "empty," intellectually rather than morally, "empty-headed," like Abimelech's hirelings, Judg. 9:4, and the "vain" man of Jas. 2:20. As condemned by Christ, Matt. 5:22, it was worse than being angry, inasmuch as an outrageous utterance is worse than a feeling unexpressed or somewhat controlled in expression; it does not indicate such a loss of self-control as the word rendered "fool," a godless, moral reprobate.

RAHAB
Hebrew:
7343 - Rachab (raw-kwawb), proud;
Rahab was a black woman from a Cannanite city called Jericho, which was surrounded by such popular Hamite cities as Gibeon, Beeroth and Jerusalem.
When Joshua sent spies into Rahab's city, she hid them in a thread stock on her roof. Rahab had heard about these Jews and their God who rescued them from Africa and subdued their foes in Canaan. Moreover, she knew her people could not withstand their strength, so out of fear, Rahab concealed the spies and began to bargain with them concerning security. She pleaded with them to spare her and other kinsmen during the seizure of Jericho. This request was approved by the two men in regard to her courtesy.
After the spies completed their mission, Rahab hauled them down by a scarlet thread through her window and advised them to hide themselves within the mountains for three days to avoid their pursuers. When the messengers journeyed to camp and notified Joshua of their experience, he instantly prepared his people to overthrow Jericho, for God had instructed him as to the manner in which to take the city. He was to march around it six times once a day. Then on the seventh day he was to encompass it seven times with the

sound of trumpets and a loud shout. So when Joshua did as told, the walls of Jericho fell to the earth, and only Rahab,"the harlot," and a few kinsmen were spared. Rahab lived among the Israelites, and there she married a Jew by the name of Salmon (an ancestor of Jesus Christ), who fathered her a child named Boaz. Gen. 9:18; Jos. 2:1; 6:1; I Chron. 2:11-13; Ruth 4:21; Matt. 1:5.

REASONABLE

English: 1. capable of reasoning; rational; 2. governed by or being in accordance with reason or sound thinking; 3. being within the bounds of common sense.

Greek: 3050 - logikos (log-ik-os) from 3056 (logos), rational, (logical), reasonable, of the word.

Pertaining to reason and therefore reasonable, or pertaining to speech as reasonable expression. In Romans 12:1 the reasonable service or worship is to be understood as that service to God which implies intelligent meditation or reflection, without heathen practices as intimated in I Cor. 12:2, and without the OT cultic worship which had become mere thoughtless habit (Is. 1:12-15). On the other hand, in I Peter 2:2, logikon gala (1051milk) cannot possibly mean reasonable milk. LOGOS from which "logikos" is derived, means God's reason or intelligence expressed in human speech in John 1:1, 14. Understanding LOGOS as the Word of God, logikon gala becomes the milk of the Word, milk to be found in the Word, The Word of God is spiritual nourishment as milk is physical nourishment. The second adj. adolos (97) unadulterated, agrees with this, meaning that the "Word of God" when not mixed with human error is nourishing. See adolons, in II Cor. 4:2, not beguiling the Word of God.

REGENERATION

3824 - paliggenesia or palingenesia (pal-ing-ghen-es-ee-ah) "new birth" (palin, "again", genesis, "birth"), is used of "spiritual regeneration," Titus 3:5, involving the communication of a new life, the two operating powers to produce which are "the word of truth", James 1:18; I Peter. 1:23, and the Holy Spirit, John 3:5,6; the loutron, "the laver, the washing", is explained in Eph. 5:26, "having cleansed it by the washing (loutron) of water with the word"

The new birth and "regeneration" do not represent successive stages in spiritual experience, they refer to the same event, but view it in different aspects. The new birth stresses the communication of spiritual life in contrast to antecedent spiritual death; "regeneration" stresses the inception of a new state of things in contrast with the old.

Also defined as "palin" 3825 and "ginomai" (1096), to become. Recovery, renovation, a new birth. Occurs in Mathew 19:28 which refers to the coming state of the whole creation, equivalent to the restoration of all things (Acts 3:21), which will occur when the Son of Man shall come in His glory. The washing of paliggenesia (Titus 3:5) refers to the regeneration of the individual soul.

REPLENISH

Hebrew:

4390 - male (maw-lay) or mala (maw-law) to fill, accomplish. The verb generally denotes the completion of something that was unfinished or the filling of something that was empty. Male was used of the termination of a set period of time (Gen. 29:27; Esth. 2:12; Dan. 9:2) or an indefinite period of an object into a receptacle, whether literally (Gen. 42:25; Josh. 9:13; I Sam. 16:1) or figuratively (Job 8:21; Ps. 71:8; Prov. 12:21).

Male depicted the act of replenishment (Gen. 1:28; Gen. 9:1; Jer. 31:25), as well as the experience of satiation (Ex. 15:9; Prov. 6:30). It could also function as the confirmation of a statement (I Kings 1:14). An interesting idomatic use of male is with the noun yad (3047), where male yad (literally, "fill a hand") is translated "consecrate."

*also means to confirm, give in, be expired, fenced in, gather (selves together), replenish, satisfy, set, space, take a [hand] full, + have wholly

REPROBATE

Greek:

96 - adokimos (ad-ok'ee-mos), signifying "not standing the test, rejected" (a, negative, dokimos, "approved"), was primarily applied to metals (cf.1:22); it is used always in the NT in a passive sense,

(a) of things, Heb. 6:8, "rejected," of land that bears thorns and thistles; (b) of persons, Rom. 1:28, of a "reprobate mind," a mind of which God cannot approve, and which must be rejected by Him, the effect of refusing "to have God in their knowledge"; In I Cor. 9:27 (for which see cast, rejected);

2 Cor. 13:5, 6, 7, where the RV rightly translates the adjective "reprobate" (KJV, "reprobates"), here the reference is to the great test as to whether Christ is in a person; in 2 Tim. 3:8 of those "reprobate concerning the faith," i.e., men whose moral sense is perverted and whose minds are beclouded with their own speculations; in Titus 1:16, of the defiled, who are "unto every good work reprobate," i.e., if they are put to the test in regard to any good work (in contrast to their profession), they can only be rejected.

REPROOF

Hebrew:

1606 - ge'arah (gheh-aw-raw), from 1605 (meaning to address harshly, scold, rebuke, reprove, threaten). a chiding:- rebuke (ing), reproof. A scolding, a threatening—2 Sam. 22:16; Job 26:11; Ecc. 7:5.

8433 - towkechah (to-kay-khaw) or towkachath (to-kakh'-ath), form 3198; chastisement; fig. (by words) correction, refutation, proof (even in defence). Justification, pleading, the act of arguing, defense, maintaining the right (Job 23:4); contradicting (Psalm 39:11; 73:14), rebuke, reproof (Prov. 1:23, 25, 30; 3:11; 5:12); complaint (Hab. 2:1)

Greek:

1650 - elegchos (el'-eng-khos); proof, conviction:-evidence, reproof, a proving. Conviction, only in 2 Timothy 3:16 and Hebrews 11:1. It implies not merely the charge on the basis of which one is convicted, but also the manifestation of the truth of that charge. The results to be reaped from that charge and the acknowledgement, (if not outwardly, yet inwardly) of its truth on the part of the accused are referred to as well.

RESIST

Hebrew:

7853 - satan (saw-tan'), a primitive root; to attack, (fig.) accuse: - (be an) adversary, resist—Zec. 3:1

Greek:

436 - anthistemi (anth-is'-tay-mee), "to set against" (anti, "against," histemi, "to cause to stand"), used in the middle (or passive) voice and in the intransitive 2nd aorist and perfect active, signifying "to withstand", oppose, resist," is translated "to resist" in Matt. 5:39; Acts 6:10, KJV (RV, "withstand"); Rom. 9:19; KJV (RV, "withstandeth"); Gal. 2:11, RV (KJV, "withstood"); 2 Tim. 3:8 (2nd part), KJV (RV, "withstand"); "to withstand" in Acts 13:8; Eph. 6:13; 2 Tim. 3:8 (1st part); to stand against—James 4:7

478 - antikathistemi - an-tee-kath-is'-tay-mee), "to stand firm against" (anti, "against," kathistemi, "to set down," kata), is translated "ye have (not) resisted" in Heb. 12:4. In the Sept. Deut. 31:21; Josh. 5:7; Mic. 2:8.

496 - antipipto (an-tee-pip'-to); lit., and primarily, "to fall against or upon" (anti, "against," pipto, "to fall"), then, "to strive against, resist," is used in Acts 7:51 of "resisting" the Holy Spirit.

498 - antitassomai - (an-tee-tas'som-ahee), anti "against," tasso, "to arrange," originally military term, "to range in battle against," and frequently so found in the papyri, is used in the middle voice signifying "to set oneself against, resist,"

(a) of men, Acts 18:6, "opposed themselves"; elsewhere "to resist," of resisting human potentates, Rom. 13:2; (b) of God, James 4:6; 5:6, negatively, of leaving persistent evildoers to pursue their self-determined course, with eventual retribution; I Peter 5:5

REVELATION
Greek:
602 - apokalupsis (ap-ok-al'-oop-sis), from 601; disclosure: - revelation (12x), be revealed (2x), to lighten, manifestation (1x) coming (1x) appearing (1x). This word is more comprehensive than epiphaneia (2015) and depicts the progressive and immediate unveiling of the otherwise unknown and unknowable God to His church. One of three words referring to the Second Coming of Christ (I Cor. 1:7; II Thess. 1:7 I Peter 1:7, 13). The other two words are epiphanieia, appearing (I Tim. 6:14), and parousia (3952), presence, coming (II Thess. 2:1). Apokalupsis, a grander and more comprehensive word, includes not merely the thing shown and seen but the interpretation, the unveiling of the same. The epiphaneiai (pi), appearings, are contained in the apokalupsis, revelation, being separate points or moments therein. Christ's first coming was an epiphaneia (II Tim. 1:10); the apokalupsis will be far more glorious.

REVELING
Greek:
2970 - komos (ko'-mos), derived form Comus, the god of feasting and reveling. His sacred rights consisted in feasting and drunkenness with impurity and obscenity of the grossest kind. Actually there were lascivious feastings with songs, music, and drinking wine. Therefore, it always presupposes a festal company and drunken revelers. Used only in the plural in the NT, riotings (Rom. 13:13); revelings (Gal. 5:21; I Pet. 4:3). A "revel, carousal," the concomitant & consequence of drunkenness. Related words methe (3178), drunkenness in the abstract sense; potos (4224), a drinking bout or banquet giving opportunity for excessive drinking but not necessarily realizing it; oinophlugia (3632), excess of wine; kraipale (2897), the sense of overfull ness of wine.

5172 - truphe (troo-fay') "luxuriousness, daintiness, reveling," is translated freely by the verb "to revel" in II Pet. 2:13, RV (KJV, "to riot"), lit., "counting reveling in the daytime a pleasure." In Luke 7:25 it is used with en, "in," and translated "delicately."

REVERENCE

Hebrew:

3372 - yare (yaw-ray) to be afraid; to fear, revere; to be feared; to be dreadful; to be reverenced; to terrify, make afraid. There are two main types of fear described by "yare" : a. the emotion and intellectual anticipation of harm, what one feels may go wrong for him; b. a very positive feeling of awe or reverence for God, which may be expressed in piety or formal worship.—Lev. 19:3; Psalm 89:7

7812 - shachah (shaw-khaw) to depress; to prostrate oneself (in homage to royalty or to God, Gen. 23:7; 37:7; to bow down (Is. 51:23); to crouch; to fall down, sink down; to humbly beseech; to do obeisance; to worship (I Sam. 15:25; Jer. 7:2) shachah was not used in the general sense of worship, but specifically to bow down, to prostrate oneself as an act of respect before a superior being. Joseph saw sheaves, representing his brothers, bowing down before his sheaf (Gen. 37:5, 9, 10) Ruth bowed before Boaz (Ruth 2:10). David bowed before Saul. This honor was shown not only to superiors, such as kings and princes (Gen. 23:7), or to equals (II Sam. 9:8), but especially in worshiping a deity. Therefore it meant to honor God with prayers (Gen. 22:5) even without prostrating the body (Gen. 47:31). However, those who used this mode of salutation often fell upon their knees and touched the ground with their foreheads (Gen. 19:1,48:12).—Lev. 26:2—in short it was a way of showing submission.

Greek:

127 - aidos (ahee-doce) bashfulness, i.e. (towards men), modesty or (towards God) awe: reverence, shamefacedness—Heb. 12:28

1788 - entrepo (en-trep-o) "to turn in" (i.e., upon oneself), "to put to shame," denotes, when used in the passive voice, "to feel respect for, to show deference to, to reverence," "to invert" in a good sense, to respect; or in a bad one, to confound: regard—Matt. 21:37; Mark 12:6

5399 - phobeo (fob-eh-o) to be in awe of, i.e. to revere: "to fear," used in the passive voice in the NT; in Eph. 5:33 of reverential fear on the part of a wife for a husband

2124 - eulabeia (yoo-lab-i-ah)" as a noun "caution, reverence," is translated "reverence" in Heb. 12:28 (1st part in the best mss; some have aidos)

REWARDER

Greek:

3406 - misthapodotes (mis-thap-od-ot'-ace), from misthos (3408) a reward, and apodidomi (591), to render; a recompenser, a rewarder; one who pays wages

RIGHT HAND

Hebrew:

3325 - yamiyn (yaw-meen) "right hand." This word has cognates attested in Ugaritic, Arabic, Syriac, Aramaic, and Ethiopic. It appears about 137 times and in all periods of biblical Hebrew.

First, it represents a body part called the "right hand" (Gen. 48:13). Second, yamiyn represents the direction, to the "right." In this use the word can specify the location of someone or something (Exod. 14:29). In other contexts yamiyn signifies "direction toward: (Gen.13:9 - the first biblical appearance). Third, yamiyn can be used of bodily parts other than the right hand. Judges 3:16 (the thigh), I Sam. 11:2 in conjunction of the eye. Fourth, used to mean "south," since the south is on one's "right" when he faces eastward (I Sam. 23:19).

* the right hand or side (leg, eye) of a person or other object (as the stronger and more dexterous.)

3233 - yemaniy (yem-aw-nee), "right hand; on the right side; the right side (of ones' body); southern." This noun appears 25 times in the OT. First appearance in Exod. 29:20 refers to a location.

8486 - teman (tay-mawn) from 3225; the south (as being on the right hand of a person facing the east):- south

RIGHTEOUS/RIGHTEOUSNESS

Hebrew:

6663 - sadaq or tsadaq (tsaw-dak)"to be righteous, be in the right, be justified, be just." This verb, which occurs almost 40 times in biblical Hebrew, is derived from the noun sedeq. Nowhere is the issue of righteous more appropriate than in the problem of the suffering of the righteous presented to us in Job, where the verb occurs 17 times. Apart from the Book of Job the frequency of sadaq in the various books is small.

The basic meaning of sadaq is "to be righteous". It is a legal term which involves the whole process of justice. God "is righteous" in all of His relations, and in comparison with Him man is not righteous. In a causative pattern, the meaning of the verb brings out more clearly the sense of a judicial pronouncement of innocence: "If there be a controversy between men, and they come unto judgment, that the judges may judge them; then they shall justify (sadaq) the righteous (saddiq), and condemn the wicked" (Deut. 25:1).

6664 - sedeq or tsedeq (tseh-dek) is a noun and it carries with it the sense of "loyalty" demonstrated by a king or priest as a servant of his own god. In these languages a form of the root is combined with other words or names, particularly with the name of a deity, in royal names. In the OT we meet the name Melchizedek ("king of righteousness"). A more limited meaning of the root is found in Arabic (a South Semitic language): "truthfulness" (of propositions). In rabbinic Hebrew the noun "sedaqah" signifies "alms: or: demonstrations of mercy."

Translators have found it difficult ot translate these two words. The older translations base their understanding on the Septuagint with the translation dikaiosune ("righteousness") and on the Vulgate iustitia ("justice"). In these translations the legal relationship of humans is transferred to God in an absolute sense as the Lawgiver and with the perfections of justice and "righteous."

Exegetes have worked hard in an attempt to understand contextually the words sedeq and sedaqah. The conclusions of the researchers indicate a twofold significance. On the one hand, the relationships among people and of a man to his God can be described as sedeq, supposing the parties are faithful to each other's expectations. It is a relational word. In Jacob's proposal to Laban, Jacob used the word sedaqah to indicate the relationship. On the other hand, "righteous" as an abstract or as the legal status of a relationship is also present in the OT. Gen. 15:6—"And he (the Lord) counted it to him (Abraham) for righteousness"

6662 - saddiq or tsaddiyq (tsad-deek) "righteous; just". adjective occurs 206 times in biblical Hebrew, and signifies "loyalty" of a king or high priest to his personal god, often represented by a gift to the god. The word is used of God in Exodus 9:27: "I have sinned this time: the Lord is righteous, and I and my people are wicked." Saddiq is used of a nation in Gen. 20:4: "And he said, Lord, wilt thou slay also a righteous nation?

Greek:

1342 - dikaios (dik-ah-yos) signifies "just," without prejudice or partiality, e.g. of the judgment of God, II Thess. 1:5; of His character as Judge, II Tim. 4:8; Rev. 16:5; of His ways and doings, Rev. 15:3.

1343 - dikaiosune (dik-ah-yos-oo-nay) is "the character or quality of being right or just"; it was formerly spelled "rightwiseness," which clearly expresses the meaning. It is used to denote an attribute of God, e.g., Rom. 3:5, the context of which shows that "the righteousness of God" means essentially the same as His faithfulness, or truthfulness, that which is consistent with His own nature and promises; Romans 3:25, 26 speaks of His "righteousness" as exhibited in the death of Christ, which is sufficient to show men that God is neither indifferent to sin nor regards it lightly. On the contrary, it demonstrates that quality of holiness in Him which must find expression in His condemnation of sin. It is found in the sayings of the Lord Jesus, (a) of whatever is right or just in itself, whatever conforms to the revealed will of God, Matt. 5:6, 10, 20; John 16:8, 10; (b) whatever has been appointed by God to be acknowledged and obeyed by man, Matt. 3:15; 21:32; (c) the sum total of the requirements of God, Matt. 6:33; (d) religious duties, Matt. 6:1 (distinguished as almsgiving, man's duty to his neighbor, vv. 2-4, prayer, his duty to God, vv. 5-15, fasting, the duty of selfcontrol, vv. 16-18).

"In preaching of the apostles" recorded in Acts the word has the same general meaning.

R.S.V.P.

French:

r.s.v.p. - respondez s'il vous plait (respond will you please)

English: please reply

RUDIMENT

Greek:

4747 - stoicheion (stoy-khi'-on), something orderly in arrangement, i.e. (by impl.) a serial (fundamental, initial) constituent (lit.), proposition, (fig.):- element, principle, rudiment.

From stoichos, row, and stoicheo (4748), to put or go in a row, one of a series. In the pl. ta stoicheia, the elements or first principles of matter from which other things proceed in order or of which they are composed (II Peter 3:10, 12). Figuratively refers to the elements of first principles of the Christian doctrine (Heb. 5:12). Paul calls the elements of the world or worldly elements (Gal. 4:3; Col. 2:8, 20). In Galatians 4:9 he calls them weak and poor elements when considered merely in themselves and in opposition to the geat realities to which they were designed to lead. These elements contain the rudiments of the knowledge of Christ. The Law, as a schoolmaster, was to bring the Jews to this knowledge (Gal. 3:24). They called worldly as consisting in outward worldly institutions (Heb. 9:1).

RULE

Hebrew:

4910 - maschal (maw-shal) to rule, reign, govern, have dominion, to manage. Gen. 1:18 indicates the prominence of the sun over the daytime and the moon over the nighttime. Part of Eve's punishment was submission to the appropriate leadership of her husband over the family (Gen. 3:16; 4:7). Joseph's rule over his brothers, the supremacy of the rich, an oppressive king, cultural domination, political leadership, self control and God's providence, all are depicted by the word "maschal". All types of authority have their source in God Himself (Rom. 13:1-7).

4475 - memshalah (mem-shaw-law) to reign as king—Gen 1:16

7287 - radah (raw-daw) to tread down (as a winepress, with the feet); to subjugate, subdue (Gen. 1:28). To rule, to cause to rule, to crumble; to oppress; to walk on a person (Ps.49:14); have dominion, reign; to prevail against, to take (honey from a hive), to scrape out (Jer. 5:31). The Talmud used the word for taking bread from an oven 8323 - sara (saw-ra') to have, exercise, get dominion—Est. 1:22

Greek:
757 - archo (ar'kho) to rule, be first in rank—Mark 10:42
746 - arche (ar-kay) beginning. Arche means a pass, beginning or an act, cause (Col. 1:18) Christ is called the beginning because He is the efficient cause of the creation; the head because He is before all things and all things were created by Him and for Him (John 1:1-3; Heb. 1:10). Arche also means extremity or outer most point (Acts 10:11); rule, authority, dominion, power (Luke 20:20). The verb archo (757) to be first or to rule. The noun archon (758) denotes a ruler; archalos (744) of ole time; archegos (747), leader.
1018 - brabeuo (brab-yoo'-o) to govern, prevail—Col. 3:15
2233 - hegeomai (hayg-eh'-om-ahee) to lead, i.e. command—Heb 13:7
2583 - kanon (kan-ohn') rule, standard—II Cor. 10:15
4165 - poimaino (poy-mah'-ee-no) to tend as a shepherd (or fig. a supervisor)— Rev. 2:27 4291 - proistemi (prok'-i-mahee) to preside; to practice—I Tim. 3:5

S

SABBATH -

Hebrew:

4868 -mishbath -(mish -bawth) cessation, i.e. - destruction: sabbath.

7673 - shabath (shaw-bath) to repose, i.e. desist from exertion; used in many implied relations; (cause to, make to) cease, celebrate, cause (make to fall), keep (sabbath) suffer to be lacking, leave, put away (down), (make to) rest, rid still, take away

7676- shabbath (shab-bawth) intermission, the sabbath

7677 - shabbathown (shab-baw—thone) a sabbatism or special holiday, rest, sabbath

Greek:

4521 - sabbaton (sab-sab-on) of Hebrew origin (7676); the sabbath, or day of weekly repose from secular avocations (also the observance or institution itself) sabbaton was transliterated from the Aramaic word, which was mistaken for a plural; hence the singular, sabbaton. The root means "to cease, desist" (Heb. shabath means to intercept, interrupt) the doubled "b" has an intensive force, implying a complete cessation or a making to cease, probably the former. The idea is not that of relaxation or refreshment, but cessation from activity. The observation of the seventh day of the week, enjoined upon Israel, was a sign between God and His earthly people, based upon the fact that after the six days of creative operations He rested. The Old Testament regulations were developed and systematized to such an extent that they became a burden upon the people (who otherwise rejoiced in the rest provided) and a byword for absurd extravagance. The effect upon current opinion explains the antagonism roused by the Lord's cures wrought on the "Sabbath". The Lord's attitude towards the "sabbath" was by way of freeing it from these vexatious traditional accretions by which it was made an end in itself, instead of a means to an end (Mark 2:27) In the Epistles the only direct mentions are in Col. 2:16, "a sabbath day", where it is listed among things that were "a shadow of things to come), example - Heb. 4:4-11, where the "sabbatismos" is appointed for believers (rest). "Vine's complete Expository Dictionary"

THE WORD WINDOW

The Heb. 4 passage cross reference is found in the Old Testament passage found in Numbers 14:30 concerning God telling the Israelites they will not enter the land to dwell (rest), because of their unbelief. Because of Christ we can now enter into God's rest

SAVE/SAVED/SALVATION

Hebrew:

389 - ak (ak) surely, at least, certainly, but, howbeit, nevertheless, only, save truly, verily

518 - im (eem) oh that, whether, when, while, yet, save, doubtless if

657 - ephec (eh-fes) no further, cease, end but (only), no more, save, (ing), uttermost part, want, without (cause)

1107 - biladey (bil-ad-ay) from word meaning apart from, except, without, besides KJV usage includes - not in me, not till, not (in), save

1115 - biltiy (bil-tee) a failure of, not, except, unless, besides, because not until, save, without, nothing

2108 - zuwlah (zoo-law) scattering, i.e. removal, but, only, save

2421 - chayah (khaw-yaw) from word meaning to show. To live, to revive, keep, quicken, recover, repair, restore (to life), be whole, give life, save

3444 - yeshuwah (yesh-oo-aw) Noun - used about 78 times - includes the idea of "salvation" through divine appointed means (but a few times as a human act), something saved - deliverance aid, victory, prosperity, health, help (ing), save, saving, welfare

3467 - yasha (yaw-shah) Verb - appears about 205 times in biblical Hebrew - it signifies to remove or seek to remove someone from a burden, oppression or danger. Sometimes from danger of defeat. To be open, wide or free, to be safe, preserve, deliver, help, be safe, bring (having), salvation, saved

3468 - yesha (yes-shah or yay-shah) Noun used about 36 times - signifies that which God will do in man's behalf, or that which has been done by Him for man. Liberty, deliverance, prosperity, safety, salvation, saving

4190 - mowshaah (mo-shaw-aw) "salvation" from (3467-deliverance) occurs 1 time

4422 - malat (maw-lat) to be smooth, to escape (as if by slipperiness), to release, or rescue, deliver (self), leap out, let go, save

7535 - raq (rak) leanness, i.e. limitation, at the least, nevertheless, nothing but, only, save, so (that), surely, in any wise

8104 - shamar (shaw-mar) to hedge about (as with thorns), to guard, or protect, attend to, take heed, observe, preserve, save

8668 teshuwah (tesh-oo-aw) Noun - used about 34 times. Frequently joined with responses of thanksgiving and rejoicing. The idea of "salvation" is that of preservation from threatened, impending and perhaps deserved danger and suffering. Rescue, deliverance, help, safety, victory.

Greek:
235 - alla (al-lah) contrariwise:- and, but (even), indeed, nay, nevertheless, no, not withstanding, save, therefore, yea, yet
1295 - diasozo (dee-as-odze-o) to save thoroughly, to cure, preserve, rescue, bring safe, escape, heal, make perfectly whole, save
1508 - ei (i-may) if not, but, except (that), more than, save (only), saving, till
2228 - e (ay) a participle of distinction between two connected terms, than, but (either), rather, save, that, what
3844 - para (par-ah) near, insight of, nigh, than, with, save, among, at, the vicinity of
4133 - pl en (plane) moreover, besides, save that, rather, yet, but, except, save, nevertheless, notwithstanding
4982 - SOZO - to save, i.e. to deliver or protect: - heal, preserve, do well, be, make whole

Acts 2:47; Mt. 1:21; Rom. 5:10; Rom. 11:26; Lk. 19:10; John 10:9; I Cor. 10:33; Mark 13:13; I Cor. 3:15; Rev. 21:24

1. used of material & temporal deliverance from danger, suffering, etc.
2. spiritual and eternal salvation granted immediately by God to those who believe on the Lord Jesus Christ
3. of the present experiences of God's power to deliver from the bondage of sin
4. of the future deliverance of believers at the second coming of Christ for His saints
5. deliverance of the nation of Israel at the second Advent of Christ
6. inclusively for all the blessings bestowed by God on men in Christ
7. of those who endure to the end of the time of the Great Tribulation
8. of the individual believer, who though losing his reward at the judgement seat of Christ hereafter, will not lose his salvation
9. of the deliverance of the nations at the Millennium

examples:
Hebrew
389-Ex.12:16 * 518-11 Chron.2:6 * 657-Deu.15:4 * 1107-Gen.14:24 1115 - Ex. 22:20 * 2108 - Deu. 1:36 * 2421 - I Sam. 10:24
3444 - Ps. 80:2, 49: 18, Isa. 12:3)
3467-Ex.2:17, Josh. 10:6, Judg.12:2, II Sam.10:11, II Sam. 10:27, PS.20:9
3468 - Gen. 49:18
4422 - I Sam. 19:11
7535 - I Kings 8:9
8668-Judg.15:18, II Sam. 11:13, Prov.11:14

Greek:
235 - Mt. 19:11 * 1295 - Acts 27:43 * 1508 - Mt. 11:27 * 2228 - Jn. 13:10 3844 -II Cor.11:24 * 4133 - Acts 20:23 * 4991 - Lk. 1 :69 * 4992 - Lk. 2:30, Ep. 6:17 4982 - Mt. 8:25; Rom. 5:9 7. Mt. 10:22.

SEALED

An engraved stamp, ring, or cylinder for making an impression which would be proof of authenticity, either the substitute for or the authenticating of a signature. Stamp seals were first used in the fourth millennium B.C. and the engraved cylinder came a little later. These were either impressed or rolled on soft clay in earliest times and in later times on wax. The Egyptian scarab was such a seal. From the Palestinian excavations have come many stamped jar handles, indicating not content by ownership. In both Testaments the word is used literally and figuratively - as well as metaphorically.

In the OT God seals up the sins of men (Deut. 32:34; Job 14:17; 33:16.) In the NT Paul's converts are God's seal on Paul's ministry (I Cor. 9:2), and believers are said to be sealed with the promised Holy Spirit and sealed for the day of redemption (Eph. 1:13; 4:30). The NT sealing of the believer is called the arrabon in Greek, a word transliterated from the Hebrew' errabon and is used in clear OT contexts which show its meaning to be "a pledge." Note - Gen. 38:12-26. The gift of the Spirit is the pledge, token, seal, earnest, that the one engifted will ultimately be fully redeemed.

SEDITIONS

Greek:

1370 - dichostasia (dee-khos-tas-ee'-ah), from a der.of 1364 and 4714; disunion, i.e. (fig.) dissension: division (2x, sediton (1x). It means literally "a standing apart" (dicha, "asunder, apart," stasis, "a standing"), "seditions" in Galatians 5:20; and "divisions" in Romans 16:17; I Cor. 3:3

SEEK

Hebrew - As a Verb

1245 - baqash (baw-kash) to search out (by any method especially in prayer or worship), to strive after: - ask beg, beseech, desire, get, make inquistion, request, require, seek, consult (used about 220 times) - to find something that is lost or missing, or at least, whose location is unknown. (Gen 37:15)

1239 - baquar (baw-kar) to plough, break forth, to inspect, admire, seek out 579 - anah (aw-naw) to seek a quarrel

1875 - darash (daw-rash) to tread or frequent: usually to follow (for the pursuit or search); by implication to seek or ask; specifically for worship, gently inquire make inquisition (used about 160 times) - to inquire of God, which sometimes indicates a private seeking of God in prayer for direction (Gen. 25:22). Also often used to describe the "seeking of" the Lord in the sense of entering into covenantal relationship with Him (Isa. 55:6)

Greek -
2212 -zeteo (dzay-teh-o) to seek: spec. to worship (God - Acts 17::27), or in a bad manner - to plot (against life - Mat. 7:7, 8)
327 - anazeto (an-ad-say-teh-o) - to search out, to seek carefully
1567 - ekzeteo (ek-say-teh-o) to search out, investigate, crave demand, worhip: to seek after (carefully, diligently) — HEBREWS 11:6

SELAH
Hebrew:
5542 - selah (seh-law) a term of unknown meaning used three times in Hab. and seventy-one times in Psalms. Some suggest it was a direction for the conductor; others that it had some liturgical function (for examples, see Ps. 3:4, 8; 4:2, 4; Hab. 3:3). Also thought to mean - to lift up, exalt (a technical musical term probably showing accentuation, pause, interruption)
5544 - cela - (seh-lah) craggy rock, fortress, the rock city of Edom. former name of Joktheel (II Kings 14:7)

SERVE/SERVANT/SERVICE
Hebrew:
582- enowsh (en-oshe) a mortal, a man in general, servant — I Sam 24:7
3027 - yad (yad) a hand, (the open one indicating power, means direction) service, side, sore, draw with strength—I Chron. 6:31
5288 - na'ar (nah-ar) a boy, from the age of infancy to adolescence; a servant, a girl of similiar lattitude in age: babe, child, damsel, lad, servant, young man— Jud. 7:10
5650 - ebed (eh-bed) a servant, bondman, (man) Gen. 9:25
5647 - abad (aw-dad) to work (in any sense), to serve, enslave, worker, bond-service, husband man, (cause to, make to) serve (ing), service, worshipper Gen 49:15
6635 - tsaba (tsaw-baw)
   tsebaah (tseb-aw-aw) a mass of persons (or fig. things), impl. a campaign, lit. or fig. (spec. hardship, worship):- host, service, soldiers Numbers 4:35
7916 - sakiyr (saw-keer) a man at wages by the day or year: hired (man, servant). hireling—Lev. 25:6; Lev. 25:40
8278 - serad (ser-awd) stitching (as pierced with a needle):- service Ex. 39:41

THE WORD WINDOW

Greek:
1248 - diakonika (dee-ak-on-ee-ah) attendance (as a servant), aid (official), minister (ing, tration, try), office relief, service (ing)—Rom. 16:1
1249 - diakonos (dee-ak-on-os) to run on errands, an attendant, a waiter (at table or in other menial duties); spec. a Chr. teacher and pastor (tech. a deacon or deaconess):- deacon, minister, servant —— Mk. 9:35
1398 - doulevo (doo-yoo-o) to be a slave to (lit. or fig), to be in bondage, (do) serve (ice) —— Mat. 6:24
1401 - doulos (doo-los) a slave, bondman, man of servile condition, one who gives himself up to anothers will—Mat. 10:25
2324 - therapon (ther-ap-ohn) a menial attendant (as if cherishing), servant— Heb 3:5
2999 - latreia (lat-ri-ah) divine service, ministration to God, i.e. worship—Heb. 9:1
3000 - latrevo (lat-ryoo-o) to minister (to God), i.e. render, religious homoage:- serve, do the service, worship —Lk. 1:74
3407 - misthios (mis-thee-os) a wage earner;- hired servant—Lk. 15:17
3610 - oiketes (oy-ket-ace) a fellow resident, i.e. menial domestic:- (household) servant ——Lk. 16:13
3816 - pais (paheece) a boy, agirl Lk. 15:26

SEVEN SAYINGS FROM THE CROSS
1. "Father, forgive them" ————Luke 23:34
2. "Today shalt thou be with me in paradise" ————Luke 23:43
3. "Woman, behold thy son" ————John 19:26
4. "My God, my God" ————Matt. 27:46
5. "I thirst" ———— John 19:28
6. "It is finished" ————John 19:30
7. "Father, into thy hands" ———— Luke 23:46

SHADOW (FOCUS ON PSALMS 23:4 & 17:8)
Hebrew:
6738 tsel (tsal e), this mas. noun comes from 6751. It means shadow, shade. There are two distinctly different connotations of this word. First, a shadow can convey the sense of protection from the heat (Job: 7:2; Is. 4:6), shelter (Gen. 19:8; Is. 30:2,3, cf. Ps. 17:8; 36:7; 91:1). Second, man's life is similar to a temporary, fleeting shadow (I chl. 29:15). In Job 17:7 the term is used to describe the failing, frail condition of an individual who is ill.
6757 - tsal maweth (tsal-maw-'veth), this fem. compound noun comes from two parts: tset (6738) and maweth (4194). It means shade of death, the shadow of death, the grave, deep darkness, terror, calamity. This is one of the few

compound Hebew words in the OT. It is a poetic term for very thick darkness (Job 3:5; 10:21; 28:3; 34:22; 38:17). Tsalmaweth appears in Psalm 23:4 which speaks of God leading His people (sheep) safely through no matter how dark a place (the experience of death) is. It is also used to describe the internal anguish of a person who has rebelled against God (Ps. 107:10-14). God promised to send His Messiah as a light (Is. 9:2).

SHEKINAH, SHECHINAH

Shekhina with the above alternative transliterations, is the English spelling of a feminine Hebrew language that means the dwelling or settling, and is used to denote the dwelling or settling presence of God, especially in the Temple in Jerusalem. It is derived from the Hebrew verb 'sakan' or 'shachan'. In Biblical Hebrew the word means literally to settle, inhabit, or dwell, and is used frequently in the Hebrew Bible (Gen 9:27, 14:13, Psalms 37:3, Jer. 33:16), as well as the weekly Shabbat blessing recited in the Temple in Jerusalem ("May He who causes His name to dwell [shochan] in this House, cause to dwell among you love and brotherliness, peace and friendship").

The word "Shekhina" also means "royalty" or "royal residence" (The Greek word 'skene' - dwelling - is thought to be derived from 'shekina' and 'sakan'. The word for Tabernacle, mishacan, is a derivative of the same root and is also used in the sense of dwelling - place in the Bible, e.g. Psalm 132:5 ("Before I find a place for God, mishcanat (dwelling-places) for the Strong One of Israel.") Accordingly, in classic Jewish thought, the Shekhina refers to a dwelling or settling in a special sense, a dwelling or settling of divine presence, to the effect that, while in proximity to the Shekhinah, the connection to God is more readily perceivable. Shechinah - a Chaldee word meaning resting-place, not found in Scripture, but used by the later Jews to designate the visible symbol of God's presence in the tabernacle, and afterwards in Solomon's temple. When the Lord led Israel out of Egypt, he went before them "in a pillar of cloud." This was the symbol of his presence with his people. God also spoke to Moses through the 'shekhinah' out of a burning bush. (Exodus 14:20; 40:34-38; Leviticus 9:23; Numbers 14:10; 16:19,42)

The shekhinah in the NT is commonly equated to the presence or indwelling of the Spirit of the Lord (generally referred to as the Holy Spirit, or Spirit of Christ) in the believer, drawing parallels to the presence of God in Solomon's Temple. Furthermore, in the same manner that the Shekhinah is linked to prophecy in Judaism, so it is in Christianity: For no prophecy ever came by the will of man: but men spake from God, being moved by the Holy Spirit. (II Peter 1:21 ASV) In a minority of Christian sects, Shekhinah is identified with Sophia, the feminine aspect of God.

When reference is made to the Shekhinah as manifestations of the glory of the Lord associated with his presence, Christians find numerous occurrences in the NT in both literal (as in Luke 2:9 which refers to the "glory of the Lord" shining on the shepherds at Jesus' birth) as well as spiritual forms John 17:22, where Jesus speaks to God of giving the "glory" that God gave to him to the people).

SHINETH

SHINETH (as used in John 1:5)

Greek:

5316 - phaino (fah'-ee-no), to shine (John 1:5; 5:35; 2 Peter 1:19; I John 2:8; Rev. 1:16; 8:12; 21:23).

In the pass., phainomai, to appear, be conspicuous, shine (Matt. 24:27); to appear, be seen (Matt. 1:20; 2:13, 19); to appear, seem (Matt. 6:5,16; 23:28); to seem, appear, be thought (Mark14:64). It indicates how a matter phenomenally shows and presents itself with no necessary assumption of any beholder at all. This suggests that something may shine without anybody necessarily seeing it, contrasted to something that exists but does not shine. Nooumenon is that which is conceived in the mind but does not have any objective existence and does not necessarily manifest itself. Phainomenon is that which manifests itself, appears or shines (phainetai), and must have a reality behind it. It cannot be just the figment of the imagination. Therefore, phainomai, is often syn. with eimi (1510), to be, and ginoma (1096), to become (Matt. 2:7; 13:26). It may also have no substance, yet presupposes one. Dokeo (1380), think, has in contrast the subj. estimate which may be formed of a thing, not the obj. showing and seeming which it may actually possess. One may dokei (think) something which may not have an objective reality. The Docetic heresy owes its name to this verb. It taught that Christ's body was not real but imaginary. However, something that shines, phainei, must exist objectively. This is where we get our word "phenomenon" - any occurrence or fact that is directly perceptible by the senses.

SHOFAR (SHOFAR -FER)

noun - Judaism. The shofar is a horn that was developed by the ancient Hebrews. It was, and is, a ceremonial item. It was used during holy rites, to call assembly or signal a sacrifice. The shofar was also used in battle by the ancient Hebrews who used it as a call to war and believed that the sound would panic their enemies. The sound of the shofar also announced the Jubilee year. Today, this ancient trumpet of Israel is used in both Jewish and Christian worship. It is most closely associated with the Jewish Holy days of Rosh Hashana (New Years) also called Yom Teru'ah (the day of blowing), and

Yom Kipurr (Day of Atonement). Outside of these religions it is not uncommon to find the shofar used in holistic ceremonies or rites associated with the earth elements. The ancient Hebrew shofar was made of animal horn. It was originally made from the horn of a domestic ram; however, horns used would have included those of domestic sheep and goat, wild mountain goat, antelope, or gazelle.

There are basically two types of trumpets used in the OT most frequently used, and consequently the Hebrew word most often in scripture, is the shofar, or trumpet made of animal horn. Any type of animal horn from a "clean" animal, except the cow or steer, could be used to make a shofar. According to Jewish tradition, God does not want to be reminded of the "golden calf incident" (Ex. 32); hence the prohibition cow horns. The ram's horn, which is most often used, is a reminder of the ram He provided to Abraham (Mount Moriah), in exchange for the life of Isaac. Realistically, in those times it was also an instrument which was readily available and could also be as a weapon in battle. The other type of trumpet referred to in the OT is the silver trumpet originally made for the Tabernacle of Moses from God's blueprint. It is a straight instrument made of cast silver with a flared end and had no valves, traditionally blown only by the priests. After the destruction of the temple, the Yemenite shofar began to be used in the synagogue as replacements. Traditionally, the ram's horn shofar could be blown by any Jewish man and was not normally blown by a woman. The Yemenite shofar and the silver trumpets were blown only by priests. Today, Christians of both sexes blow the shofar (either the ram's horn or Yemenite shofar), since under the New Covenant we are all " ... a chosen generation, a royal priesthood, an holy nation, a peculiar people; (I Pet. 2:9)

Uses:
announce the beginning of the festivals or feasts (Num. 10:10); announce the beginning day of each month (short blasts); announce the beginning of Rosh Hashanah (Ps.82:1-3) blessing for the people (Num 6:24-26); call to battle, and call to signal battle was over (Joshua 6; Judges 7); coronation of kings (I Kings 1:34, 39); musical instrument in worship (Ps. 98:6); alarm or warning (Ezek. 33:3-6); call an assembly (Judges 3:27); call to repentance (Is. 58:1); reminder that God is sovereign (Ps.37:5); sound the year of Jubilee (Lev. 25:9-10). Prophetically, the shofar will be blown: to usher in the day of the Lord (Joel 2:1); the resurrection of the dead (I Thess. 4:16), and God judges the earth (Rev. 8 & 9).

SIMEON THAT WAS CALLED NIGER
One of the prophets and teachers in the Christian community at Antioch. He is also called Niger, which was the gentile name he had assumed, Simeon being Hebrew. He was among those who set apart Paul and Barnabas for their missionary work (Acts 13:1,2)

SIMON THE CANAANITE
Simon was one of Jesus' twelve apostles, who was honorably called a Canaanite because of his descent from Ham through Canaan (Gen. 10:6). named the Canaanite (Matt. 10:4; Mk. 3:18 KJV) or "the Cananean RSV or "Zelotes" (Luke 6:15); Acts 1:13 KJV or the "Zealot" RSV

The designation "Cananean" is regarded as a political rather than of geographical significance. The zealots were a faction headed by Judas of Galilee who bitterly opposed the increase of taxation and were against the Messianic prophecy.

The "Hamitic" Simon was a Jew by nationality and culture, not through genealogy, since he was a descendant of Ham. (Ham was the youngest son of Noah and is the father of Canaan. His name means black or dark and he and his son's populated the northern parts of Africa [except Canaan - Palestine]. Canaanite was who Simon was - Zealot was how he lived.

SIMON OF CYRENE
Simon, a black man, helped the Messiah bear his cross to Mt. Calvary. He was probably visiting Israel preceeding the trial and crucifixion, since blacks themselves had their own synagogue in Jerusalem. Simon was presumably standing among the crowd as Jesus struggled with the cross near him. There he was compelled to share Christ's burden toward the place of the skull.

Nothing more is said in the Scriptures about him, except for the mention of his two sons Alexander and Rufus, who became leaders in the Christian church. The Apostle Paul saluted Rufus because of his devoted ministry and for laying his life on the line for Paul. Sirnon and his brothers Cyrenians (or Libyans) were called Hebraist Jews (a person studying Hebrew rituals); from this with other documentation, we know that Africa had black Jews (including from Abraham) over two thousand years ago.

The Jewish philosopher Philo (40 B.C. to 40 A.D.) says that in his lifetime, there were one million Jews living in central and northern Africa.

Matt. 27:32; Mark 15:21; Luke 23:26; Acts 6:9; Ro. 16:4, 13.

SOLOMON
The king of Israel throughout Israel's finest years of prosperity, was a son and successor to King David. His lineage can be scripturally traced as far back

as Rahab the "black Canaanite," or harlot, who was a descendant of Ham's fourth-born Canaan. Solomon was anointed king at Gihon by his stricken father's request. He rose to power when Israel was an empire, with a desire to serve God as had his father David. When the Lord appeared to him in a dream, saying: "Ask what I shall give thee," the young king asked for an understanding heart to judge his people and to discern between good and bad. This choice by Solomon prompted God to bless him beyond his wishes. Solomon was granted riches as well as wisdom.

As years passed, Israel became a strong nation and enjoyed a Golden Age, culturally, under Solomon. Her wealth increased because of Solomon's ties with God and his wisdom in social and political affairs. He was full of wisdom and people came from far away to see and question him. He excelled in subjects such as literature, science and political policies. Solomon wrote most of the Book of Proverbs. He was one of Judah's earliest kings to have Negro blood in his veins. His great-great, etc., grandmother was Rahab the "black Canaanite," who was an offspring of Ham (Gen. 10:6, 15; 45:17; Num. 13:17; 21:3; Joshua 2:1; 6:17,23,25). She married a Jew named Salmon, having a child named Boaz, who was an ancestor of David, Solomon, Jehoram, etc. (Ruth 4:21-22; Matt. 1:5-6; Luke 3:31-32). Solomon's glamorous black wives played a major role to his downfall (I Kings 11:5, 33). His wish to serve their gods generated a split between him and Jehovah. The intermarriages between the two races were not an unusual circumstance (I Kings 11:1, 13, 31-33). The most severe laws throughout Israel failed to prevent or curtail black and Jew matrimony.

THE SONS OF NOAH

"These are the three sons of Noah: and of them was the whole earth overspread." Gen. 9:19,10:1-32. JAPHETH (Caucasian) the father of the Gentile nations.

Gen. 10:1-5 (in most revised Bibles the word Gentile, in relation to Japheth, has been removed).

Gomer - Cimmerians
Magog - (Europeans)
Madai - Medians
Kavan - Grecians
Tubal and Meschech -   Russians
Tiras - Thracians
Ashkenaz - Germans
Tarshish - Spaniards

HAM (Hamitic) Cush, Mizraim, Phut, Canaan -
SHEM (Semitic)
Elam Asshur Lud Aram

Ethiopians Egyptians Libyans
Canaanites
Persians Assyrians Lydians Syrians

According to Sir Arthur Keith, M. Fishberg, G. Massey, the Greek Herodotus, and the Roman Tacitus, because of centuries of miscegenation, the Semites (including the Hebrews) and Hamites (Blacks or Negroes) were largely a blend of one race.

SORCERER:
Greek - 3097 - magos (mag-os) a magician, i.e. a scientist, sorcerer, a wise man. A wizard, a pretender to magic powers, a professor of the arts of witchcraft. The name Magus, "the magician" was originally applied to Persian priests.

5333 - pharmakos (far-mak-os) same as 5332, spell giving potion); a druggist ("pharmacist") or poisioner, a magician, a sorcerer

SORCERY
Greek:
5331 - pharmakia (far-mak-i-ah) medication ("pharmacy") primarily signified the use of medicine, drugs, spells; then, posioning; then, sorcery, (Gal. 5:20). Mentioned as one of the works of the flesh.

In sorcery, the use of drugs, whether simple or potent, was generally accompanied by incantations and appeals to occult powers, with the provision of various charms, amulets, etc., PROFESSEDLY DESIGNED TO KEEP THE APPLICANT OR PATIENT FROM THE ATTENTION AND POWER OF DEMONS, BUT ACTUALLY TO IMPRESS THE APPLICANT WITH THE MYSTERIOUS RESOURCES AND POWERS OF THE SORCERER.

SOUL ("SELF; LIFE; PERSON; HEART")
Hebrew:
Noun
5315 - nepes/nephesh (neh-fesh) a very common term in ancient and modern Semitic languages. It occurs over 780 times in the OT and is evenly distributed in all periods of the text with a particularly high frequency in poetic passages.

The basic meaning is apparently related to the rare verbal for, napas (the verb). The noun refers to the essence of life, the act of breathing, taking breath.

However, from that concrete concept, a number of more abstract meanings were developed. In its primary sense the noun appears in its first occurrence in Gen. 1:20: "the moving creature that hath life," and in its second occurrence in Gen. 2:7: "living soul." However, in over 400 later occurrences it is translated "soul." While this serves to make sense in most passages, it is an unfortunate mistranslation of the term. The real difficulty of the term is seen in the inability of almost all English translations to find a consistent equivalent or even a small group of high-frequency equivalents for the term. The KJV alone uses over 28 different English terms for this one Hebrew word.

The problem with the English term "soul" is that no actual equivalent of the term or the idea behind it is represented in the Hebrew language. The Hebrew system of thought does not include the combination or opposition of the terms "body" and "soul," which are really Greek and Latin in origin. The Hebrew contrasts two other concepts which are not found in the Greek and Latin tradition: "the inner self" and the "outer appearance" or, as viewed in a different context, "what one is to oneself" as opposed to "what one appears to be to one's observers.: The inner person is nepes, while the outer person, or reputation, is sem, most commonly translated "name." In narrative or historical passages of the OT, nepes can be translated as "life" or "self," as in Lev. 17:11: "For the life of the flesh is in the blood: and I have given it to you upon the altar to make an atonement for [yourselves] .... " Needless to say, the reading "soul": is meaningless in such a text.

But the situation in the numerous parallel poetic passages in which the term appears is much more difficult. The Greek Septuagint and the Latin Vulgate both simply use the Greek and Latin equivalent "soul," especially in the Psalms.

napas - the verb form means "to breathe; respire; be refreshed." This verb, which is apparently related to the noun nepes, appears 3 times in the OT (Exod. 23:12; 31:17). The other appearance is in II Sam. 16:14:

"And the king, and all the people that were with him, came weary, and refreshed themselves there,"

5082- nediybah (ned-ee-baw) nobility, i.e. reputation:- soul —— Job 30:15

Greek:

5590 - psuche (psoo-khay) denotes "the breath, the breath of life,: then "the soul," in its various meanings. The NT uses "may be analyzed approximately as follows:

(a) the natural life of the body, Matt. 2:20; Luke 12:22; Acts 20:10; Rev. 8:9; 12:11; cf. Lev. 17:11; I Sam. 14:7;

Esth. 8:11   (b) the immaterial, invisible part of man, Matt. 10:28; Acts 2:27; cf. I Kings 17:21;

THE WORD WINDOW

(c) the disembodied (or "unclothed" or "naked," I Cor. 5:3, 4) man, Rev.6:9; (d) the seat of personality, Luke 9:24, explained as = "own self," v. 25; Heb. 6:19; (e) the seat of sentiment element in man, that by which he perceives, reflects, feels, desires, Matt. 11:29. (f) the seat of will and purpose, Matt. 22:37; (g) the seat of appetite, Rev. 18:14; (h) persons, individuals, Acts 2:41, 43; Rom. 2:9; James 5:20; (i) the equivalent of the personal pronoun, used for emphasis and effect:- 1st person, John 10:24 ("us"); (j) an animate creature, human or other, I Cor. 15:45; Rev. 16:3, ct. Gen 1:24; 2:7, 19; (k) "the inward man," the seat of the new life, Luke 21:19; (cf. Matt. 10:39); I Peter 2:11; III John 2

SOVEREIGN

One of the attributes of God.

Supreme or highest power; superior to all others; chief; as our sovereign prince.

Independent of, and unlimited by, any other; possessing, or entitled to, original authority or jurisdiction; a sovereign state, a sovereign discretion.

Princely; royal. Predominant; greatest; utmost; paramount. Efficacious in the highest degree; effectual; controlling; as, a sovereign remedy. The person, body, or state in which independent and supreme authority is vested; especially in a monarchy, a king, queen, or emperor. A gold coin of Great Britain. A butterfly

STEDFAST

Hebrew:

539 - aman (aw-man), from a root word meaning to build up or support; to foster as a parent or nurse; fig. to render or be firm or faithful, to trust or believe, to be permanent or quiet; to be true or certain; to go to the right hand:- hence assurance, bring up, establish, be faithful (of long continuance), stedfast, sure, surely, trusty, verfied, trust, turn to the right—Ps 78:8; 78:37

3332 - yatsaq (yaw-tsak'), from root word to pour out; by implication to melt or cast as metal; to place firmly, to stiffen or grow hard:-cast, cleave fast, be (as) firm, grow, be hard, layout, molten, overflow, pour (out), run out, set down, stedfast ••• Job 11:15

7011 - qiyam (kah-yawm'), stedfast, sure—Dan. 6:26

Greek:

949 - bebaios (beb-ah-yos), "firm, secure" is translated "steadfast" in 2 Cor. 1:7; Heb. 2:2.

- 1476 - hedraios (hed-rah'-yos), primarily denotes "seated" (hedra, "a seat"); hence, "steadfast," metaphorical of moral fixity, I Cor. 7:37; Col. 1:23, RV (KJV "settled").
- 4733 - stereoma (ster-eh-o-mah), "a support, foundation," denotes "strength, steadfastness," Col. 2:5. In the Septuagint, in Gen. 1, and Ezek. 1:22, it is used of the firmament which was believed to be a solid canopy. The corresponding Heb. word raqia means "expanse," rom raqa', "to spread out.
- 4740 - sterigmos (stay-rig-mos) a setting firmly, supporting," then "fixedness, steadfastness" (akin to sterizo "to establish"), is used in 2 Peter 3:17.

STOUT (WITH FOCUS ON MALACHI 3:13)

Hebrew:

2388 - chazaq (khaw-zak'), to (fig. courageous, causal. strengthen, cure, help, repair, fortify), ostinate; to bind, restrain, conquer:-aid amend, cleave, confirm, be constant, constrain, continue, be of good (take) courage, encourage (self), be established, fasten, force, make hard, (in a bad sense), harden, become (wax) mighty, prevail, be recovered, be sure, play the man, take (hold), be urgent, behave self valiantly, withstand, stout, arrogance, proud. —Malachi 3:13—Your words have been stout against me, saith the Lord. Yet ye say, What have we spoken so much against thee? Your words have been spoken proudly against me. Their hearts had become hard (like Pharoah's).

STRIPES

Hebrew:

2250 - chabbuwrah (khab-boo-raw) a wale (or black and blue mark itself): blueness, bruise, hurt, stripe, wound

Greek: 3468 - molops (mo-lopes) bruise, wale, wound that trickles with blood

STRUCK (FOCUS ON LUKE 22:64)

Greek:

5180 - tupto (toop' to), a prim. verb (in a strengthened form),; to "thump", i.e. cudgel (a short heavy club) or pummel (prop. with a stick or bastinado), but in any case by repeated blows; thus differing from 3817 and 3960, which denote a [usually single] blow with the hand or any instrument, or 4141 with the fist [or a hammer], or 4474 with the palm; as well as from 5177, an accidental collision; by impL to punish; figurtively to offend (the conscience):- beat, smite, strike, wound. To strike, smite with the hand, stick, or other instrument (Matt. 27:30; Mark 15:19; Luke 6:29; 18:13; Luke 22:64; 23:48;

Acts 23:2,3); to beat (Matt. 24:49; Luke 12:45); to smite, strike, punish (Acts 23:3); to hurt, wound spiritually (I Cor. 8:12).

STUDY
Hebrew:
3854 - lahag (lah-hag) to be eager; intense mental application: - study

Greek:
5389 - philotimeomai (fil-ot-im-eh-om-ahee) from root word to be friendly, to be fond of honor, to be eager or earnest to do something, labor, strive, study
4704 - spoudazo - (spoo-dad-zo) from root words meaning speed, haste, urge on, be diligent, to make effort, be prompt or earnest, business, forwardness, be diligent (forward), endeavor, labor, study
3854 - Ecc. 12:12
5389 - I Thess. 4:11 4704 - II Tim. 2:15

SUBDUE
Hebrew:
1696 - dabar (daw-bar) to arrange (but used fig. of words) to speak, declare, converse, command, promise, warn, threaten, sing, to lead away, to put to flight, to subdue —Ps. 18:47
2827 - chashal (khash-al) Aramaic word meaning to subdue, crush, shatter
3533 - kabash (kaw-bash) to subject, subdue, force, keep under, bring into bondage, to bring into bondage, make subservient; violate; dominate, tread down—Gen. 1:28
3665 - kana (kaw-nah) to humble oneself; to be humbled; be subdued; to be brought down, be low, be under, be brought into subjection—Judges 4:23
7286 - radad (raw-dad) to beat down, beat out; subdue—-Isaiah 45:1
8214- shaphal (shef-al) Aramaic word meaning to be or bring low, humble— Daniel 7:24 (humble 1 x, abase 1 x, subdue 1 x, put down 1 x)

Greek:
2610- katagonizomai (kat-ag—nid-zom-ahee) to stumble, to overcome—Hebrew 11:12
5293 - hupotasso (hoop-ot-as-so) to arrange under, to subordinate, to subject, put in subjection, to subject one's self, obey, to submit one's self control—I Cor. 15:28
*A Military term meaning "to arrange (troop divisions) in a military fashion under command of a leader. "In non-military use, it was "a voluntary attitude of giving in, cooperating, assuming responsibility, and carrying a burden)

THE WORD WINDOW

SUBSTANCE

Hebrew:

202 - own (one) ability, power; wealth
1564 - golem (go-lem) embryo
1942 - havvah (hav-vaw) desire; craving
1952 - hown (hone) wealth
2428 - chayil (khah-yil) wealth, virtue; valor; strength
3351 - yequwm (yek-oom) living thing
3581 - koach (ko-ach) force, might; strength
4678 - matstsebeth (mats-tseh-beth) stock of a tree
4735 - miqneh (mik-neh) stock
6108 - ostsem (o-tsem) power; framework of the body
7009 - qiym (keem) opponent
7075 - qinyan (kin-yawn) acquisition, purchase
7399 - rekuwsh (rek-oosh) property
7738 - shavah (shaw-vaw) to destroy

Greek:

3776 - ousia (oo-see-ah) wealth, property, possessions
5223 - huparxis (hoop-arx-is) property, possessions
5224 - huparchonta (hoop-ar-khon-tah) property, or possessions
5287 - hupostsis (hoop-os-tas-is) a setting or placing under
   a. thing put under substructure, foundation 2. that which has a foundation is firm
a. that which has actual existence 1. a substance, real being
b. the substantial (quality, nature, of a person)
c. the steadfastness of mind, firmness, courage, resolution
1. confidence, firm trust, assurance
In general, something which has been put under; therefore, used as a basis or foundation subsistence, existence; frequently applied by the church fathers as a distinct person in the Godhead (Heb. 1:3); applied to the mind, firm confidence, constancy (II Cor. 9:4; 11:17; Heb. 3:14), confidence or confident expectation (Heb. 11:1)

SUBVERT

Hebrew:

5791 - avath (aw-vath), to wrestle, bend make crooked; to pervert the cause of someone (Job 19:6; Ps. 119:78; Lam. 3:36), deal perversely; to falsify; to corrupt, seduce, lead someone astray (Ps. 146:9), subvert, turn upside down; to be crooked, be curved; to bend oneself, stoop; to overthrow. Avath denotes something shaky and unreliable, like the legs of an elderly man (Ecc. 12:3).

The word pertains to dishonest business transactions in Amos 8:5. Bildad (Job 8:3) and Elihu (Job 34:12) argued that if Job were innocent, that would be tantamount to accusing God of perverting justice. Job's answer is found in Job 19:6,7. This world simply contains moral crookedness, and we have to accept that fact (Ecc. 1:15; 7:13). The psalmist appealed to God (Ps. 119:78).

Greek:
396 - anatrepo (an-at-rep'o), to overturn (fig.) : - overthrow, subvert—Titus 1:11
1612 - ekstrepho (ek-stref-o), to pervert (fig.):- subvert—Titus 3:11
384 - anaskeuazo (an-ask-yoo-ad'-zo), to upset: subvert —Acts 15:24
2692 - katastrophe (kat-as-trof-ay'), an overturn ("catastrophe"), i.e. demolition; fig. apostasy: - overthow, subverting—2 Tim. 2:14

SUFFICIENT, SUFFICIENCY
Hebrew:
1767 - day (dah-ee) sufficiency, enough (a) enough; (b) for, according to the abundance of, out of the abundance of, as often as—Ex. 36:7
4078 - madday (mad-dah-ee) what is enough, sufficiency—II Chron. 30:3
5607 - cepheq (say-fek) handclapping, mocking, mockery, scorn, (a) meaning dubious—Job 20:22 7654 - sob'ah (sob-aw) satisfaction, satiety, one's fill—Isaiah 23:18

Greek:
713 - arketos (ar-ket-os) sufficient, enough—Matt. 6:34
714 - arkeo (ar-keh-o) to be possessed of unfailing strength, (a) to be strong, to suffice, to be enough 1. to defend, ward off (b) to be satisfied, to be contented ——II Cor. 12:9
2425 - hikanos (hik-an-os) sufficient (a) many enough, enough; (b) sufficient in ability, (meet, fit)—II Cor. 2:6
2426 - hikanotes (hik-an-ot-ace) sufficient, ability or competency to do a thing—II Cor. 3:5

SUNDRY TIMES
Greek:
4181- polumeros (pol-oo-mer-oce) adv. meaning in many portions, i.e. variously as to time and agency (piecemeal): - at sundry times (1x). It means by portions, by many times and in many ways, yet all connected. It is many pieces; hence, all of God's means of revelation still have Him, the One God as their source—Hebrews 1:1

SUPPLICATION

Hebrew:

2420 - chiydah (khee-daw) a puzzle; hence a trick, conundrum (riddle in which a fanciful question is answered in a pun). A hard question, proverb, dark saying (sentence, speech)

2603 - chanan (khaw-nan) to bend or stoop in kindness to an inferior, to favor, to bestow, to move to favor by petition:- beseech, entreat, (to ask earnestly)

2604 - chanan (khan-an) A CHALDEAN WORD - to favor, show mercy, to entreat

6419 - palal (paw-lal) to judge (officially or mentally), to intercede, pray

8467 - techinnah (tekh-in-naw) supplication; graciousness, favor, grace

Greek

1162 - deesis (deh-ay-sis) from 1189 to beg (as binding oneself), a petition; prayer, request

2428 - hiketeria (hik-et-ay-ree-a) from a base word (through the idea of approaching for a favor)

In 1162- deesis - supplication or prayer for particular benefits (Luke 1:13; I Tim. 2:1).

Proseuche (4335) is a more general request directed to God in particular. "Deesis" can be a request for specific benefits from God or anyone else. Therefore, proseuche is a more sacred word

In 2428 - hiketeria - a suppliant, which is from hikomai, to come, approach, particularly as suppliant, from the act hiko, to come. Supplication, equivalent to a supplication or humble and earnest prayer (Heb. 5:7). Related words: euche (2171), wish; proseuche (4335), prayer; "deesis" (1162), supplication for a particular need; enteuxis (1783), intercession; eucharisitia (2169), thanksgiving; aitema (155), petition

SURFEITING

Greek

2897 - kraipale (krahee-pal'-ay), signifies "the giddiness and headache resulting from excessive wine-bibbing, a drunken nausea," a headache (as a seizure of pain) from drunkeness:- "surfeiting," Luke 21:34. *synonyms: methe, drunkenness," oinophlugia, "wine-bibbling" (KJV, "excess of wine," I Peter 4:3).

TALLIT OR TALLET

A prayer shawl "cloak" that is worn during the morning Jewish services (the Shacharit Prayers) in Judaism. It has special twined tzitzit and knotted "fringes" attached to its four corners. The tallit is sometimes also referred to as the arba kantot, meaning the four wings (in connotation of four corners).

According to classical Rabbinical Judaism only boys and men are required to wear it at various points of their lives as Jews, and many regard it as compulsory. This is still practiced by orthodox Judaism.

Historically, women have been either permitted (mainly Sephardi and western Ashkenazi Rishonim), seen as obligated to (Karaites), or it has been frowned upon for those women (mainly eastern Ashkenazim) who wear it. Many modern, mainly non-orthodox groups have allowed women to wear them is they desire.

TANAKH

Hebrew

Tanakh is an acronym, based on the letters T (for "Torah"), N (for "Neviim," the Prophets), and K (for "Ketuvim," the Sacred Writings). It is the compendium of the teachings of G-d to human beings in document form.

How does G-d teach Man? In the Torah, He did it by direct communciation with Moshe, the "Master of the Prophets," whereby Moshe literally received "dictation from Heaven" for every word of the Torah. In the "Neviim," HaShem "spoke," as it were, with the great and holy Prophets and Prophetesses of the Jewish People, and His Messages were transmitted by them to the Jewish People, for the most part, and sometimes to others nations. In the Sacred Writings, great individuals were inspired by "Ruach HaKodesh," the Holy Spirit, to produce great and holy works. The composition of the "TANAKH" was determined by the "Anshei K'nesset HaGedolah," the Men of the Great Assembly, under the influence of the "Holy Spirit." It consists of twenty-four "books," where first and second volumes of one work are counted as one, and where all the twelve "Books" of the "Trei Asar," the Twelve Prophets, are also considered as one.

The twenty-four "Books" are as follows:
1-5 The Five Books of Moses: Bereshit (Genesis), Shemot (Exodus), VaYikra (Leviticus), BaMidbar (Numbers), Devarim (Deuteronomy).
6-9: The "Neviim Rishonim," the Early Prophets: Yehoshua, "Shoftim"/Judges, Shmuel I and II, "Melachim"/Kings I and II.
10-13: The "Neviim Acharonim," the Later Prophets: Yeshayahu, Yirmiyahu, Yechezkel, "Trei Asar": Books and Prophets within "Trei Asar": Hoshea, Yoel, Amos, Ovadiah, Yonah, Michah, Nachum, Chavakuk, Tzefaniah, Chaggai, Zechariah, Malachi.
14~16: The "Sifrei Emet," Books of Truth": "Tehilim"/Psalms, "Mishlei"/Proverbs, "Iyov"/Job.
17-21: The "Five Megilot" or "Five Scrolls": "Shir HaShirim"/Song of Songs, Ruth, "Eichah"/Lamentations, "Kohelet"/Ecclesiastes, Esther.
22-24": The "Other Writings": Daniel, Ezra-Nechemiah, "Divrei HaYamim"/Chronicles I and II

TEACH/TEACHER (WITH A TOUCH OF LEARN)

Although several Hebrew words are translated "teach" in English translations of the Old Testament, two words predominate: yara (yaw-raw) 3384 - to point out, to lay or throw, to teach, to instruct, to shew, through, teach (er, -ing)

lamad (law-mad); 3925 - to goad, to teach (the rod being the original incentive), instruct learn, skilful, teach (er) to be accustomed to, to be taught, be trained, - has the idea of training & educating — the Greek required 2 words to achieve what the Hebrew does in one word "manthano" (3129) to learn—and "didasko" (1321) to teach

Greek more frequently used Disdasko - to teach

Katecheo - to instruct systematically matheteuo - to train disciples - (from 3101)

paideuo - to train, instruct

noutheteo - to correct, counsel - to put in mind, to caution, warn, admonish

parangello - to command, order

paradido - to hand down tradition

1321 - didasko (did-as-ko) to know or teach. To teach, instruct by word of mouth (Mat. 28:15, 20); Luke 11:1). Didasko has inherent in it the calculation of the increase in understanding of pupil. Its counterparts are "akouo (191) - to hear for the purpose of understanding, and "manthano" (3129) - to learn, from which "mathetes (3101) - learner, pupil, disciple, is derived. The one teaches, and the other learns or assimilates as part of himself "matheteuo" (Mat. 10:24). "Kerusso" (2784), to preach, proclaim, does not inherently have the same expectation of learning and assimilation a "didasko" does (Mat. 4:23). The thing aimed at when teaching "didasko" is the shaping of the will of the pupil (Mat. 5:19; Acts 21:21). "Didasko" is used absolutely of Christ's teaching in the Christian faith and Christian teaching (Acts 11:26; Rom. 12:7; Col. 1:28; Heb. 5:12)

3100 - matheteuo - from (3101) to become a pupil, to disciple - to enroll as scholar, to instruct, teach

3101 - mathetes - a learner, pupil, disciple

3129 - mathano - to learn, to be appraised

1. to increase one's knowledge, to be increased in knowledge; 2. to hear, be informed; 3. to learn by use and practice (to be in the habit of, accustomed to)

TEMPERANCE

Greek: noun

1466 - egkrateia (eng-krat'-i-ah), from kratos "strength," occurs in Acts 24:25; Gal. 5:23; 2 Pet. 1:6 (twice), in all of which it is rendered "temperance"; the RV marg., "self control" is the preferable rendering, as "temperance" now limited to one form of self-control; the various powers bestowed by God upon man are capable of abuse; the right use demands the controlling power of the will under the operation of the Spirit of God; in Acts 24:25 the word follows "righteousness," which represents God's claims, selfcontrol being man's response thereto; in 2 Peter 1:6, it follows "knowledge," suggesting that what is learned requires to be put into practice.

adjective

1468 - egkrates (eng-krat-ace'), akin to enkrateia, denotes "exercising self-control," rendered "temperate" in Titus 1:8.

3524 - nephalios (nay-fal'-eh-os), for which see sober, is translated "temperate" in I Tim. 3:2, RV (KJV, "vigilant"); in 3:11 and Titus 2:2, RV (KJV, "sober")

Note: In Titus 2:2, KJV, sophron, "sober," is rendered "temperate" (RV "soberminded")

verb

1467 - egkrateuomai (eng-krat-yoo-om-ahee), akin to both egkrateia & egkrates, rendered "is temperate" in I Cor. 9:25, is used figuratively of the rigid self-control practiced by athletes with a view to gaining the prize.

TESTAMENT

Greek:

1242 - diatheke (dee-ath-ay-kay) testament, covenant. In Classic Greek it always meant the disposition which a person makes of his property in prospect of death, that is his testament. This is the meaning when used either in the singular or plural. The plural also means the testamentary arrangements of a person. It should be understood that the disposition of God becomes an institution of God. In the NT it means a solemn disposition, institution or appointment of God to man (Heb. 9:16 -18), to which our word dispensation answers adequately; for the religious dispensation or institution which God appointed to Abraham and the patriarchs (Acts 3:25); for the dispensation begun at Sinai (Heb. 8:9); for the dispensation of faith and free justification of which Christ is the mediator (Heb. 7:22; 8:6) and which is called new (kaine - 2537, qualitatively new), in that it is a dispensation of faith in respect of the old, the old being the Sinaitical one (II Cor. 3:6); Heb 9:15).

On the other hand the old dispensation is called palaia - (3820) "diatheke" and should be distinguished from archaia (744) which is related to arche (746) referring to the beginning. Palaia, which relates to the OT, is not the original testament and dispensation of God but is simply the old contrasted to the new and refers to the dispensation contained in the books of Moses (II Cor. 3:14).

Diatheke, translated covenant, gives the misleading idea that God came to an agreement with fallen man as if signing a contract. Rather, it involves only the declaration of God's unconditional disposition as given to Abraham in regard to Israel as a nation (Gen. 13:14 - 17; 15 - 18; 17:7, 8; 17:19 - 20 - 23; Heb. 12:18 - 21) which God made for the Jews only if they obeyed. In the NT God provided His Son in the execution of His plan and dispensation, but not as a result of the obedience to any rule that He preset. However, the giving of eternal life to individuals is presupposed on the acceptance of that sacrifice of the Son of God. It also means a solemn disposition or appointment of man (Gal. 3:15). Deriv. "tithemi" (5087), to set, place, lay. The term the covenant of the new testament may be understood as personally referring to Christ (Mat. 26:28; Mark 14:24). The same meaning would pertain to the blood of His covenant which would be the blood of His promise, the blood of His own body (Heb. 9:20; 10:29). (covenant 20 times, testament 13 times)

The word testament is not found in the NIV, where the Greek word "diatheke" is rather rendered by "covenant" (I Cor. 11:25; Heb. 9:15-20)

Why was New Testament originally written in Greek?

The New Testament - sometimes called the Greek Testament or Greek Scriptures, and sometimes also called the New Covenant which is the literal translation of the Greek, it is the name given to the final portion of the Bible. It was written by various authors after 45 A.D. and before 140 A.D. Its books were gradually collected into a single volume over a period of several centuries. Some believe the Eng. term NT ultimately comes from the Hebrew language. NT is taken from the Latin - Vovum Testamentum, first coined by Tertullian (1st to use the terms Novum Testamentum and Vetus Testamentum - NT & OT). Some believe this in turn is a translation of the earlier koine Greek (pronounced in post classic Greek as Keni Dhiathiki (see Testament). Though commonly called New Covenant, this word is found even earlier in the Greek translation of the OT that is called the Septuagint. In Jer. 31:31, the Septuagint translated this term into Greek from the original Hebrew. The Hebrew term is usually also translated into Eng. as New Covenant. Most modern English versions of the NT are based on critical reconstructions of the Greek text.

During the classical period, the Greek lang. was divided into a number of dialects. The Attic dialect was the lang. of Athens in her glory.

Macedonia was not originally a Greek kingdom, but adopted the dominant civilization of the day, which was the civilization of Athens.

The tutor of Phillip's son, Alexander the Great, was Aristotle, the Greek philosopher. Alexander made himself master of the whole eastern world, and the triumphs of Macedonian. After his death the kingdoms divided, but the governing classes stayed as Greek kingdoms.

When the Romans, in the last two centuries before Christ, conquered the eastern part of the Mediterranean world, they kept the Greek language.

Thus in the first century after Christ Greek had become a world language. Other languages continued to exist, but side by side with Greek.

Paul's letter to the Roman Church is written not in Latin, but in Greek.

The new lang. which prevailed after Alexander has been called "Koine". The word means "common". It is a common medium of exchange for diverse peoples.

The Koine, then, is the Greek world language that prevailed from about 300 B.C. to the close of ancient history at about A.D. - The NT was written within this Koine period. It is united in every close way with the Greek translation of the OT called the "Septuagint", which was made at Alexandria in the centuries just preceeding the Christian era.

THANKSGIVING

Also called Turkey Day

A celebration of being thankful for Significance what one has and the bounty of the previous year.

Parades, Spending Time with Celebrations Family, Eating Large Dinners, Football (Canada and USA) games .

Thanksgiving, or Thanksgiving Day, is an annual one-day holiday to give thanks (traditionally to God), for the things one has at the close of the harvest season. In the United States, Thanksgiving is celebrated on the fourth Thursday of November, and in Canada it is celebrated on the second Monday in October. In the United Kingdom, Thanksgiving is another name for the Harvest festival, held in churches across the country on a relevant Sunday to mark the end of the local harvest, though it is not thought of as a major event (compared to Christmas or Easter) as it is in North America, where this tradition taken by early settlers became much more important. Other European countries, such as Germany, also have harvest-thanks (Erntedank) celebrations which are perceived to be rather minor and mostly rural holidays.

THEOPHANY
Greek:

theo - (God) & phaneia (to show oneself, appear); the visible appearance of God to a human being; manisfestation of God, usually to his people - by voice (Gen. 3:8; Matt. 17:5); by the burning bush (Ex. 3:2-6); by the pillar and cloud; by thunder, lightning, dark black smoke (Ex. 19:16); by the Angel of the Lord. Jesus Christ was not only an appearance of God, but God himself (John 1:1). God became flesh and lived among mankind (John 1:14). The one seeing Jesus has seen the Father (John 14:9). God has only shown himself to man in the form of the Son, Jesus Christ both carnate and preincarnate Matt. 11:27). However, God has revealed his power and invisible attributes in all that He has created (Romans 1:20; Col. 1:16).

The Orthodox celebrates A Feast of Theophany (Jan. 6). "It commemorates the baptism of the Lord Jesus Christ and much more, as its name implies ... the Holy Trinity was made manifest after His baptism (when He came out of the water)."

THRONE
Greek:

2362 - thronos (thron-os) a throne seat

a. chair of state having a footstool; b. assigned in the NT to Kings, hence, kingly power or royalty

1. metaph. - to God, the governor of the world; 2. to the Messiah, Christ, the partner and assistant in the divine administration, hence divine power belonging to Christ

1. to judges i.e. tribunal or bench; 2. to elders

*of God e.g. Heb. 4:16, "the throne of grace *of Christ e.g. Heb 1:8 "His seat of authority"

968 - bema - (bay-ma) see "JUDGEMENT SEAT"—Romans 14:10 and II Cor. 5:10

A symbol of majesty and authority on which kings, governors, judges and high priest would sit (Gen. 41:40; Ps. 9:7). God is pictured as seated on a throne (Is. 6:1-3); Da. 7:9; Rev.4:2-11). In the end of days the Messiah and the twelve apostles will be seated on thrones (MT. 25:31)

TIME (AS USED IN I TIMOTHY 6:15)
Greek:

2540 -kairos (kahee-ros), season, time, but not merely as a succession moments which is chronos (5550). Kairos implies that which time gives the opportunity to do. Related to eukairia (2120), from eu (2095), good, and kairos, opportune time, opportunity.

Kairos, however, implies not the convenience of the season, but the necessity of the task at hand whether the time provides a good, convenient opportunity or not (Mark 1:15); Col. 4:5). When used in the pl. with chronoi (times), it is translated as seasons, times at which certain foreordained events take place or necessary accomplishments need to take place.

TITTLE
Greek:
2762-keraia or kerea (ker-ah-yah) "a little horn" (keras, "a horn"), was used to denote the small stroke distinguishing one Hebrew letter from another (fig. the least particle): tittle. The rabbis attached great importance to these; hence the significance of the Lord's statements Matt. 5:18 and Luke 16:17, charging the Pharisees with hypocrisy, because, while professing the most scrupulous reverence to the Law, they violated its spirit. Grammarians used the word to denote the accents in Greek words.

TO BE UNCLEAN
Hebrew:
2930 - tame (taw-may), to be foul especially in a ceremonial sense (contaminated). This root is limited to Hebrew, Aramaic, and Arabic. The verb occurs 160 times in biblical Hebrew and mainly in Leviticus, as in Lev. 11:26. Tame is the opposite of taher, to be pure."
2932 - tumah (toom-aw), "uncleanness." noun - derived from tame. Tumah occurs 37 times in biblical Hebrew. One is Num.5:19 (sexual uncleanness). It occurs twice in Le. 16:16 and refers to ethical and religious "uncleanness."
2931 - tame (taw-may'), the adjective; "unclean" occurs 89 times in the OT. The frequency of the word is high in Leviticus. The usage of tame in the OT resembles that of tahor, "pure." First, uncleannesses a state of being. The leper was compelled to announce his uncleanness wherever he went (Lev. 13:45); however, even here there is a religious overtone, in that his uncleanness was ritual. Hence it is more appropriate to recognize that the second usage is most basic. Tame in the religio-cultic sense is a technical term denoting a state of being ceremonially unfit. Animals, carcases, unclean people, and objects conveyed the impurity to those who touched them (Num.19:22).
The Greek Septuagint translations are: akathartos ("impure; unclean") and maino ("stain; defile"). The KJV gives these translations: "unclean; defiled; polluted."

TONGUE/TONGUES
Hebrew:
762 - aramiyth (ar-aw-meeth) in Syrian language (tongue)
2013 - hacah (haw-saw) to hush:-hold your peace (tongue), keep silence, still, be silent 2790 - charash (khaw-rash) to scratch, to engrave, plough; to fabricate,

to devise (in a bad sense), to be silent, to let alone; to be deaf (as an accompaniment of dumbness), cease, conceal, be deaf, devise, ear, imagine, leave of speaking, hold peace, be quiet, keep silence, practice secretly, speak not a word, be still, hold tongue, worker

3956 - lashown or lashon (law-shone) the tongue (of man or animals) used as an instrument of licking, eating or speech. a fork of flame, a cove of water: - babbler, evil speaker, language, talker, tongue, wedge —— occurs 115 times in OT mainly in poetic and some prophetic books

"Tongue" with the meaning "speech" has a synonym peh, "mouth" (Ps. 66:17), and more rarely sapah, "lip" (Job 27:4). A further extension of meaning is "language". In Hebrew both sapah and lason denote a foreign "language": "For with stammering lips and another tongue will he speak to this people" (Isa. 33:19). THE GREEK TRANSLATION IS GLOSSA (1100)

Greek:

1100 - glossa (gloce-sah) tongue, the tongue of a man (Mark 7:33, 35); used for the fiery tongues appearing upon the apostles on the day of Pentecost (Acts 2:3); a tongue, language (Acts 2:4, 11; 10:46); people of different languages (Rev. 5:9); a foreign or strange language which one has not learned but yet is enabled to speak as a result of the supernatural intervention of the Holy Spirit, particularly in what the NT calls the baptism in the Holy Spirit by Jesus Christ. The historic events of speaking in foreign tongues or dialects came with the Jews at Pentecost in Acts 2:4, 11, the Gentiles at Caesarea in Acts 10:46, and the disciples of John the Baptist at Ephesus in Acts 19:6. These were all languages unknown to the speakers, spoken at that particular time in demonstration of their being baptized into the body of Jesus Christ (I Cor. 12:13). These are the same languages demonstrated as charismata (the result of the grace of God in the human heart) spoken of by Paul in I Cor. 12:10, 30). Paul refers to speaking in "glossais", languages or tongues. He meant the languages which he already knew or the ones that he was enabled to speak by the Holy Spirit when and if so needed. The plural "glossai" with a singular. pronoun or subject refers to known, understandable languages (Acts 2:3, 8, 11) not to an unknown tongue as practiced in Corinth. But even when utilizing these one must make sure he is understood by those who hear him otherwise he will be taken as a maniac, "mainomai" (3105), be beside oneself, mad (I Cor. 14:26). Whenever the word "glossa" in the singular with a sing. subject or pronoun is used, translated in the KJV as unknown tongue (I Cor. 14:2), 4, 13, 14, 19, 26, 27), it refers to the Corinthian practice of ecstatic utterances not comprehended by anyone and therefore, not an ordinarily spoken language. In I Cor. 14:26 it may refer to a language foreign to the hearers and uninterpreted.

1258 - dialektos (dee-al-ek-tos) discourse, i.e. "dialect" - language, tongue (Acts 1:19; 2:6, 8; 21:40; 22:2; 26:14)

1447 - hebraisti (heb-rah-is-tee) Hebraistically or in the Jewish (Chaldee) language: - in (the) Hebrew (tongue) (Rev. 16:16)

2084 - heteroglossos (het-er-og-loce-sos) a foreigner: - man of other tongue (I Cor. 14:21)

To TRANSFIGURE

Greek:

3345 - metaschematizo (met-askh-ay-mat-id'-so), to disguise:-transfer, transform (self); to change.

From meta (3326), denoting change of condition, and schema (4976), form, fashion. To transfigure. Occurs only in I Corinthians 4:6; II Corinthians 11:13-15; Philippians 3:21. The difference between metaschematizo and metamorphoo is best illustrated in this way. If one were to change a Dutch garden into an Italian one, this would be metaschematizo. But if one were to transform a garden into something wholly different, as into a ball field, it is metamorphoo (3339), from morphe (3444). It is possible for Satan to metaschematizo, transform himself into an angel of light (i.e., he can change his whole outward semblance), but to any such change it would be impossible to apply the word metamorphoo, for this would imply an internal change, a change not of appearance but of essence, which lies beyond his power. In the metaschematismos, a transformation of the bodies (I Cor. 15:53; Phil. 3:21) there is to be seen a transition but no absolute dissolution of continuity. The outer physical transformation of believers at the end of the days (I Cor. 15:44, 51) is called metaschematizo by Paul in Phillippians 3:21, but such transformation has already begun in this life from within.

TWELVE TRIBES OF ISRAEL

Jacob fathered 12 sons. They are the ancestors of the tribes of Israel, and the ones for whom the tribes are names. Each occupied a separate territory (except the tribes of Levi, which was set apart to serve in religious duties, and Joseph, who was set over all of the tribes). Genesis 48 and 49.

The Eastern Tribes - Judah, Issachar, Zebulun

The Southern Tribes - Reuben, Simeon, Gad

The Western Tribes - Ephraim, Manasseh, Benjamin The Northern Tribes- Dan, Asher, Naphtali

* Joseph didn't get a tribe, he was set over all of the tribes. His son's - Ephraim and Menasseh, were given the status of independent tribes

U

UNBELIEF/UNBELIEVER
Greek: 543 - apeitheia (ap-i-thi-ah) from the neg. a (1), without, and peitho (3982), to persuade. Disobedience (Heb. 4:6). In the NT it corresponds with the verb unbelief which opposes the gracious word and purpose of God. It is a stronger term than the syn. apistia (570) unbelief. Hence we have the sons of apeitheias, disobedience (Rom. 11:30, Eph. 2:2; 5:6; Col. 3:6)

570 - apistia - (ap-is-tee-ah) faithlessness or uncertainty, distrust, unbelief. In the NT, the lack of acknowledgment of Christ (Matt. 13:58; Mark 6:6); want of confidence in Christ's power (Matt. 17:20; Mark 9:24). In general a want of trust in the God of promise (Rom. 4:20; Heb. 3:12,19)

571 - apistos (ap-is-tos) adjective, is used as a noun, rendered "unbeliever" in II Cor. 6:15 and I Tim. 5:8, RV.; plural in I Cor. 6:6 and II Cor. 6:14; KJV only, Luke 12:46 ("unfaithful")

UNCLEANNESS
Greek: 167 - akatharsia (ak-ath-ar-see'-a), from 169 (impure), whether physical or moral; uncleanness; From the neg. a (1), and kathairo (2508), to cleanse. Uncleanness, filth, in a natural or physical sense (Matt. 23:27); moral uncleanness, lewdness, I Thess. 2:3; 4:7); any kind of uncleanness different from whoredom (II Cor. 12:21); any unnatural pollution, whether acted out by oneself (Gal. 5:19, Col. 3:5), or with another (Roman 1:24)

USURP
English: to seize and hold (the power or rights of another, for example) by force and without legal authority. 2. to take over or occupy without right; to seize another's place, authority, or possession wrongfully.

Greek: 831 - authenteo (aw-then-teh-o), to dominate, to seize and take hold of 1. one who with his own hands kills another or himself; 2. one who acts on his own authority, autocratic; 3. an absolute master; 4. to govern; exercise dominion over one. Note: In I Timothy 2:12 the meaning of the word is attached to the words "usurp authority over", with the word "authority being (831) authenteo

VARIANCE
Greek:

2054 - eris (er'-is), a quarrel, i.e. (by implication) wrangling:- contention (2x), debate 2x), strife (4x) variance (1x). Eris, "strife, contention" is the (1) expression of "enmity," Rom. 1:29, "debate"; 13:13; I Cor. 1:11, "contentions"; 3:3; II Cor. 12:20, "debates"; Gal. 5:20, "variance"; Phil. 1:15; I Tim. 6:4; Titus 3:9, "contentions".

(2) the stress in this word is on rivialry

VERITY
Hebrew:

571 - 'emeth (eh'-meth) as a noun means firmness, stability (Is. 39:8; Jer. 33:6), continuance; faithfulness (of man, Neh. 7:2; of God, Ps. 71:22), sureness (Prov. 11:18); truth (Deut. 22:20); as an adjective, truly (Ps. 145:18; Jer. 10:10). being derived from 'aman (539), 'emeth has firmness or stability as its basic meaning. In the sense of faithfulness it is used frequently of God and expresses one of His key OT attributes. It is the principal Hebrew word for truth, which is quite often how it is translated in our English translations.

VIRTUE
Greek:

703 - arete (ar-et-ay) a virtuous course of thought, feeling and action, virtue, moral goodness; any particular moral excellence, as modesty, purity; excellency, being pleasing to God, the excellence of God revealed in the work of salvation. Arete denotes in a moral sense what gives man his worth, his efficiency. In the NT: virtue, excellency, perfection (I Peter 2:9); the virtue as a force or energy of the Holy Spirit accompanying the preaching of the glorious Gospel, called glory in II Peter 1:3; human virtue in general (Phil. 4:8); courage, foritude, resolution (II Pet. 1:5)

1411 - dunamis (doo-nam-is) strength power, ability, inherent power, power residing in a thing by virtue of its nature, or which a person or thing exerts and

THE WORD WINDOW

puts forth; power for perfoming miracles; moral power and excellence of soul; the power and influence which belong to riches and wealth; power and resources arising from numbers; power consisting in or resting upon armies, forces, hosts

All the words derived from the stem duna- have the basic meaning of being able, capable. Contrast ischus (2479) which stresses the factuality of the ability. It may even mean to will. Dunatos (1410), to be able; dunateo (1414) to have great ability (II Cor. 13:3); dunamoo (1412) and endunamoo (1743), to strengthen (Col. 1:11). Nouns: dunastes (1413), one who exercises dominion authority; dunameis (pl). powers, miracles coming out of that mighty power of God inherent in Christ and which power was lent to His witnesses and ambassadors.—Mark 5:30; Luke 6:19; Luke 8:46 ...

WAITETH (WITH SPECIAL FOCUS AS USED IN PSALM 65:1)
Hebrew:
1747- duwmiyah (doo-me-yaw) silently; quiet, trust, stillness; waiteth, silent, from root word 1820 - damah (daw-maw) to be dumb or silent; hence to fail or perish, cease to be —— "Psalm 65:1" Psalm 62:1

2442 - chakah (khaw-kaw) await; hope for—Psalm 33:20

3176 - yachal (yaw-cal) to wait; to be patient, hope—Micah 5:7

8104 - shamar (shaw-mar) to watch, to hedge about, to guard, attend, to protect, observe, preserve, regard, save (self), sure, (that lay) wait (for)—Job 24:15

Greek:
553 - apekdechomai (ap-ek-dekh-om-ahee) to expect fully, await—Romans 8:19

1551 - ekdechomai (ek-dekh-om-ahee) to await, expect—James 5:7

WEARY
Hebrew:
3019 - yagiva (yaw-ghee-ah) weary, tired—Job 3:17

3021 - yaga (yaw-gah) to gasp; hence to be exhausted, to tire, to toil; faint (make to labor), be weary, to grow weary—Isaiah 40:31

3023 - yagea (yaw-gay-ah) weary, wearisome—Deu. 25:18

3286 - yaaph (yaw-af) to be or grow weary, be fatigued, be faint, wearied—Jud. 8:15

3811 - laah (law-aw) to be weary, impatient, be grieved, be offended, be tired of something, (grieve, faint, loath)—Isaiah 16:12

5774 - uwph (oof) to fly; fly about; fly away, hover, light upon, to fly to and fro, to cover; be dark, gloom—Judges 4:21

5889 - ayeph (aw-yafe) faint, weary, exhausted—Jer. 31:25

6973 - quwts (koots) to be grieved, to loath, abhor, feel loathing or sickening dread, to cause sickening dread, (distressed, vex, grieved)—Gen. 27:46

7646 - saba (saw-bah) to be satisfied, be sated, be fulfilled, to have one's fill of (have desire satisfied); to be weary of (fig)—Proverb 25:17

Greek:

1573 - elkakeo (ek-kak-eh-o) to be utterly spiritless, to be wearied out; exhausted—Gal. 6:9 II Thessalonians 3:13

5299 - hupopiaze (hoop-o-pee-ad-zo) to beat black and blue, to smite so as to cause bruises and livid spots (a) like a boxer one buffets his body, handle it roughly, discipline by hardship (2) to give tolerable annoyance (a) be one out (b) wear one out—-Lk. 18:5

WICKED

Hebrew:

7489 - Ra a (raw-ah) verb—to be bad, be evil

a. displeasing; to be sad; to be injurious; be evil; b. to do an injury or hurt; to do evil or wickedly; mischief; to break, shatter

(evil 20, evildoer 10, hurt 7, wickedly 5, worse 5, afflicts 5, wicked 4, break 3, doer 3, ill 3, harm 3, displease 2)

WILDERNESS

Greek:

2047 - eremia (er-ay-mee-ah) an uninhabited place, is translated "wilderness" in the KJV of Matt. 15:33 and Mark 8:4 (RV, a desert place); RV and KJV, "wilderness" in II Cor. 11:26.

2048 - eremos (er-ay-mos) an adjective signifying "desolate, deserted, lonely," used as noun, and rendered "wilderness" 32 times in the KJV; in Matt. 24:26 and John 6:31, RV, "wilderness" (KJV, "desert")

WILES

Hebrew:

5231 - nekel (nay'-kel), from 5230 (which means to be deceitful, crafty, to beguile), cunning, wiliness, craft, knavery, deceit,:- wile—Num. 25:18

Greek:

3180 - methodeia (meth-od-i'-ah), from methodos, method; the following or pursuing of orderly and technical procedure in the handling of a subject. In the NT connected with evil-doing, a device, article, art, artificial method, or wile (Ephesians 4:14; 6:11). Verb methodeuo, to go systematically to work, to do or pursue something methodically and according to the rules; traveling over, i.e. travesty (trickery):- wile, lie in wait.

WINE

Hebrew:

2562 - chamar (kham-ar), corresp. to 2561; wine (6x)—Dan. 5:2

3196 - yayin (yah'-yin), from an unused root meaning to effervesce; wine (as fermented); by implication intoxication: - banqueting (1x), wine (138x), winebibbers (1x). Commonly drank for refreshment; used in rejoicing before the Lord; offered to God as a ritual. Pagans used wine in their worship, but "their wine is the poison of dragons, and the cruel venom of asps" (Deut. 32:33); means drunkenness (Gen. 9:24), it is a synonym of tirosh (8492), "new wine", in Hos 4:11, where it is evident that both can be intoxicating; tirosh is distinguished from yayin by referring only to new wine not full fermented; yayin includes wine at any stage

3342 - yeqeb (yeh'-keb), from an unused root meaning to excavate; a trough (as dug out); spec. a wine vat; wine presses (10x)—Deut. 16:13

6071 - aciyc (aw-sees), from 6072; must or fresh grape-juice - (as just trodden out):- new wine—Joel 1:5 8492 - tiyrowsh (tee-roshe); or tiyrosh (tee-roshe), in the sense of expulsion; must or fresh grape-juice (as just squeezed out) ferment wine: -(new, sweet) wine (38x)—Gen. 27:28

Greek

1098 - gleukos (glyoo-kos), akin to 1099; sweet wine, must (fresh juice), but used of the more saccharine (and therefore highly inebriating) fermented wine: - new wine. Gleukos denotes sweet "new wine", Acts 2:13, where the accusation shows that it was intoxicant and must have been undergoing fermentation some time

3631 -oinos (oy'nos), a primary word "wine" (32x). Oinos is the general word for "wine." The mention of the busting of the wineskins, Mt. 9:17; implies fermentation. See also Eph. 5:18 (cf. Jn. 2:10). In Mt. 27:34 is translated "vinegar" the result of complete fermentation

3943 - paroinos (par'-oy-nos), from 3844 and 3631; staying near wine, i.e. tippling (a toper):- given to wine. Paroinos, as an adjective, literally means "tarrying at wine, give to wine" (I Tim. 3:3; Titus 1:7 with the second sense, of the effects of wine bibbling , abusive brawling

WINTERED

Greek:

NOTE The Strongs Concordance lists the number as-

3916 - parachrema (par-akh-ray'-mah), at the thing itself, ie., instantly:- forthwith, immediately, presently, straightway, soon—Acts 28:11 . However, further research shows another (and what appears to be better) definition as-

3914 - paracheimazo (par-akh-i-mad'zo), translates as winter 4 times; to "winter", pass winter, with one or at a place; near, i.e. stay with over the rainy season: - winter—Acts 28:11 - And after three months we departed in a ship of Alexandria, which had wintered in the isle, whose sign was Castor and Pollux. (KN)

WISDOM

Hebrew:

2451 - chokhmah (khok-maw) originates from 2449. It means wisdom, knowledge, experience, intelligence, insight, judgment. It is always used in a positive sense.

True wisdom leads to reverence for the Lord (Job 28:28;) Therefore, skeptics will never find this kind of wisdom (see James 3:13-18), and they will never know the true meaning of life (Prov. 14:6, 7). Chokhmah is used to describe an entire range of human experience: embroidering (Ex. 28:3), metal working (Ex. 31:2, 6), military strategy (Is. 10:13), diplomacy (Deut. 34:9; II Sam. 14:20; Ezek 28:4, 5), shrewdness (II Sam. 20:22), prudence (Ps. 37:30); 90:12); and practical spirituality (Is. 33:6). God is all-powerful and all-knowing. Therefore, all wisdom has its source in Him (Job 11:6; 12:13; 28:20; Prov. 2:6). Chokhmah is personified only to a point- it does not have a separate existence (Prov. 1:20; 8:1-31). The figure of wisdom was never regarded as independent of God. It is only one of His attributes.

998 - biynah (bee-naw) from 995 meaning to separate mentally (or distinquish); understanding: - knowledge, meaning, wisdom—Job 39:17

3820 - leb (labe) the heart: also very widely for the feelings, the will and even the intellect: likewise for the center of anything, willingly, wisdom—Prov. 11:2; Ecc. 10:3

6195 - ormah (or-maw) trickery: or (in a good sense) discretion:- guile, prudence, subtilty, will, wisdom—Prov. 8:5

7922 - sekel (seh-kel) intelligence: success:- knowledge, policy, prudence, sense, wise, understanding, wisdom—I Chron. 22:12

Greek:

4678 - sophia (so-fee-ah) is used with reference to (a) God, Rom 11:33; I Cor. 1:21, 24; (b) Christ, Matt. 13:54; Mark 6:2; Luke 2:40, 52; (c) "wisdom" personified, Matt. 11:19; (d) human "wisdom" (1) in spiritual things, Luke 21:15; Acts 6:3, 10. - wisdom - (higher or lower, worldly or spiritual)

5428 - phronesis (fron-ay-sis) from mental action or activity, i.e. intellectual or insight:prudence, wisdom—the mind is translated "wisdom" in Luke 1:17.

*Note: "While sophia is the insight into the true nature of things, phronesis is the ability to discern modes of action with a view to their results; while sophia is theoretical, phronesis is practical". Sunesis, "understanding, intelligence," is the critical faculty; this and phronesis are particular applications of sophia

WIZARD
Hebrew:

3049 - yidde'oni (yid-deh-o-nee) from 3045 (yada -to perceive, acquire knowledge).

A knowing one; spec. a conjurer; (by impl.) a ghost-wizard

   This adjective which is used as a substitute means sorcerer, magician, wizard, prophesying spirit. The Berkeley Translation and the NASB translate it as "fortune-teller." The NEB has "familiar spirit." It comes from 3045. Therefore, an occultist possessed the esoteric knowledge of his craft which he would not share with commoners. It was forbidden by God to consult them (Lev. 19:31; 20:6; 27, Deut. 18:11) or other diviners. The good kings did not do so (II Kings 23:24). Isaiah denounced them (Is. 8:19; 19:3).

One who speaks to the dead (Is. 8:19). Wizards were readily available but unreliable (I Sam. 28:3 -19). The Bible strictly forbids seeking advice from wizards, also called mediums.

WORD
Hebrew:

561 - emer (ay-mer) - something said: answer, saying, speech, word 562 - omer (o-mer) - promise, speech, thing, word

565 - imriy (im-ree) - fem. to 561 something said: answer, commandment, speech, word

1697 - dabar (daw-bawr) - a word, a matter (as spoken of) or thing, a cause: act, advice, affair, answer, song, spoken, thought, tidings, what (soever), wherewith, which, word, work

3983 - memar (may-mar) - appointment, word

4405- millah (mil-law) - masculine as if from root word meaning to speak -mostly poetic-, or say, speak milleh (mil-leh) - a word, a discourse, a topic, mater anything to say, to speak talking, command, or commandment, thing

6310 - peh - the mouth as the means of blowing, whether literally or fig.), according to

6600 -pithgam (pith-gawn) - a word, answer, letter or response, decree, word

Greek:

518 - apaggello (ap-ang-el-lo) - to announce: bring word, declare, report, show (again) tell

3056 - logos (log-os) - something said (including the thought): by implication a topic (subject or discourse), divine expression (i.e. Christ), account, cause, communication, tidings, treatise, utterance, word, work

4487 - rhema (hray-mah) - an utterance (individual, collectively, or specific); a matter or topic, a saying, word Logos (3056) denotes 1. the expression of thought - not the mere name of an object - a. as embodying a conception or idea; b. a saying or statement

logos - one of the titles of our Lord, found only in the writings of John (1:1-14, I John 1:1, and Rev 9:13) Christ is the revealing of God. His office is to make God Known. Christ is the bosom of the Father (He declared Him - John 1:18) Everything that God wanted man to be —Christ is!!!

examples: Hebrew: 565- Deu. 30:14
1697 - Gen. 15:1, Gen 15:4 3983 - Dan. 4:17
4406 - Dan. 3:28 & 4:31
6310 - I Kings 13:26   Joshua 19:50 & Joshua 22:9
6600 - Ezra 6:11
examples: Greek: 518 - Matt. 2:8
3056 - John 1:1, etc. (hundreds of others)
4487 - Matt. 26:75; Matt. 4:4

WOUNDED

Hebrew: 2490 - chalal (khaw-lal) to profane, defile, pollute; to prostitute; to make common; to loose; to break. The core meaning of this root and its history in cognate languages is rather uncertain. Originally, the word was to refer to sexual defilement (Gen.49:4) or incest. Generally speaking, chalal refers to doing violence to the established law of God (Ps. 55:20). It is a desecration of something which is holy. Chalal also means to be pierced, perforated, wounded (Ex. 32:26, Ezek. 28:9).
THIS IS ALSO HOW USED IN- Isaiah 53:5

WRATH

Hebrew:

2534 - hemah (khay-maw) "wrath; heat; rage; anger. "This noun occurs in Semitic languages with meanings "heat, wrath, poison, venom." The noun, as well as the verb yaham denotes a strong emotional state. The noun is used 120 times, predominantly in the poetic and prophetic literature, especially Ezekiel. The word indicates a state of anger. Most of the usage involves God's "anger".

Greek: The Septuagint gives the following translations: orge and thumos
3709 - orge (or-gay), to desire eagerly or earnestly. Wrath, anger as a state of

mind. Contrast thumos (2372) indignation, wrath as an outburst of that state of mind with the purpose of revenge, Aristotle says orge is desire with grief, cf Mark 3:5. The Stoics considered it as a desire to punish one who seems to have hurt them in a manner he ought not. The anger, wrath of man (Eph, 4:31; Col. 3:8; James 1:19, 20), or of God (Heb. 3:11; 4:3); the effect of anger or wrath, that is punishment from man (Rom. 2:5; Eph. 5:6; I Thess. 1: 10; 5:9). Any violent emotion, but esp. anger. Anger exhibited in punishment, hence used for punishment itself. Punishment inflicted by magistrates; violent passion, abhorence by implication punishment:- anger, indignation, vengeance, wrath.

2372 - thumos (thoo-mos), from thuo, to move impetuously, particularly as the air or wind; a violent motion, or passion of the mind; as ascribed to God (Rev. 14:10); to man (Luke 4:28), to the devil (Rev. 12:12).

Found together with orge (Rom. 2:8), indignation; Eph (4:31). wrath; Col. 3:8). which means the more abiding and settled habit of mind, whereas thumos is the more passionate and, at the same time, more temporary character of anger and wrath. Thumos is an outburst of orge, anger

Y

YEA & YES

Hebrew:

432 - illuw (il-loo), nay, i.e. (softened) if:- but if, yea though—Ecc. 6:6

637 - aph (af), a prim. particle; mean. accession (used as an adv.or conj.); also or yea; adversatively though:also, but, even, how much less (more, rather than), moreover, with, yea—Isaiah 45:21

834 - asher (ash-er'), who, which, what, that; also (as adv. and conjunc.) when, where, how, because, in order that, etc. (however, forasmuch, wherein, though)—I Sam. 15:20

1571- gam (gam), by contr. from an unused root mean. to gather; prop. assemblage; used only adv. also, even, yea, though; often repeated as correl. both ... and:-again, alike, also, (so much) as (soon), both ... (so) ... and, but, either ... or, even for all, (in) likewise (manner), moreover, nay ... neither, one, then, though, what, with, yes— Ps. 23:4; Mal.2:2

3588 - kiy (kee), a prim. particle. very widely used as a rel. conj. or adv.; often largely modified by other particles annexed:- and, (forasmuch,inasmuch, where) as, assured (ly), even for, how (because, in, so, than) that, now rightly, seeing, since, surely, then, when, whether, while, whom, yea, yet—Prov. 2:3; Jer. 27:21; Hos. 9:12

Greek:

3483 - nai (nahee), a particle of affirmation, as used (a) in answer to a question, (ex. Matt. 9:28; 11:9; 13:51) (b) in assentato an assertion, Matt. 15:27, RV (KJV, "truth"); (c) in confirmation of an assertion, Matt. 11 :26 and Luke 10:21, RV (KJV, "even so"); Luke 11:51 RV (KJV, "verily"), (d) in solemn asseveration, Rev. 1:7 (KJV and RV, "even so"); (e) in repetition for emphasis, Matt. 5:37; singly in contrast to no, "nay," 2 Cor. 1:18,19 (twice), 20, "(the) yea," RV. Strong affirmation; yes:even so, surely, truth, verily, yea

235 - alla (al-lah), "but," is translated "yea" in John 16:2; Rom. 3:31, KJV (RV, "nay"), contrariwise (in many) applications:- and, but (even), howbeit, indeed, nevertheless, no, notwithstanding, save, therefore, yet

2532 - kai (kahee), "and, even," is rendered "yea: e.g., Luke 2:35; John 16:32; in Acts 7:43, KJV (RV, "and") but, even, for, if, indeed, likewise, moreover, or, so that, then therefore, when, yes, yet

3304 - menounge (men-oon'-geh), "yea rather," occurs, e.g. Luke 11:28; in Rom. 10:18, "yea (KJV, yes) verily"; in Phil. 3:8, RV, "yea verily" (KJV, "yea doubtless').

*Notes" (1) In 1 Cor. 15:15 the RV translates kai by "and" (KJV, "yea"). (2) In Luke 24:22 the RV translates alla kai "moreover" (KJV, "yea ... and"), (3) In 1 Cor. 16:6, (KJV, e kai, "or even" (RV), is translated "yea, and."). (4) In 2 Cor. 5:16, KJV, the phrase ei kai (some texts have ei de kai) is translated "yea, though, (RV, "even though"). (5) In Phil. 2:8, RV the particle de, "but," is translated "yea" (KJV, "even").

YEAR

Hebrew:

8141 - shanah (shaw-naw') from 8138; "year." Biblical Hebrew attests it about 877 times and in every period.

The word signifies "year": "And God said, Let there be lights in the firmament of the heaven to divide the day from the night; and let them be for signs, and for seasons, and for days, and years" (Gen. 1:14 - the first biblical occurrence of the word).

There are several ways of determining what a "year" is. First - may be based on the relationship between the seasons and the sun, the solar year or agricultural year. Second - based on a correlation of the seasons and the moon (lunar year). Third - may be decided on the basis of the correlation between the movement of the earth and the stars (stellar year). At many points the people of the OT period set the seasons according to climatic or agricultural events; the year ended with the grape and fruit harvest in the month Elul: "Thou shalt keep] the feast of harvest, the first fruits of thy labors, which thou hast sown in the field: and the feast of ingathering, which is in the end of the year, when thou hast gathered in thy labors out of the field" (Ex. 23:16)

The Gezer calendar shows that by the time it was written (about the tenth century B.C.) some in Palestine were using the lunar calendar, since it exhibits an attempt to correlate the agricultural and lunar systems. The lunar calendar began in the spring (the month Nisan, March - April) and had twelve lunations, or periods between new moons. It was necessary periodically to add a thirteenth month in order to synchronize lunar calendar and the number of days in a solar year.

Greek:

2094 - etos (et-os), is used (a) to mark a point of time at or from which events take place, e.g., Luke 3:1

(dates were frequently reckoned from the time when a monarch began to reign); in Gal. 3:17 the time of the giving of the Law is stated as 430 "years" after the covenant of promise given to Abraham;

(b) to mark a space of time, e.g., Mat. 9:20; Luke 12:19; Acts 7:6, where the 400 "years" mark not merely the time that Israel was in bondage in Egypt, but the time that they sojourned or were strangers there;

(c) to date an event from one's birth, e.g. Mark 5:42; (d) to mark recurring events, Luke 2:4;

(e) of an unlimited number, Heb. 1:12.

Note: In Heb. 11:24, ginomai, "to become," with megas, "great" is rendered "when he was come to years"

YIELD

Hebrew:

5414 - nathan (naw-than), to give, used with great latitude of application (put, make, etc.):- add, apply, appoint, ascribe, bestow, bring, cause, charge, come, commit distribute, without fail, fasten frame, occupy, offer, ordain, pay, perform, place, pour, print, store, send (out), thrust, trade, turn, willingly,+ withdraw,+ would (to) God, yield—(ex. Gen. 4:12; Lev. 26:4)

6213 - asah (aw-saw), to do or make, in the broadest sense and widest application (as follows):accomplish, advance, appoint, apt, be at, become, bear, bestow, bring forth, bruise, be busy, have the charge of, commit, deal (with), execute, exercise, fashion, fulfil, furnish, gather, get, go about, govern, grant, observe, be occupied, offer, prepare, provide, sacrifice, serve, set, shew, take, work, (man), yield, use—(ex. Heb. 3:17; Isaiah 5:10)

Greek:

591 - apodidomi (ap-od-eed'-o-mee), "to give up or back," is translated "to yield" in Heb.12:11; Rev. 22:2 (in each case, of bearing fruit). See deliver

863 - aphiemi (af-ee—ay-mee), "to send away," is translated "yielded up (His spirit)" in Matt. 27:50 (cf. paratithemi, "I commend," Luke 23:46, and paraidomi, "He gave up," John 19:30). See forgive. 1325 - didomi (did-o-mee), "to give", is translated "to yield," i.e., "to produce," in Matt. 18:8, RV (KJV, "brought forth"); Mark 4:7,8. See give

3936 - paristemi (par-is—tay-mee) or paristano (par-is-tan-o), to stand beside, recommend, substantiate; to be at hand (or ready), aid:- assist, bring before, command, commend, give presently, present, prove, provide, shew, stand (before, by here, up, with), yield — translated "to yield" in Rom. 6:13 (twice), 16,19 (twice), RV, "to present," in each place. See commend.

3982- peitho (pi-tho), "to persuade," in the passive voice, "to be persuaded," is translated "do (not) thou yield, to convince (by argument, true or false); to assent (to evidence or authority), to rely (by inward certainty):- agree, assure, believe, have confidence, be (wax) confident, make friend, obey, trust, yield. (Acts 23:21). See persuaded

4160 - poieo (poy-eh'-o)), "to make to do", is translated "yield" in James 3:12.

REFERENCES AND RESOURCES

*All Scripture quotations, unless otherwise noted, are taken from the King James Version of the Bible.

Hebrew-Greek Key Word Study Bible, King James Version, (1991). AMG International, Inc.

The Revised Standard Version of the Bible, (1973). Division of Christian Education of the National Council of the Churches of Christ in the U.S.A.

The New American Standard Bible, (1977). The Lockman Foundation

Holy Bible: The New International Version, (1978). The New York International Bible Society. Zondervan Bible Publishers

Strong's Exhaustive Concordance of the Bible, (1990). Thomas Nelson Publishers

Vine's Complete Expository Dictionary of Old and New Testament Words, (1996). Thomas Nelson, Inc.

The Student Bible Dictionary, (2000). Barbour Publishing, Inc.

The Black Biblical Heritage, (1993). Winston-Derek Publishers, Inc.

Young's Compact Bible Dictionary, (1989). Tyndale House Publishers.

The Complete Book of Bible Answers, (1997). Harvest House Publishers

The Complete Book of Bible Literacy, (1992). Tyndale House Publishers

The American Heritage Dictionary of the English Language, (1978). Houghton Mifflin Company

Crosswalk.com. www.crosswalk.com

Strong's Concordance with Hebrew and Greek Lexicon. www.eliyah.com/lexicon.htm

Study Light – The New Testament Greek Lexicon. www.studylight.org/lex/grk/

ABASE 7	COMPLAIN 33	FEEL/FEELING/FELT 57	INTERPRET/
ACCOMPLISHED ...7	COMPROMISE 33	FELLOWSHIP 58	INTEPRETATION/
ADDICTED 8	CONFIRMATION .34		INTERPRETER .80
ADO 8	CONFUSION (with	FERVENT/	ISHMAEL 81
ADOPTION 8	focus on author of	FERVENTLY 59	ISSUE (OF BLOOD) 81
AGAIN (emphasis on	confusion) 34	FINISHER 59	JEBUS 83
- be born again) 9	CONSECRATE 35	FIRST FRUIT(S) 60	JEHOVAH (written as
AGNOSTIC 10	CONSECRATION 35	FOES 61	YHWH) 83
ALTAR 10	CONSIST 35	FORSAKE 62	JESUS 85
ANOINTED ONE..11	CORNERSTONE ..36	FRANKINCENSE ..62	JOT 85
ANOINTING 11	COUNTENANCE .37	FULLERS SOAP 63	JOUDHOUR (Roots
APOCRYPHA - 12	COVENANT 38	GAP THEORY 64	of Ham 86
APPLE 13	CRUCIFIXION,	GENESIS 64	JUDGMENT SEAT 86
APPREHEND &	CRUCIFY 39	GENTLENESS 65	KEEPER 87
APPREHENDED 13	DART/DARTS 40	GENTiIe/GENTiIeS	LASCIVIOUSNESS 88
AUTHOR 13	DEAD SEA	64	LEARN 88
Acknowledgements..2	SCROLLS 40	GIANT(S) 66	LEAVEN 89
BAAL 15	DERIDE 41	GLUTTON 66	LEVITICUS 89
BESEECH 16	DIADEM 41	GLUTTONOUS 66	LINQUA FRANCA 90
BIBLE VERSIONS	DISCERN 42	GNASH 66	LIST......................92
(Most read) 16	DISCIPLE/	GODHEAD 67	LONGSUFFERING 92
BIBLICAL PRAYERS 18	DISCIPLESHIP .42	GODLY 67	LUCIUS OF CYRENE 92
BIND UP (focus on	THE DIVIDED	GOODNESS 68	MAJESTY 93
Isaiah 61) 18	KINGDOM 43	GREAT WHITE	MALEFACTOR(S) ..93
BOAST 18	DROPSY 44	THRONE 68	MANSION 94
BOAZ 19	DRUNK WITH WINE	GREEK ALPHABET .68	MARANATHA 94
BORN/BEGET/BEGAT	... EXCESS 44	GROSS (to wax) ...70	MARK 95
/ BEAR............20	DUMB 45	HALLOWED..........71	MATRIX 95
BREATH, BREATHE 20	EARTH 46	HAM 71	MEEK/MEEKNESS 95
BRUISED 21	EASTER 46	HAM'S	MELCHIZEDEC ...96
BUFFET 21	EFFECTUAL 47	DESCENDANTS	MEMORIAL DAY ..96
BULWARKS 22	EFFEMINATE 48	72	MERCY 97
BURDEN 22	EFFULGENCE 48	HARDENED (in	MINISTER/
C.E. and B.C.E. ...26	ELI ELI LAMA	dealing with	MINISTERED/
CANAAN 24	SABACHTHANI	Pharaoh) 73	MINISTERS/
CANON 25	"ELOI ELOI" ...48	HEALING 73	MINISTRY 98
CAPHTOR -	EMMANUEL -	HEARING 74	MIRY 99
KAPHTOR 25	IMMANUEL -	HEBREW ALPHABET	MIZRAIM 99
CHASTEN/	IMMANUW'EL 49	74	MODEST 100
CHASTENING/	EMULATIONS 50	HEIR—JOINT HEIR	NATURAL/
CHASTISE/	ENEMIES..............50	75	NATURALLY .101
CHASTISEMENT .	ENOCH 50	HERESY 76	NETHINIMS 101
.....................27	ERR 51	Hebrew Alphabet	NIGER 102
CHRISTMAS 28	THE ETHIOPIAN	(continued)......75	NIMROD 102
CHURCH 29	EUNUCH 51	INDIGNATION 77	OF LIKE PASSIONS
CIRCUMSPECT/CIRC	EXCESS 52	INFIRMITY—	(Acts 14:15)..104
UMSPECTLY ...30	EXEGESIS 52	INFIRMITIES ...77	OG 104
CLEAN and	EXPRESS IMAGE	INIQUITY 78	ONE (focus on John
UNCLEAN 30	(Hebrews 1:3) 53	INTEGRITY 79	10:30) 105
COMELY 31	FACE 54	INTERCESSION/	ONE HUNDRED
COMFORT/	FAITH 54	INTERCESSIONS	FORTY FOUR
COMFORTER/	FAITHFULNESS 55	79	THOUSAND ..105
COMFORTLESS 32	FAMILIAR 55		ONLY BEGOTTEN ...
COMMODIOUS ..32	FAVOR/FAVORED 56		............105, 106

THE WORD WINDOW 175

PARABLE 107	SAVE/SAVED/	TANAKH 151
PASSETH 107	SALVATION ..133	TEACH/TEACHER
PATIENCE/PATIENT/	SEALED 135	(with a touch of
PATIENTLY 108	SEDITIONS 135	learn) 152
PERADVENTURE 109	SEEK 135	TEMPERANCE 153
PERFECT 109	SELAH 136	TESTAMENT 153
PHARAOH'S	SERVE/SERVANT/	THE SONS OF
DAUGHTER .110	SERVICE 136	NOAH 142
PHARISEES 111	SEVEN SAYINGS	THEOPHANY 156
PHUT 112	FROM THE	THRONE 156
PICNIC 112	CROSS 137	TIME (as used in I
POSSESS 112	SHADOW (focus on	Timothy 6:15) .....
PRAISE 113	Psalms 23:4 &	156
PRAY/PRAYER 114	17:8) 137	TITTLE 157
PRECEPT 115	SHEKINAH/	TO ANOINT 10
PRECIOUS 116	SHECHINAH 138	TO BE UNCLEAN .157
PREDESTINATE ..117	SHINETH 139	TO COUNSEL (verb)
PRESUMPTION &	SHOFAR (shofar -fer)	37
PRESUMPTUOUS	139	TO FORGIVE 61
....................117	SIMEON THAT WAS	TONGUE/TONGUES
PRIEST/	CALLED NIGER ..	157
PRIESTHOOD 118	141	TWELVE TRIBES OF
PROPHECY/	SIMON OF CYRENE	ISRAEL 159
PROPHESY/	141	Thanksgiving 155
PROPHESYING ..	SIMON THE	To ANOINT 10
....................119	CANAANITE .141	To TRANSFIGURE .....
QUEEN CANDACE	SOLOMON 141	159
"QUEEN" 120	SORCERER: 143	
QUEEN OF SHEBA ..	SORCERY 143	UNBELIEF/
....................120	SOUL ("self; life;	UNBELIEVER .160
QUICKEN 121	person; heart") ...	UNCLEANNESS .160
R.S.V.P...............130	143	USURP 160
RACA 122	SOVEREIGN 145	VARIANCE 161
RAHAB 122	STEDFAST 145	VERITY 161
REASONABLE 123	STOUT (with focus on	VIRTUE 161
REGENERATION 123	Malachi 3:13)	WAITETH (with special
REPLENISH 124	146	focus as used in
REPROBATE 124	STRIPES 146	Psalm 65:1) .163
REPROOF 125	STRUCK (focus on	WEARY 163
RESIST 125	Luke 22:64) .146	WICKED 164
REVELATION 126	STUDY - 147	WILDERNESS 164
REVELING 126	SUBDUE 147	WILES 164
REVERENCE 127	SUBSTANCE 148	WINE 165
REWARDER 127	SUBVERT 148	WINTERED 165
RIGHT HAND 128	SUFFICIENT/	WISDOM 166
RIGHTEOUS/	SUFFICIENCY	WIZARD 167
RIGHTEOUSNESS	149	WORD...............167
....................128	SUNDRY TIMES ..149	WOUNDED 168
RUDIMENT 130	SUPPLICATION ..150	WRATH 168
RULE 130	SURFEITING 150	YEA & YES 170
SABBATH 132	TALLIT or TALLET 151	YEAR 171
		YIELD 172